The Four I's

The Four I's

Interviewing, Interrogation, Investigating, and Intelligence in Criminal Justice

Gabe Morales and Korey Cooper

cognella®

SAN DIEGO

Bassim Hamadeh, CEO and Publisher
Carolyn Meier, Publisher
Amy Smith, Senior Project Editor
Jeanine Rees, Production Editor
Emely Villavicencio, Senior Graphic Designer
JoHannah McDonald, Licensing Coordinator
Natalie Piccotti, Director of Marketing
Kassie Graves, Senior Vice President, Editorial

cognella® | ACADEMIC PUBLISHING
320 South Cedros Ave., Ste. 400, Solana Beach, CA 92075

Brief Contents

Detailed Contents

CHAPTER 3   Conducting Interviews 37

CHAPTER 4   The Statement 55

PART II. INTERROGATION

PART III. INVESTIGATIONS

PART II. INTERROGATION

PART III. INVESTIGATIONS

Acknowledgments

The authors would like to give thanks and appreciation to the following people:

Scott Abbott, Felix Aguirre, Tami Jo Aiken, Efren Almodovar, Robert Almonte, Antonia Alvarado-Jackson, Robert Almonte, David Anderson, Paul Annetts, Nelson Arriaga, J.R. Auten, Tony Avendorph, David Au, Zach Baggett, Guy Baker, Kimberly Bell, Robert Belshay, Barry Belt, Ron "Cook" Barrett, Rick Bishop, Chris Blatchford, Robert Borg, Chris Brandon, Matt Browning, "Buck" Buchanan, Sam Buentello, Justin Cagle, Pablo Cajigal, Marylou Carrillo, Tony Casas, Bob Cepeda, David Chan, Morgan Chappelle, George Chavez, Columbia (TN) Police Department, Francisco Cisneros, Roy & Diane Daubney, David Contreras, Katlyn Cooper, Seth Cooper, Suzanne Cooper, Shirley Cooper, Eduardo Cordero, Ernest Cuthbertson, Maryanne Denner, Todd DePalma, Adrian Diaz, Frank Diaz, Jose Diaz, Franco Domma, Kyle Dombroski, Todd Drew, Bill Dunn, Steve Duncan, Jeff Duncan, "Rocky" Dyer, Jim Dyment Sr., Marc Espinoza, Jimmy Eubank, Andy Eways, Enrique Franco, Marcus Frank, Bill Fogarty, Dan Foley, Russell Fonoimoana, Joe Gagliardi, Emil Garza, Joe Garza, Jeff Gibson, Mark Gibson, F. Hunter Glass, Seth Gonzalez, Chris Grant, Ben Griego, Steve Haley, Rick Handel, Bill Hankins, Harry Hanson, Rod Hardin, Chuck Hastings, Johnny Hawkins, Devan Hawkes, Johnny Hawkins, Dave Harris, Don Harris, Joe Harris, Jeremy Haywood, Carter Hickman, Alberto Hidalgo, Lindsey Houghton, Tom Howard, Rondo Jackson, Brandon James, Lawrence Jaramillo, Al Jensen, Marc Johnson, Michelle Jordan, Mike Kash, Kristy Kelley, "TJ" Leyden, Paul Lozada, Steve Lucero, Tagaloa Manu, Robert Marquez, Frank Marcell, Mike Martinez, Pablo Martinez, Robert Mateo, Chris Mouzis, Mario Molina, Joe Moody, Wes McBride, Keiron McConnell, Larry Mead, Mike Merrill, Dave Miranda, Mario Molina, Jeri Moomaw, Tony Moreno, Marcial Morales, Roy Morales, Robert Morrill, MSAB, John Myrick, Art Nakamura, Von Narcisse, Jack Nasworthy, Patrick Natividad, Brian Novotny, Robert Nylen, Michele Ochoa, Jim Ortiz, Mike Oster, Tony Ostos, Larry Parham, Tony Parker, Brian Parry, Eric Patao, Jeff Paynter, Kerry Pople, Joseph Preciado, Mike Prill, Celso Rangel, Dave Reardon, Darin Reedy, Chris Register, Melissa Rendon, Todd Reiswig, Brad Richmond, John Ringer, Yvonne Rios, Ruben Rivera, Antonio Rodriguez, Clem Rodriguez, Dave Rodriguez, Martin Rodriguez, Luis Rosa, Jesse Ruelas, Jeffrey P. Rush, Randall Russness, Roger Russness, Joe Ryan, Claudio Saa, Robert Saavetasi, Ruben Salamanca, Jesse Salazar, Joe Salazar, Johnny Salazar, Mark Salazar, Natalie Salazar, Armando Saldate, Joe Salinas, Jason Sanders, Edwin Santana, Miko Santiago, Dwayne Santistevan, Ken Sanz, Lou Savelli, John Scaduto, Adam Schniper, Chuck Schoville, the late Roy Sellers, Lowell Smith, David Schilling, Joe Sparks, Dennis Spice, Ron Stallworth, Jeffrey Stamm, Ramon Suarez, Dennis Sullivan, Tennessee Law Enforcement Training Academy, Kris Tenpas, "Smokey" Thomas, Aaron Thompson, Dale Thrush, Edwin Torres, Tom Trindad, Kerry Tripp, Tim Turmezei, Justin Tuttle, Bill Valentine, Mero Valenzuela, Angel Vasquez, Danny Vasquez, Richard Valdemar Larry Visitacion, Nga Vuong-Sandoval, Scott Wilder, Shawn Williams, Sherman Wilkins, Jason Wilke, Gary Williams, Daniel P. Wilson, Earl "Austin" Wozniak, Arthur Wynn, Christopher Young, Ed Yee, Paul Zamarripa, and Chris Zimmer.

CHAPTER 1

Introduction

The Four I's

Purpose

The four I's are interviewing, interrogation, investigations, and intelligence. The four I's will break down the fundamentals of communication in a way that's easy to understand. We will categorize each of the four I's and show their connection to one another in criminal investigations. This book will cover all major aspects of interviewing, interrogation, investigations, and intelligence, and it is designed to improve your understanding of the problems encountered as well as potential actions you can take to resolve these problems. Today, people skills are more important than ever. Today's technology has created a gap in our interpersonal communication skills. Communication is critical. These are perishable skills. If we do not practice them daily, we often will see them diminish. We will connect traditional techniques and interpersonal communication with some of the technological advancement.

We will cover each of the four I's in detail throughout this book and explain their purpose. We will explain the differences between interviewing and interrogating, or interrogating and investigating. We break each main topic down in easy to digest ways; however, be aware some areas may overlap. The approach we took in reviewing them was to reassess everything we know, reveal the major issues to you, and reviewed them again to make sure nothing was left out. In addition, we will cover some of the common challenges people in the field face that make understanding the four I's important in your work. We will include some scientific studies and our own empirical evidence that shows individuals with a proper understanding of these elements perform better in their jobs, have higher rates of effectiveness, and can achieve better results.

Interviewing

Interviewing is crucial to police and corrections investigations. It can build a strong foundation to future work and approaches on a case. The main goal of an investigative interview and process is to obtain accurate, reliable, and actionable follow-up information you and others involved can use in a most beneficial way. The proper interviewing of victims, witnesses, and suspects nd in the best environment possible will form an important part of your investigations into criminal activities and supplemental reports. The quality and fairness of those interviews often determine whether or not justice will be served in a proper manner.

Process Overview

There are many types of interviews. Some interviews that we will discuss include interviews related to criminal investigations, such as victim interviews, witness interviews, suspect interviews, and field interviews. Interviews may be conducted in a correctional setting and in the field, such as street side questioning (or field interviews) and/or more formal interviews at the police station. One common goal or purpose of interviewing is fact seeking (i.e., uncover the truth). Each interview will be different. It should be noted that an interview of a suspect could turn into an interrogation. We will discuss this in more detail throughout the text.

When conducting an interview, one of the first things to consider is the general purpose of the interview. It is also important to consider environmental factors, such as whether the interview is being conducted in a police station versus out on the street or whether the interview is with a single individual in a parole hearing room or involving multiple witnesses from a prison fight. It's also important to consider the approach of the interview and to be prepared to adjust that approach should things not work out as intended. Considering these elements in advance and taking things such as time limits into consideration helps to achieve the most effective investigation. Finally, you'll want to review your work and make sure you've connected the dots, crossed your T's and dotted your I's.

The most effective interviewers aren't just naturally good but have trained and worked at it—constantly honing and re-honing their skill set. Reading body language during interviews can be an important tool or skill. We will show you how to better interpret a person's behavior and answers during your interview for greater results.

Environmental Factors

Many times, you will be put into situations that are less than ideal. You may even want to give up sometimes in frustration, but an effective investigator does not let roadblocks stop them as long as what they are doing is not illegal and not against written policy. An effective investigator does not let roadblocks such as uncooperative witnesses, minimal physical evidence, or the lack of leads stop them. They use approved legal methods that adhere to written policy and procedures to achieve results. Those methods can be things like technological advancements, such as cellular telephone data (e.g., tolls, records, and location information) to develop leads.

Many times, investigators fail to simply canvass the area of the crime scene. That's when effective interview skills are valuable. By conducting door-to-door canvassing and interviewing neighbors, you may develop evidence and leads that will help solve the crime. Nowadays, many residences use surveillance cameras to monitor their property. Those cameras can also record activity, such as foot traffic or passing cars, that can assist with investigations. Neighborhood canvassing can also provide eyewitnesses who otherwise may not have been identified without the canvass. And last but certainly not least, time can be an asset. Sometimes, effective investigations are developed in time by not forcing theories or evidence to fit a preconceived notion or early belief.

In today's world of technology, you may have access to lots of information at your fingertips—so much so that, at times, it may be hard to sift through. You may have forensic scientists or access to detailed databases that have provided you information. Some of this information may be highly complex or written in language that only users are familiar with, and it will be your job to decipher it and break it down into terms a prosecutor, jury, or other parties will understand.

For example, you can gather information from Regional Information Sharing Systems (RISS) on a particular subject or property. RISS is a private entity that "assists local, state, federal, and tribal criminal justice agencies by providing adaptive solutions and service that facilitate information sharing, support criminal investigations, and promote officer safety" (RISS, n.d., para. 1). RISS networks can provide historical and detailed information on your "target." The information provided can be in bulk and complex in nature. The data is collected from various open record databases, such as court records, vehicle registrations, utility applications, and creditors, just to name a few. If you have access to an intelligence analyst, they can sift through the data and provide the investigator with the most valuable information for their specific investigation.

You may encounter veteran interviewers who have poor communication skills and thus get poor results. You will probably meet or already know other interviewers who are highly skilled at their jobs and usually get great results. Poor interview skills are often the result of learning poor communication skills by untrained individuals or sometimes even veterans of the field may fall into bad habits. In the age of technology, we are starting to see a generation of officers/investigators with less interpersonal communication skills. This may be a result of the uses of different platforms of electronic communication. Communication skill are a must-have in the realm of criminal investigations. Auditory, visual, and hands-on skills are often learned through academy training or taking courses using books such as this, then those skills are honed according to each interviewer's style and technique.

The best interviewers developed their skill through training; they were not born a great interviewer. While persistence often pays off in this field, often there are time constraints and pressure by supervisors and administrators to interview a certain number of individuals (often referred to as a **quota**). Often, there are ideal times and places to interview that may be missed and result in a far less effective interview down the road.

So, you must consider potential roadblocks and hurdles: Am I safe? Is the interviewee safe? If I were to conduct my interview right now, is the environment suitable? Can I conduct my interview in a better location? Am I fully prepared to conduct the interview right now? Can I gather some initial information if I am fairly certain I will have access to the individual later? Is the subject tired, high, drunk, or otherwise under the influence in a manner that might affect the quality of my interview? What other environmental factors might impact my interview?

Approaches

One of the first things you'll want is confidence in yourself. Be confident in what the purpose of your interview is and how you want to best approach it. Some of the different approaches related to interviewing in law enforcement are general conversations, structured interviews, and spontaneous/impromptu interviews, to name a few. Each requires a different approach.

Many successful veterans consider an interview to be a conversation between them and another individual for the aims of achieving a specific purpose. This differentiates a professional interview from a casual conversation of chitchat. While your approach will be focused, there may be occasions where you may allow the subject to delve off into tangents unrelated to your interview if it relaxes them. But you will come to a point, sometimes quickly, where you will move to refocus them to get back on track to accomplish your goals. You do not want to appear to be a question-and-answer machine, like a robot, but you will also need to guide them in order to obtain the most truthful and accurate information you can gather in a timely manner without appearing to rush them or disrespect them.

Interrogations

Interrogations can sometimes be confused with interviews. While there are some similarities, one primary difference is custody. An interrogation is custodial. Typically, an interrogation is accusatory as well. Best practice is to conduct an interview prior to an interrogation for information seeking details that can be corroborated in the interrogation.

Process Overview

Interrogations can take several forms depending on the environment, mission, and end goals. For instance, in a correctional facility there are often disciplinary hearings on inmates who may or may not be charged in criminal court but may face in-house disciplinary sanctions for in-custody rule violations such as assault, verbal abuse of staff, or a walk-away from work release which is still considered an escape.

In these situations, it is not always necessary to advise inmates of Miranda Rights because it may not be legally required for a hearing where only in-house sanctions may result. *Miranda v. Arizona* (1966) was a major Supreme Court case that gave certain rights to criminal suspects, called the **Miranda warning**. During these types of hearings, there may be incident reports along with supplemental information provided that can be reviewed by the hearing officer(s). Inmates who appear before the hearing often go through a process that is very similar to police interrogations; however, the judge and jury is the hearing officer or hearing committee. Courts have cited that there is not the burden of proof in these hearings that may apply in a criminal case. The inmate is still read certain due process rights and gets a copy of the main report and time to defend themselves.

During these hearings, the inmate is asked to plead guilty or not guilty to the rule violation offenses. Offenders in custody may be reluctant to be truthful about events. Your job is to get at the truth of what occurred in order to determine guilt or innocence and the degree of that guilt or innocence. Again, there is not the level of burden of proof that would exist during a criminal trial; there just has to be a "preponderance of the evidence."

If the inmate pleads not guilty, witnesses may be called, such as staff and other inmates. The accused inmate does not have the right to call witnesses, although they may be considered if it is believed they may have information relevant to the incident. The inmate is then asked questions, interrogated, to determine their guilt or innocence. One a finding has been determined, they have the right to appeal. Once that

process has been exhausted or if they don't appeal, they serve their sanction that can consist of anything from a verbal warning, to disciplinary segregation, to loss of programs.

If it was suspected during the investigation that a felony crime was committed (e.g., murder, assault, introduction of a substantial amount of drugs, etc.), the inmate may be referred to a county prosecutor. In some high-profile cases, federal authorities may decide to charge them also.

Just as in police work, corrections staff assigned to an internal investigations unit (IIU) may also use interrogation techniques if a staff member is suspected of violating major rules or possibly has committed a crime. We will not elaborate on these types of interrogations here, as they vary from agency to agency and have union protections but can be similar in nature. In criminal interrogations, many officers and investigators get interviews and interrogations mixed up. Interviews are used for fact seeking and involve more open-ended questioning. Interrogations are different. An interrogation is more accusatory, and questions should not be directed toward what occurred but why it occurred. Typically, an interrogation is also custodial, with the subject in custody (or under arrest). An interrogation should be controlled by the investigator, not the subject or suspect.

There are legal considerations that need to be considered with interrogations, which will be discussed in Chapter 5. One obvious legal consideration is the Miranda warning, as mentioned above. We will discuss when the warning should be used and the legal aspects as it relates to interviews and interrogations. Effective investigators must decide when or if deception tactics should be used. We will discuss tactics related to using false evidence ploys to create confessions. Can false evidence ploys cause false confessions? Both pros and cons related to this tactic will be further discussed.

Another legal aspect that we will discuss later in detail is coercion. Effective investigators will not utilize coercive techniques to gain a confession. At times, there may be a fine line between what is and isn't considered coercion. We will discuss cases where investigators used tactics that the courts decided were coercion, thus suppressing the statements from interrogations. Investigators should always err on the side of caution on anything that may be considered coercion.

Most interrogations come after some type of interview. Rarely are interrogations conducted without a previous interview. That's why an initial suspect interview is important. The initial interview establishes a baseline and a foundation for questioning. Additionally, evidence and other interviews—from victim(s) and witnesses—should be available for the investigator's review during the interrogation. While this material is not always shared with the suspect, it can be used by the investigator to ask questions during the interrogation.

Environmental Factors

Ultimately, the goal of any interrogation is to corroborate evidence in a criminal investigation and/or gain a confession from the suspect. Whether in a correctional environment or outside criminal investigations, many environmental factors can affect the outcome of an interrogation. Typically, it is best to conduct interrogations in a controlled environment, such as a police station. You want the suspect outside of their comfort zone. Many of the same environmental factors that are associated with interviews also apply to interrogations. In Chapters 5 and 6, we will discuss this in more depth.

Rapport is very important. The investigator needs to have outstanding rapport with the suspect, especially when dealing with career criminals. Many of them have nothing to lose, especially if the interview is conducted in a correctional setting. Many inmates already have lengthy sentences. They look forward to being paroled and do not want anything to hinder their release. It's important for investigators to take time to connect with the suspect to build trust and rapport.

An effective investigator must also be aware of false confessions and the factors that cause them. Over the years, false confessions have led to wrongful convictions. This has been uncovered more in recent years with advancements in **deoxyribonucleic acid (DNA)** technology. Innocent people can provide self-incriminating statements during the police interrogation process. That's why it is critical to use all resources available, such as interviews, intelligence, evidence, and other investigative techniques when conducting interrogations.

Approaches

The best approach to any interrogation is planning and preparation. The three other I's of this book cover the best planning techniques to complete a successful interrogation. You must be an active listener, observant of body language, and patient to be an effective investigator. When conducting interrogations, investigators should research the subject prior to the interrogation. The more you know about the person you're interrogating, the better off you'll be. Research all aspects of the case being investigated. While a motive is not necessary to conduct an investigation, it is helpful to understand why a suspect committed the crime(s) and thus benefit in the interrogation process.

Investigations

A criminal investigation involves collecting information and evidence to identify, eventually arrest or apprehend, and convict a suspected offender involved in a criminal offense. Private investigations focus more on a civil process than is not criminal in nature. Both types of investigation involve being thorough and detail oriented to be successful.

Process Overview

We will cover the proper use of investigative and behavior-provoking questions, as well as recommendations for carefully evaluating the accuracy and credibility of an allegation. We will discuss proper use of follow-up and possible bait questions, considering the pros and cons of each.

We will cover recent advancements in DNA evidence, incident review and solvability factors, past and new terrorism and homeland security issues, electronic data searches and privacy concerns, and new case law that impact investigations. We will discuss use of body cameras and hidden cameras, ethics issues, as well as increasing standards of proof for personal stops and associated legal issues. We will give you easy-to-learn pointers and practical tools you can use to further refine investigative techniques and skills in your toolbox.

Investigations can encompass the private sector and the field of criminal justice. Private investigations include civil matters such as personal, legal, and/or family issues. These investigations typically aren't connected to criminal offenses. One example of a personal private investigation would be surveillance on a boyfriend or girlfriend suspected of cheating. Corporations may use private investigators to investigate issues related to an employee's insurance or medical claim. Child custody disputes are common for private investigators as well. There are times, however, when a private investigator connects to a criminal investigation.

A private investigator may be hired by an attorney or private citizen to collect additional evidence in criminal cases. Some examples are electronic forensics of computers, mobile devices, or extended surveillance to present as defense in a criminal case. Private investigators may also conduct background checks or investigations, research analyses, and/or interviews as part of their duties.

For the purpose of this text, the investigations that we will focus on are related to criminal activity. Effective investigations start the moment of the initial complaint. Whether it's the call received by a dispatcher or the response of the first officer on the scene, the first minutes are often the most critical components to the effectiveness of any investigation.

Environmental Factors

The attention to detail and thorough reporting by the first responding officers are valuable to a successful criminal prosecution. The initial handling can dictate the overall track of an investigation. First and foremost, you must determine whether nor not a crime occurred. Once you've determined that a crime has occurred, then the fact seeking begins. Criminal investigators must keep an open mind and not subject themselves to preconceived notions or anything that can alter their ability to focus on the facts.

A criminal investigation involves the collection of information and evidence to identify, apprehend, and eventually convict suspected offenders. It should also be noted that excluding/clearing suspects through an investigation is just as important. An effective investigator is a fact seeker who lets the evidence lead them to a conclusion as to what specifically occurred in the course of the criminal activity. You should ask yourself what happened and how it happened. You must corroborate your conclusion with facts and/or evidence.

Investigations can sometime be tough due to the pressures of the media, true-crime television (i.e., the "CSI effect"), and ever-changing technology advancements. Victims and jurors often expect investigators to produce scientific evidence like they see in the media. Unfortunately, the cost of such scientific methods and technological advancements is far higher than the limited budgets for most agencies. Therefore, effective investigators must seek to adapt their investigations and evidence-collection techniques to the increased expectations of the layperson. One example is searching for public and private video or surveillance cameras. Today's technology allows for inexpensive live and recorded camera footage to be more readily available. But investigators must seek to identify potential video evidence in a timely manner. Most video footage is only captured and saved for a limited timeframe.

Approaches

Investigators should seek advanced training and skills in evidence collection, including DNA, electronic media (e.g., processing cellular phones and geo-tracking), and many other scientific methods. You should stay up to date with technology and the different types of evidence that can identify and/or exclude suspects in criminal investigations. Remember, jurors will look for advanced procedures in criminal trials, so you should think outside the box to provide more than a basic investigation at trial.

Case management is also important. Investigators should utilize a team effort while conducting criminal investigations. Communication is key. Utilize all your available resources. For example, interagency communication with patrol and specialized units (boots on the ground) is effective. Another suggestion is to have frequent discussions with the prosecutor's office. For more complex investigations, a case management checklist or template can be used to ensure all possible sources of information and evidence are sought. A crime scene checklist can also be used, which will prevent valuable information from being overlooked. Additionally, a crime scene checklist severs as an excellent source of documentation and guide to refresh the investigators memory.

Intelligence

Intelligence is an important aspect to any interview, interrogation, or investigation. Although, an interview can be used as an information-seeking session to develop intelligence for an investigation or interrogation. Developing intelligence is a process of checks and balances to validate information gathered. The intelligence cycle will be discussed and we will show the importance of the intelligence process.

Overview: Connecting the Dots

Intelligence strategies in the criminal justice system are valuable. Many practitioners in criminal justice confuse "information" with "intelligence." What most believe is intelligence actually is simply just information. By understanding the intelligence cycle (collection, processing, collation, analysis, reporting, dissemination, and reevaluation), you will see that validated information creates intelligence (see Figure 1.1). Intelligence collection requires sifting through all available **data** or raw information to eliminate unusable, worthless, or inaccurate information and to put data in logical order. This is also known as "connecting the dots."

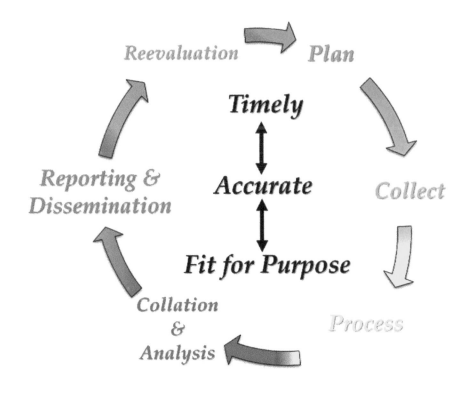

FIGURE 1.1 The Intelligence Cycle

Intelligence analysis can be divided into two categories: strategic and tactical analysis. Examples of strategic analysis include crime trends, statistical reports, and analyses of criminal activity or specific situations. Tactical analysis can develop characteristics such as modus operandi (MO), crime mapping, and link analysis.

We will show you how to properly gather, store, and disseminate intelligence.

Environmental Factors

Intelligence gathering has some limitations and legal aspects. Information to develop intelligence products must be collected lawfully. Open-source collection from sources such as social media, the internet, or public access area are available. In the United States, citizens' rights are protected from unlawful collection. Citizens should remain free of government surveillance without reasonable suspicion of criminal activity. For example, 28 CFR Part 23, states, "Operators shall collect and maintain criminal intelligence information concerning an individual only if there is reasonable suspicion that the individual is involved in criminal conduct or activity and the information is relevant to that criminal conduct or activity" (part a). The first amendment of the U.S. Constitution is a protected act. Law enforcement must err on the side of caution when collecting information for intelligence purposes that may be protected by the first amendment.

In addition, an operator must never collect private information about a person's views, behaviors, religion, social circles, work, and so on if it does not relate to an investigation. Moreover, "reasonable suspicion" cannot exist if there is no evidence of criminal activity to back it up (28 CFR § 23.20).

Approaches

Intelligence-led policing is a concept that was developed after the historic September 11, 2001, terroristic attack where airplanes were hijacked and flown into the World Trade Center in New York City. This produced the fusion center process, which created intelligence centers made up of multiple state, local, and federal law enforcement agencies collaborating and sharing information to develop intelligence products. Community and problem-solving policing integrated with intelligence-led policing provides planning strategies to reduce crime in targeted communities. Intelligence-led policing uses information and data gathered from law enforcement incident reports to generate actionable intelligence to solve crime. The intelligence can also provide data to recognize crime trends and patterns to prevent or reduce criminal activity in a **proactive** manner by anticipating or stepping in front of a known law enforcement issue, problem, and/or crime by collecting information and data.

Historically, intelligence-led policing involved some aspect of the correctional system. Just because someone is "locked up" doesn't mean they are not still involved in criminal activity, to include activity on the streets. That's why it's important to include the correctional function with intelligence-led policing on the streets.

There is also a need to focus on intelligence specific to correctional facilities in an effort to reduce contraband introduction and violence within those facilities. This book will do just that. It will use information derived from correctional incident reports, investigations, open sources, and cell phone extractions. The possession of cell phones by inmates is typically a violation of law and departmental inmate policies. Therefore, no expectation of privacy is protected. A wealth of information can be derived from correctional facilities (jails or prisons), which can be a source for intelligence-led policing as well as intelligence-led

The Office of the Federal Register, Selection from "Operating Principles," Code of Federal Regulations, 2023.

corrections. There is always a nexus to criminal activity within a correction environment to the streets, such as contraband introductions through visitation or "throw overs." A *throw over* is a when package(s) of prohibited material or contraband are thrown over a secured correctional area (fence) by someone who is not incarcerated. This occurs in an effort to provide prohibited material (e.g., drugs, tobacco, paraphernalia, cell phones, etc.) to inmates. The use of correctional intelligence will reduce criminal activity within a correctional setting.

Information and intelligence gathering is task that take pieces of information from multiple sources directed toward a plan with a criminal predicate. The raw information is sifted for valuable information specific to the plan or target, and useless information is discarded. The remaining information is analyzed and processed to form a tentative conclusion. Then the conclusive information and its sources are evaluated for validity, reliability, and the ability to be corroborated. If it is found to be valid, the information is developed into intelligence and disseminated as a product on a need-to-know basis. The product is continuously evaluated for changes in validity and reliability, as well as feedback. If information within the product changes, the process, or intelligence cycle, must be completed again. As previously mentioned, this process is referred to as connecting the dots.

PERSONAL EXPERIENCES

Morales

I was conducting a lot of interviews one day. Inmates were overflowing in the receiving unit, and we were under decent decree due to a lawsuit to keep maximum capacity under 160 inmates in that unit. The unit could be over that limit for no more than 72 hours or face repercussions. I gathered a list of inmates who had been there the longest as well as inmates who were "frequent flyers," who had been in custody before and who I knew well. In fact, some I had interviewed on a different booking only weeks before. In this manner, I could interview, classify, and move inmates out of the receiving unit as quickly as possible.

I was very familiar with many inmates who were caught in the "revolving door" of corrections. They were constantly in and out of jail. Because of that, I sometimes fell into the bad habit of treating an interview as "routine," barely updating the last booking file entries. Sometimes I knew more about what happened to these individuals in the last week than I did my own kids.

I was just finishing the last person, a "regular customer," when the unit officer sent me another inmate on a list that I provided him. I caught a slight view of the inmate out of the corner of my eye. He was very dark-skinned with dreadlocks and appeared to be one of the local gang members I dealt with often. I stated, "Have a seat Brah, I'll be right with you." This very casual greeting may have been OK with the individual I thought it was who had been interviewed by me many times, but this was not him. The inmate felt very offended and in a thick British-like accent responded, "Sir, I am not your brother!"

Boy, did I feel dumb.

I apologized for my rudeness and properly introduced myself and explained the purpose for my interview. I asked him for his name and inmate number and restarted the conversation.

The moral of this story is never to forget your purpose, be professional, be polite, and treat each person like it was the first time you've ever spoken to them.

You are probably familiar with the saying, " You never get a second chance to make a first impression." Be sure to start off on the right foot using a professional demeanor and etiquette. Establish a rapport with politeness, but do not become overfamiliar. Send a message that this is business even if you've known the individual through previous contact. Make sure you have a specific objective, and be prepared to ask open-ended questions so you don't just get a yes-or-no answer. Take note of not just the answer but the tone and body language of the person you are interviewing. Make sure to make eye contact; do not just write on your notepad or plug away on the computer. In fact, if you are able to legally record the interview without documenting it right then and there, that is even better.

You will often notice the subject trying to take a peek at your writing notes, or they may ask you what you are doing on the computer. This may trigger a reluctance to answer or even shut them down. People who have previous bad experiences with government officials already don't trust them. Be sure to use tact when discussing sensitive issues. Outline requirements that must be covered by your department's standard operating procedures (SOPs) and develop your own system. Most employers are OK with you conducting an interview using your own style and experience; this is why they hired you and not a robot to eventually get to the goal and objective.

Cooper

Throughout my 29-year career, I have been fortunate enough to be involved in a variety of fields within the criminal justice system. I have worked in corrections as a correctional officer and a director of a criminal investigative and intelligence unit. I've worked in law enforcement as a street cop and investigator (narcotics, criminal investigations, and gangs) and have been part of a canine unit, tactical unit, and more. This has provided me with experiences that I can share with readers as it related to the four I's.

Whether on the street, in a correctional facility, or when investigating a crime (on the street or in a prison), interviews are conducted on a daily basis. Every call for service that is answered on the street involves some sort of interview. When an inmate is booked into jail, an interview is conducted. Interviews continue during incarceration for multiple purposes: classification, daily accountability, investigations, and so on. Obviously, interviews are an important part of an investigator's duties. Of the four I's discussed in this book, interviews are what I believe to be the most critical. Interviews develop the other three I's (intelligence, interrogations, and investigations). For example, an interview can provide collaborating information to link or develop intelligence. Interviews provide details for interrogations and leads for investigations.

Take the information that we discuss here and use it as a basic foundation to develop advanced skills and seek advanced training opportunities. Interviews and interrogations go hand in hand. I believe that goes without saying. Investigations are the core piece of the four I's. An investigation cannot stand alone without utilizing any of the other I's. Some aspect of an interview must be used in an investigation. An interrogation and intelligence can enhance the investigation, but neither are "required" to complete an investigation. I would, however, suggest that an interrogation be conducted after the subject of an investigation has been arrested.

I've had successful interrogations that resulted in confessions and admissions. I've also had interrogations that resulted in omissions or lies that could be proven as such with evidence. There have also been cases where the interrogation ended without anything. It's important to understand that the interrogation stage must be a result of a fact-based investigation, not assumptions or pressures to make an arrest. Otherwise, considerations of false confessions are developed.

Intelligence is one of the four I's that will be used least often. That's because several agencies do not know how to properly utilize the intelligence process. Many agencies do not have the availability to an intelligence unit function. The intelligence process is a great tool. The process helps develop information or leads that can be processed and evaluated for accurate and valuable information. While we will discuss intelligence as the last of the four I's, it can be placed anywhere in between the others as well. If the intelligence process is used properly and an experienced intelligence analyst is utilized, the intelligence function is the key to any successful investigation, interview, or interrogation.

References

Miranda v. Arizona, 384 U.S. 436 (1966). https://www.oyez.org/cases/1965/759

Regional Information Sharing Systems. (n.d.). *About us*. https://www.riss.net/about-us/

Part I

Interviewing

CHAPTER 2

Interview Preparation

IMAGE 2.1

Types of Interviews

The best source of information is people. Interviews consist of talking to people, asking questions, and obtaining information or facts. In criminal investigations, the primary source of information is the complainant, victims, witnesses, and sometimes even the offenders. All are considered eyewitnesses. Interviews may be conducted on the street, in buildings, in houses, at the police station, or in a correctional environment.

Sometimes interviews are impromptu and conducted at the spur of the moment, such as at crime scenes and during field interviews. Other times, investigators have time to prepare for interviews, such as during an investigation or in a correctional environment. To be successful in obtaining or gathering information is to distinguish between an interview and an interrogation. An **interview** is typically a noncustodial fact-finding and truth-seeking discussion. **Open-ended questions** are commonly asked during interviews. The goal of most interviews is to gather information about investigations to develop leads and/or motives. Interviews may be conducted with suspects, victims, and witnesses. An interrogation, which will be detailed in the next section, is custodial and directed toward the suspect(s) of a crime.

The investigator needs to have outstanding rapport with the subject, especially when dealing with career criminals. Rapport is the key to a successful interview. Gaining rapport may take some time prior to asking any questions that pertain to the "goal" of your interview. This is where gathering as much information as you can about the subject you are interviewing helps. The more you know about a subject prior to speaking with them, the more prepared you will be. Gathering information such as the number of children they have and their children's age(s), their occupation, any family issues, and so on is an excellent start to preparing for an interview. An interview should be portrayed as more of a discussion. A good interviewer can sit down, speak to someone, have a good general conversation, and gather information from the conversation without the subject feeling that interviewer is trying to get information from them. For example, a street officer could approach a subject standing around at a crime scene and start a conversation:

Subject: What happened? (Note: People are nosy and always ask, right?)

Officer: I'm not exactly sure yet, but I hope everyone is okay.

Subject: Me too.

Officer: Do you live around here?

Subject: Yeah, I live at the corner in that red brick house.

Officer: This is a nice area. I haven't heard of much crime occurring around here.

Subject: It's rather quiet here, but there have been some problems since a group of kids moved in close to where that ambulance is parked.

Officer: Problems?

Subject: Yeah, I believe they're dealing drugs there. A couple of days ago, there was a blue car that drove by that house and just started shooting at the house.

Officer: That's crazy.

Subject: I know, right? There are always people coming and going from that house at late hours.

From the conversation, can an officer or investigator develop leads? Absolutely. This was not a formal interview, but more of a general conversation. However, the officer was able to develop enough of a rapport with the subject, which created conversation. What you should gather from this is that an interview does not always have to be a formal line of questioning from police to citizen. A good officer or investigator can have the "gift of gab" and conduct an interview without the subject really knowing they're being interviewed. That can lead to further questioning. At some point, the officer may need to get the subject's identification and contact information. This should include their phone number(s), address, and so forth. This could lead to a follow-up interview with detectives. It may be as easy as this:

Officer: Hey, it was great talking to you (as the officer reaches out to shake the subject's hand). Here's my business card. My name is Officer John Doe. What's yours?

Subject: Thanks. My name's John Q. Public. Have a good night, officer.

Some may call this an impromptu interview. Others will consider this a field interview. Call it what you want, but it's an interview. At this point, the officer could gather the person's contact information. The information the officer gathered could provide leads or motive for an investigation.

Being able to effectively communicate and build rapport is amongst the most important tools a police officer can have. Along with that, the use of active listening skills (ALS) is also very important. Many officers hear, but do they actually listen? If we can learn as officers and investigators to listen and be able to pick out fine details, then we most certainly will hear that everyone wants to tell the truth, whether that be a conscious decision or a subconscious one (K. Barbour, personal communication, October 15, 2021).

Inside Correctional Setting Versus Outside Setting (Free World)

Probably the best thing about conducting an interview in a correctional setting is you usually have a "captive audience." No pun intended!

Remember, some inmates may feel they have nothing to lose, especially when they are doing life without the possibility of parole. Conversely, many look forward to being paroled and do not want anything to hinder or delay their release. What has been successful for most of us who are experts in this area is keeping our word and not lying to these inmates.

A correctional setting can have some advantages and some disadvantages. For one, you are usually able to locate your interviewee relatively quickly. Even then, when dealing with large agencies, you will probably want to call ahead and verify they have not been transferred out. Most modern correctional agencies can assist you with online inmate locator systems. These are the same systems their families use to visit them and that lawyers use to speak to their clients. Even then, with experience, you will usually find out quickly when are good times and not-so-good times for your interview, such as busy times between shift changes, during meals, and so on.

Most of us in this field have to make sure that we have a good system for our confidential informants to ensure we do not compromise them. Scheduling interviews and other tricks of the trade are very important so that we don't "put a jacket" on these inmates or compromise their safety by conducting frequent interviews with them and interviewing the rest of the inmates in their pod. Thus, a disadvantage for interviewing in a correctional setting may be the lack of privacy. Inmates have a saying: "Snitches get stitches."

Unless you are within earshot of other offenders, they usually won't know what was said unless your interviewee tells them. In their own best interest, these individuals usually keep information sharing with their fellow inmates on what occurred to the bare minimum. If you are getting a confession, you probably don't want to give the inmate the legal paperwork right then and there, and their lawyer will likely need to be involved during plea bargaining. Still, they will often have a great fear of being found out as providing unknown information to authorities. Once you become familiar with the corrections environment and staff, they may be able to provide you with a semiprivate location.

Another disadvantage in interviewing at jails and prisons is speaking to subjects too soon after arrest. They may still be under the influence of drugs and/or alcohol that may taint the interview. They may still be angry at their arrest or not on their psych meds. It may come as a surprise to some outsiders, but drugs and inmate-manufactured alcohol are often readily available inside institutions. Offenders in that condition may not function well in an interview either. You also don't want to wait too long and violate rights or court and legal procedures. For example, you have 72 hours to charge somebody with a crime for probable cause. If you let time periods lapse, there can be negative repercussions and your bosses will not be very happy with you.

Keep in mind that inmate life can be extremely boring and confining. You may be the first person who has visited them in a long time—maybe the only person who has visited them. They may ask questions about loved ones, what time of day it is, who really won the World Series, or a number of questions that may seem unrelated to your interview. They may not want to stop talking during the interview, and it will be up to you to decide how much is enough or too much. As long as you don't put your interviewee or confidential information at risk, it may be OK to "shoot the breeze" with them for a minute. This is all part of gaining rapport (Hochstetler et al., 2010). This will be covered in detail in Chapter 3.

Informants can be found in almost any corrections institution, be it jail or prison, work release, or a prison camp. If you want to keep good informants, you won't want to "front them off." All inmates talk, but not getting caught talking to "the Man" is the name of the game. Keep in mind that most informants are very manipulative. Know their motives and know yours.

The information they give—or don't give—can be validated through "triangulation" (Lindegard, 2010). It is no big surprise to most veteran officers that inmates lie and can be very convincing at first. They may lie for a variety of reasons, including being intentionally misleading, re-remembering events, or changing their minds about the sequence of events or other factors. This is why many interviewers come back for further questioning, whether it be for follow-up questions, reclassification needs, or a police officer interviewing an inmate in custody.

You'll want to minimize distractions so they can concentrate and accurate answer your questions. Ideally, a private room outside of the comfort zone of the interviewee is best. Unfortunately, that may not always be possible. Use the most secluded area that you can to protect the interviewee and the information they are providing.

Field Interviews

A **field interview** can be conducted anywhere outside of a corrections institution. But just as with inside institutions, there are more ideal places to conduct your interview and less than ideal places. Once again, the less eyes and ears within sight and earshot of the interview, the better. While the person you are interviewing may not be a paid informant, they may still lie and manipulate. Unless they may be named as a suspect, you'll want to reassure them that the information they are offering is voluntary. Be up-front about whether they can provide information to you anonymously or you are obligated by policy or law to document information they give you in order to avoid any potential mistrust issues. You will quickly get a reputation as somebody who is fair or somebody who burns people or puts them in bad light. They may not like the truth, but at least if you are always fair, they know that you are being forthcoming and leveling with them.

So why should they talk to you at all? You can remind them that a crime or incident has taken place and that somebody has or could be harmed. You can ask them how they'd feel if it was them, their family, or their friends it happened to and there was nobody who cared enough to investigate it. Harp on the need for justice.

A Terry stop can be considered a field interview. A *Terry stop* is based on a decision of the U.S. Supreme Court in *Terry v. Ohio* (1968). This case set the standard in the United States for investigative stops or field interviews based on articulatable facts. While the case focuses on a Fourth Amendment seizure of John Terry, it is important to understand the difference between a consensual contact or interview and a Terry stop.

According to the *Terry v. Ohio* (1968) court documents, on October 31, 1963, in Cleveland, Ohio, Detective Martin McFadden stopped two men named John Terry and Richard Chilton. Detective McFadden was assigned to look for pickpockets and shoplifters in the area and noticed the two men who "didn't look right to him." This was based off his experience of 39 years as a law enforcement officer, 35 of which as an investigator. Detective McFadden observed the two men peeking in the window of a store in the downtown area. They would walk away but returned multiple times to look in the same window. This occurred more than 20 times. A third man, later identified as Katz, was observed at least once speaking to the two men after one of their peeks inside the store. Katz walked away "swiftly" after speaking to Terry and Chilton. Detective McFadden suspected the two men were "casing" the place (i.e., planning a robbery). With this in mind, Detective McFadden followed Terry and Chilton and saw them meet Katz a couple of blocks away in front of a different store. Detective McFadden approached the three men, identified himself as a policeman, and asked their names. The only response was a "mumble." Detective McFadden grabbed Terry and spun him around between the others and patted down the outside of Terry's clothing. McFadden felt a gun. McFadden ordered Chilton and Katz to go inside the store to keep them away from Terry. Detective McFadden removed the gun from Terry's pocket. He then ordered Chilton and Katz to face the wall and raise their hands. They complied, and McFadden recovered a gun from Chilton after patting his outer garments. Katz was also patted down, but a weapon was not felt. Ultimately, Terry and Chilton were arrested and charged with carrying a concealed weapon.

The stop and pat-down in *Terry v. Ohio* (1968) were challenged all the way up to the U.S. Supreme Court. It was concluded that Detective McFadden, through his experience, had "reasonable cause to believe" the three men were acting suspiciously. Based on this reasonable suspicion, stopping the three men for an investigative stop was reasonable. The court held that Detective McFadden had the right to pat down the men for his protection based on the reasonable and articulable facts the men could be planning a robbery and may be armed, which lead to locating concealed weapons. Once the weapons were found, this established probable cause for an arrest for possession of concealed weapons related to Terry and Chilton. This case distinguishes the difference between an investigative stop and an arrest. Detective McFadden didn't have probable cause to arrest the men until after the pat-downs and ultimate recovery of the weapons on the men.

Terry v. Ohio (1968) has long been accepted as a historic court opinion to define investigative stops, detention, seizures, and searches for law enforcement. Field interviews that are based on reasonable and articulable facts will be judged by the Terry stop factors. A consensual approach and conversation between a law enforcement officer and a citizen is different. In these cases, the difference is seizure. You must ask yourself, "Does this citizen have the right to walk away?" If so, the field interview is a consensual contact. If not, the field interview should be based off of a Terry stop.

Victims

Many victims of crimes fear retribution by their victimizers. Witness intimidation is real, and there have been many documented cases where victims of crimes have been further victimized, even killed, for giving information to authorities. You'll want to reassure them of your understanding of their fears but also reassure them that justice should be done and that they are doing the right thing by cooperating. Do not make false promises: You will lose their trust, and in our experience, they will tell people they know about their experiences with you and authorities in general. Integrity in law enforcement is important. **Integrity** is "firm adherence to a code of especially moral or artist values" (Merriam-Webster, n.d.). If your integrity is tainted, you're practically worthless in the criminal justice field. You want everyone to trust you and the profession. Although the courts have accepted law enforcement deception in interviews, we only recommend it on a last-resort basis. **Honesty** is always the best route to take.

First responding officers should be careful when interviewing and/or questioning victims of a crime, especially those who have experienced trauma. One of the first jobs while preparing for victim interviews is to separate all victims and witnesses as soon as possible. If you don't separate these parties, they could influence each other's thoughts and perspectives of what they witnessed. As human beings, we each think and view things differently. If they are left together, they will talk to each other and likely compare each other's statements, thoughts, views, and so on. Interviewing separately will provide many different viewpoints.

Trauma affects humans physically and emotionally. Victims may find themselves in situations where it may be difficult to answer specific questions in an order that establishes the fact and circumstance of a crime. The initial officer should refrain from asking victim's questions that begin with "why" or "tell me how." Using chronological questions can also be a problem because it leads to questions such as "What happened next?" The initial officer should ask open-ended questions to give the victim the opportunity to share more information from their own recall or memory. This provides a traumatized victim a better opportunity to recount a time when they were victimized and had no control over the incident in which they were victimized. One of the best initial interviews techniques for a traumatized victim is to allow them to feel some control over the direction of the interview. One way to start questioning is "Where would you like to start?" Another open-ended beginning question is "Would you tell me what you are able to remember about your experience?" Initial responding officers need to understand that their interview should be basic. Investigators or detectives should follow up with a more detailed interview. **Trauma-informed interviews** should be conducted over time, at least 24-hours after the incident or experience. Trauma-informed interviews should be conducted by investigators or forensic interviewers. Interviews involving trauma that are conducted too soon or by improperly trained interviewers may not provide as valuable information and could harm the process of the investigation.

Failure to separate victims and/or witnesses early can cause investigations to focus in the wrong direction. For example, two victims of a robbery may be standing side by side. However, they can each view the crime and circumstances differently. If the two are kept together and not separated immediately, one can influence the other's thoughts and perspectives of what they actually witnessed or felt. If Victim 1 thought the offender was wearing a blue shirt and Victim 2 thought the offender's shirt was green, one or the other

can influence the other's story. Victim 2 can be charismatic and influence Victim 1 solely because of their confident appearance. If the two victims are kept together, Victim 2 and their confident demeanor could create doubt in Victim 1's belief that the offender was wearing a blue shirt. In that scenario, if Victim 1 tells the responding officer that the shirt was green to match Victim 2, then that may produce problems. If the offender was in fact wearing a blue shirt, the information is tainted early on in the investigation, which could be detrimental to the investigation.

Cognitive Interviews

The cognitive interview technique for crime victims (to include officers) has been empirically supported for years but is a rarely used method. The purpose of a **cognitive interview** is to help the interviewee recall, from memory, what happened. Memory is fickle. Cognitive interviews are designed to reduce leading questions and frequent interruptions by the officer/investigator. Additionally, the cognitive interview technique reduced the use of close-ended questions. Investigators must be very careful to consider how their language can influence a witness statement. For instance, a study has shown that investigators' use of "crashed into" rather than "collided" caused a group of study participants to significantly increase their reporting of the speed a vehicle was traveling prior to a collision. In a study by D. Blake (personal communication, October 15, 2021), investigators asked different groups questions about what they witnessed at a traffic collision. In one question, it was asked how fast the car was traveling when it went through a "yield sign" when, in fact, no sign was present. The participants added the yield sign to their memories of what occurred.

Using cognitive interview techniques can an interviewer help gain rapport because they are less officer-centered and rely more on the subject being interviewed. Once the subject is comfortable talking to the interviewer (for our purposes, law enforcement), their ability to recall and reconstruct circumstances of an incident is better. While the cognitive interview technique can be effective, many officers/investigators don't use the technique fully, because they don't understand it. Most don't ask questions in a logical sequence, which reduces the subject's retrieval of event memory. Additionally, many interviewers interrupt the subject during their answer and deflect the cognitive recall for the subject.

Officers and investigators need to consider children who are victims of crime. Should children be interviewed differently than adults? Absolutely. As an initial responding officer, limited question should be asked of children. Children can be influenced by adults and may feel obligated to give information that they think you "want to hear" and expect them to say. A common procedure for the initial officer is to ask children basic and simple closed-ended questions that don't ask for details. Some of the reasons for such limited information from children include avoiding multiple interviews with different personnel and, most importantly, not revictimizing the child by asking detailed questions. If you must interview a child beyond some basic questions, consider using other resources, such as child advocacy centers, to assist with the interview. Some states offer assistance through their department of children's services. Best practice is to utilize resources that are specially geared to interviewing children.

Children who are victims should go through a forensic interview follow-up process to obtain accurate and detailed information. A **forensic interview** is an open-ended conversation with a child that is conducted by a trained professional, commonly a child psychologist or child specialist, that is not leading and related to possible traumatic events that the child may have experienced or witnessed. Children are placed in a controlled but comfortable environment with the interviewer. The environment is child-friendly and may contain toys or books to help comfort the child.

Victim interviews are critical in any investigation. However, first responders and investigators should understand the importance of trauma-informed interviews, cognitive interview techniques, and forensic interviews. In our experience, these can be overlooked and may jeopardize the officer's/investigator's ability to gather the most accurate information in their investigation.

In summary, you'll want to ensure your interviews yield good results and accurate information. The facts you gain from an interview may later be used during an interrogation, an investigation, and intelligence sharing.

The purpose of the interview is to identify leads to additional evidence. It should support existing physical evidence and facts that are critical to the investigation that will later likely need to be proved in court or in a hearing. Experienced investigators often fail to adequately assist victims, witnesses, and suspects to accurately recall incidents, which, in turn, reduces the quality of information received and put out. To gain the most from an interview, you'll want to prepare as much as you can in advance. Try to avoid bad habits and shortcuts that can lead to you missing important details.

Many interviewers attempt to rush the interview, which results in inaccurate information and unhappy interviewees. When interviewing, you should always listen carefully to everything the interviewee has to say. Listening selectively for key statements may cause you to overlook vital information and cause the interviewee to feel like you don't value their time and energy.

Likewise, allow the interviewee to speak, even if you don't think they're saying anything useful or relevant. You can't listen well if you are doing most of the talking, and the interviewee might feel like they can't get a word in edgewise. Finally, keep your and their emotions down. People often struggle to communicate when they are agitated or in a heightened state of emotions (Holmes, 2013).

Cognitive interviews have been proven highly effective. McLeod (2010) found that witnesses recalled 60% more information through this process. Holmes (2013) has identified six phases to cognitive interviews:

1. introduction: Be sure to let the interviewer know why you speaking with them. Your goal is to help them settle in and emphasize the importance of providing accurate information.

2. establishing rapport: Don't just jump straight into the interview! Taking a few minutes to ask the interviewee a few personal questions will help you show empathy and establish a foundational relationship with the interviewee. Always strive to listen carefully and find similarities between yourself and the person you interview.

3. interview: Once you begin the interview proper, continue to actively listen. You might prompt the interviewee to begin with an open-ended question that will provide a narrative response, like "Tell me what happened." Other useful tools include having them draw the scene or having them close their eyes to better visualize what happened.

4. follow-up: Ask neutral questions to clarify information as needed. You don't want to lead the interviewee. For example, you might ask, "Is there anything you can remember that we haven't already covered?" Tip: Try having the interviewee recall events in reverse order. This will provide a new perspective and may help them remember new details.

5. challenge: Are details not lining up? Don't be afraid to respectfully challenge any contradictions that arise. Just be sure to remain calm, respectful, and neutral.

6. closing: Don't end abruptly. You want to retain the rapport you have developed throughout the interview and encourage them to reach out if they remember anything later. Thank them for their time and gently emphasize how critical this information is.

Witnesses

Information gathering takes place even before your interview. You will want to find out as much as you can, time permitting, about your witness. Again, reviewing all reports may assist you with your interview, but keep an open mind. Most people feel a little nervous about talking to authorities. This can be due to not wanting to be branded as a "snitch" or real fears for their safety due to possible retaliation. Try to calm down any anxiety. If legally allowed, record the interview. If not allowed, try not to take notes immediately. Write down only what you need. Many of the same factors that were mentioned in victim interviews can also be applied to witness interviews.

Let them do most of the talking. You are on a fact-finding mission, so you will do everything you can do to encourage them to use their memory as accurately as possible to respond in detail to your questioning. Ask open-ended questions that require more than a yes-or-no answer or an easy answer, such as "How tall was he?" or "What race would you say he was?" Instead ask, "What did he look like?" Let them go into details.

Tailoring your questioning to their answers so that they maintain their train of thought is sometimes called "being on a roll." Do not "lead" the witness. You've probably seen in court or on TV where a defense attorney protests, "Objection, Your Honor! He's leading the witness!" and the judge throws that testimony out. You want your information to be obtained without prejudice. Understand that not all witnesses may have viewed an incident or condition in the same way. It does not necessarily mean they are lying. If the witness is a child, they may not be able to verbalize things in detail, but they can still point to a picture and make hand and body gestures that may be important to the case. You'll want to review all witness statements for consistencies, especially on key points, and chalk minor discrepancies up to differences in location/viewpoint, time, and effect. This underlines the importance of having good and accurate witness and incident reports. We have a saying in the business: "Garbage in, garbage out." The quality of your work and case will suffer and you and your agency could even be sued if you do not ensure quality. On the other hand, if your report and peers are too close, you may be accused of collusion and corruption to cloud the facts.

Only refocus their conversation, and do it tactfully, if they are getting way off topic and they start repeating themselves more than once. Repeat back what they've said periodically to verify that's what they meant and ask follow-up questions if necessary. Then let them go into more detail. Repeat this process until you feel satisfied you have gained the most accurate information you can.

You'll want to ask them not to discuss your conversation with other people to avoid tainting the case. While some people are very talkative, as described previously, witness intimidation can be a major factor, so you may be surprised how many people won't say much or anything. Remember, most people don't want to be branded a snitch or informant for their own good.

Always finish up the interview by asking if there is anything else they'd like to say. Give them your card and number if appropriate and let them know they can call you if they remember anything else. You'd be surprised how often they call you back or become a future witness in a different incident. Good witnesses are hard to come by, so that contact can come in handy later.

Interview Conduct

When interviewing witnesses, you will want to appear professional. You do not want to have a scowl on your face, but you don't want be overly familiar either. Most interviews in police and corrections work are for serious matters.

Make sure you introduce yourself properly and explain the purpose of the interview. You've probably heard the phrase "A good impression is a lasting impression." Also, to take a wise saying from poet Maya Angelou, "People won't remember what you said, they'll remember how you made them feel." It is important to speak to people you are interviewing with dignity and respect.

It should go something like this: "Hello, Mr./Mrs. ____. My name is Gabe Morales, and my job is to ____. We need to talk so we can ____." Only give general background, such as "Last Monday, January 25th, there was an assault at ____. What can you tell me about that?"

In this manner, you can cut off most argumentized reasons for not cooperating. You are being polite and getting right down to the point. Some people will still become verbally combative and are quick to escalate not matter how good you are. Make it clear that they can get out of the interview a lot quicker with cooperation. Of course, factors such as whether the interview is in a controlled environment will also come into play. You want to be at an advantage during the process no matter where it occurs. I can recall several instances where an inmate was very agitated. To continue with the interview may have escalated into a physical use of force incident, so I rescheduled it: "I, Gabe Morales, during the initial classification process, attempted to interview ____. The subject was not cooperative, so I asked them to return to their unit. Subject did so without further incident."

In most of these cases, I had 72 hours, not counting weekends, to get them classified. They could not get into programs or get extra privileges, order commissary, and so on until they were classified, so word got around to most offenders that it was to their own advantage to cooperate.

Another way to gain cooperation and rapport is to compliment people you're interviewing. This is a form of manipulation. They do it; we do it. This should not be confused with harassment or unwanted looks or conversation. I would often mirror their body movements, such as hand gestures, or lean back in my chair a little more to gain unconscious trust and rapport.

Usually, when people feel good about themselves, they feel more confident about questioning. My interactions would often go something like this:

Officer: So, how are you? What have you been up to lately?

Interviewee: Oh, I was in rehab ... was doing good but got depressed and relapsed.

Officer: That's too bad, but you can get back on your feet again. Let's see if we can get you into a program that might help after I'm done here.

Interviewee: Thanks, Mr. Morales! I need some help, man. I need to get my life back together.

Officer: That's good to hear. I hope you do that. Now let's get through a few questions.

I was sincere, genuine, and showed some empathy for them and their situation. I offered to help, and they in return were more than happy to cooperate. This harmonic technique of give and take is sometimes called "neuro-linguistic programming" (Bandler & Grinder, 1988).

It is also important to recognize that we all learn and process information in different ways. Some of us are auditory learners. Others are visual learners. Still others are mostly hands-on learners or even a combination of these three main ways of understanding and relaying information. It is OK to ask what their main learning style is and to relay information in a way they feel most comfortable. For instance, a visual learner may not be able to explain something as well as they can draw it or make a map of where certain individuals or things were during an incident in question. Even investigators often use these techniques, in addition to reports, for others to better understand what actually occurred.

Consider how any physical evidence or crime scene forensics may contrast with witness statements. Also remember, in spite of all the technological advances in policing, most cases are still solved because of good interviews and interrogations. Your interview skills will become better with practice, but don't fret if you're a novice. Veteran investigators and counselor often become too comfortable and make sloppy mistakes. Learn good basics, improve on them, and never be too old to learn new and better methods of doing business.

Many times, we have a failure to ask questions that account for human attention. We often ask, "Did you see X?" They may have seen X, or they may not have, but sometimes *when* you saw X is most important. So, the question should be prefaced with, "What was your focus of attention during X time span? Did you see X? Were you focused on X the entire time, or were you scanning and looking at other things?" The issue is that the environment can change in the blink of an eye. Witnesses often divide their attention amongst various things and don't always see the entirety: They see pieces and then—due to proven human memory issues—the witness may just fill in the blanks. This is a problem in some cases.

Suspects

Suspect interviews are nonaccusatory—that is, an interview process that is not accusing a subject of specific wrongdoing. Nonaccusatory interviews allow the subject of the interview to be more comfortable. To prepare for suspect interviews, first determine what the goal of the interview is. The goal of any interview is to seek the facts. A common goal for interviewing a suspect in an investigation is to link evidence to the suspect or connect the suspect to a crime or crimes. It should be noted that not all suspects are the ones who committed the crime being investigated. Therefore, it is equally important to eliminate them as a suspect, and an interview is the first step. If the suspect's interview can corroborate that they weren't involved, it's a successful interview too. Questioning should not be confrontational. It's an opportunity to establish rapport with the potential suspect. A good interviewer will be a good listener, who asks open-ended questions. An open-ended question allows for an explanation to the answer. Interviews can also establish a baseline of the suspect's behavior. A formal interview will be the first documented statement by a suspect. This establishes a foundation of events from the suspect's perspective. While most investigators seek an admission or confession before the initial interview, proving omissions from the first interviews is just as beneficial. For example, suppose a suspect tells you that he was out of town on the day of the crime, but you have video surveillance from a local business near the crime scene of the suspect that proves otherwise. The ability to use evidence to disprove the suspect's statement from their first interview can be just as beneficial as an admission. It shows the suspect is lying.

You'll want to review prior reports, photographs, and information in the case file before conducting a suspect interview, including reviewing their personal information. The more information that can be gained about the person you plan to interview, they better prepared you will be. This information may not always be related to the crime or investigation. Personal information, such as their history (e.g., family, work, crime, etc.) and their lifestyle, educational background, and so on is important, especially to develop rapport. Some things to keep in mind while preparing for or during the interview include the following:

- Discover as much information as possible about the suspect, including if they have children or not. If they have children and so do you, you can build rapport by discussing this and comparing experiences.

- Relay little to no information about the case initially to the suspect.

- Pay close attention to the answers. How did they respond?

  - Look at their body language. Did their head go down in a defeated posture? This could include obvious indicators of truthfulness and concern.

  - Do they respond with answers based on their knowledge, or is it what "someone" told them?

  - Listen for the verbiage they use.

- If there is a missing child or other victim, are they referring to them in the past tense? If a body hasn't been found yet, why would they assume they are dead?

Information Gathering

Among the most important traits in information seeking and in order to be a successful interviewer are empathy, communication and professionalism. All three of these characteristics send a message to the subject that the interviewer is an honorable trustworthy person, who has all of the necessary evidence, and understands the feelings of anxiety and possible guilt within the subject. Your primary initial purpose is to gather as much information as possible to make sure you, and individuals who later review your case in a trial or hearing, have an accurate picture of what occurred. The interviewee may also feel defensive so you can say things like, "You and I know this looks bad. Help me clear your name by being as truthful now as you can be. I only want to find out who did it and get the right person."

Purpose

The purpose for interviews is to gather information to develop leads, motives, suspects, and other evidence of criminal activity. Interviews can be formal or informal in nature. Interviews are nothing more than a gathering of information. When conducting interviews, you must be careful to listen and gather information rather than talk too much and divulge information to the interviewee, whether it's a victim, witness, suspect, or offender. Typically, an interview should complete the five "W's" (Who, What, When Why, and Where?) and one "H" (How?).

Background

Knowledge is power. As many attorneys will say, "Never ask a question you don't know the answer to." Many investigators go into an interview with inadequate information on both the person they are talking to as well as the subject matter they will discuss. This prevents rapport. With no rapport and no plan, you're talking in circles with a person. Using our four I's, investigate what has happened first, gather as much intelligence about the incident and the people who are either involved and/or witnesses, then enter an interview and/or interrogation with the mindset that your their "old friend" just trying to catch up on what happened (J. Sparks, personal communication, February 2023).

If time is available, it is best to obtain background information on the person(s) being interviewed. Various sources can be utilized to develop as much background information as possible on the interviewee. First, law enforcement personnel should always review their in-house incident reports, as well as local agency reports where the subject is known to frequent. Obtaining a driver's license status and history, criminal history, and vehicle information may also be helpful. There are privately operated databases that have open record information available. Most of those databases are subscriber-based and may charge an agency or investigator to use the system.

You may need to obtain background information about a victim before interviewing a suspect. **Victimology**, the study of a victim, their trends or patterns, social status, and interacts, may develop leads and/or motives to a criminal investigation to link the victim to an offender. In our experience, the more information that you can gather about the victim at the time of crime, the more likely you are to solve the case.

Evidence

One consideration is the use of evidence during an interview. However, evidence is tangible. It's not suggested to have evidence laying out for the interviewee to see, touch, or risk destroying. If you plan to discuss evidence during an interview, the use of photographs of evidence is recommended. Some investigators may display mounds of evidence to intimidate the interviewee. This tactic could have positive and negative effects on the outcome of the interview. One may feel the evidence is stacked against them after seeing a mound of evidence boxes or envelopes, which could lead to a confession during the interview process. Using this same example, just the opposite may occur; it could lead to the subject not being willing to speak at all. Another potential problem when a subject sees a mound of evidence at the table is their attempt to get the investigator to "show their cards." The suspect may challenge a suggestion or allegation by saying, "Show me the evidence that I committed the crime." If the subject believes the investigator is bluffing, they may ask for evidence (that should be on the table) to show proof of the allegation. Since an interview is a fact-seeking mission, displaying evidence (even as a prop, which will be discussed later) is not recommended.

Case File

You'll want to create a new case file for your interview and/or investigation. Having the case file and investigative documents readily available during an interview is optional. While it's not required to have a prepared case file during an interview, having a folder in hand while conducting an interview on a suspect is recommended. It may indicate preparedness. If a case file is available, an investigator may refer to the file during the interview's question-and-answer phase to reference or gauge the answers given. Just remember the interview is fact seeking, not confrontational. Using a case file could direct an investigator to be more confrontational, especially if the information from the interview is contradictory to the information in the case file. Interviews are neither the time nor place to confront inconsistencies. In those cases, the investigator may leak out valuable information to confront the inconsistent statement(s). Below is a list of some possible documents commonly kept in an investigative case file:

- Initial incident report
- Supplement reports
  - Reports from all law enforcement involved in the investigation
- Investigative actions
  - To-do list
  - Timeline
  - Index of investigative resources
- Background information
  - On the incident
  - On the victim, potential witness, and/or suspects
- List of evidence
  - Index of evidence
  - Lab reports
  - Photographs or videos
- Intelligence or information gathered
- Correspondence or news articles related to the case
- Written statements
- Court documents
  - Search warrants, arrest warrants, court orders, and the like

Props

Using props during an interview is optional. **Props** are material used to give an appearance that there is more meaning or purpose than there actually is. Props could be video tapes, CDs, DVDs, digital media

storage devices, and so on. Props are sometimes used by investigators to give the appearance that the investigation is full or has a wealth of evidence. Props are typically a form of deception. While the Supreme Court has upheld the use of deceptive props during interviews (*United States v. Russell*, 1973), it's not always recommended. Props, such as a stack of video tapes or multiple media storage devices to portray evidence of surveillance video of a crime or a recording of an accomplice's admission of guilt, have been used to illicit information from a suspect. The props give the impression that there is evidence to support the investigator's conclusion. One other common prop is a fingerprint that the investigator may indicate was recovered from a crime scene and is (falsely) identified as the suspect's, thus putting the suspect at the scene of the crime. In *Oregon v. Mathiason* (1977), this strategy was used. Officers falsely told a burglary suspect they had lifted his fingerprints at the crime scene. The suspect eventually confessed to the crime. In fact, the officers had not recovered the suspect's fingerprints. The court held that the confession was admissible although it was obtained by a false statement about nonexistent evidence.

Locations

The location of an interview can be critical to its success. Interviews can be conducted in various locations. A field interview on the street is common for police officers. Detectives conduct interviews to follow-up on investigations at many different locations, including but not limited to homes, businesses, the street, hospitals, etc. Interviews are also conducted in jails and prisons; it may be during the booking process or for many other institutional needs.

Institution

Interviews in a correctional setting may be a little more difficult since many of the interviewees are hardened criminals. Correctional interviews have been discussed previously in this chapter. This section provides information that pertains to the institution as the setting of the interview versus interviews conducted outside of a controlled environment. Institutions or correctional settings can provide some limitations. This section will provide details from a violent crime that occurred in a correctional facility. This real-life example is of a criminal investigation that involved interviewing over 100 inmates after a gang-related inmate-on-inmate homicide in a prison. One inmate was brutally stabbed in the chest by a group of inmates. The victim inmate had confronted a group of rival gang members and told them that they had to leave to "compound," or housing unit. A physical confrontation occurred resulting in the death of one inmate.

To properly investigate the crime, each inmate in the prison pod was interviewed. As you could imagine, many of the inmates didn't want to be involved or labeled as a "snitch." The strategy that worked best was to allow each inmate a designated time allotted to be interviewed. If an inmate told an investigator that they didn't see or hear anything, it was documented, but they weren't allowed to just stand up and walk away. It was explained that everyone was given an allotted time to speak with investigators. It was further explained that for the safety of each inmate and the institution, each inmate would stay in the interview room until the allotted time was fulfilled. Most inmates could not sit quietly for a few minutes without saying anything. This technique was used on over 100 inmates. Some even had to be stopped from continuing their statement because their time had elapsed. In those instances, the inmate was told that they may be removed from the housing unit at a later date or transferred to another facility so an investigator

FIGURE 2.1 Photo Taken by Coauthor Korey Cooper in an Interview in a Correctional Facility After a Gang Fight

could follow-up with them. When violent incidents occurred, it was not uncommon for the housing unit to be transferred to different facilities. Therefore, the cooperating inmates couldn't be immediately identified as cooperators just because they were transferred. By the end of the housing unit interviews, investigators had identified all of the offenders involved in the homicide. Additionally, the weapon that was used was also recovered and the inmate that provided the homemade weapon was identified.

Even in a correctional institution, most of the inmates want to do what's right, but cooperating with the investigators comes at a cost sometimes. However, if the investigators gain rapport and are upfront and honest with the inmate, many will talk and do the right thing to help the investigation. The inmates were told that they were witnesses to a crime and if the case went to trial, they were subject to being called to testify. They already knew that; they are criminals themselves. In a jail or prison environment, interviews can be successful. Most of the time, it takes initiative and effort.

Controlled Environment

If you are conducting an interview in the police station or detective's office, ensure that seating arrangements allow for reading body language and eye contact. These "play an important part in good communications" (University of Illinois, n.d.). Body language is important. **Body language** is nonverbal communication a person's body exhibits through movement or gestures. This movement can be conscious or nonconscious communication throughout the body, including eyes, posture, body, and limbs. It is estimated that nonverbal communication is about 90% of human communication, which includes 60% body language and 30% tone or voice projection. **Nonverbal communication** is the communication of information through channels other than written or spoken word. The other 10% is verbal or the message (Wicklander & Zulawski, 2007). That's why it's so important to understand body language when you are interviewing someone. It's not always about what the subject is saying but how they are saying it. A good investigator may watch the subject's actions more than they listen to what they are saying.

You'll want to separate the witnesses out of sight and hearing distance away from each other into a controlled environment, if possible. If you can transport them separately to avoid them getting together and collaborating their story, then all the better We realize in some small departments this may not always be possible. If it has been documented that the witness has previously been reliable in past cases, that is important to note for credibility reasons. You should control the access of multiple victims, witnesses, and/or suspects in any case. Be mindful of your obligations (or lack thereof) by law to restrict any of these persons. From our experience, we suggest that you separate anyone that can provide information in your investigation in order to obtain the best information from their perspective. If you don't have legal right to seize a person, this could affect your ability to separate multiple people in an investigation. You must understand the consequences if you cannot separate potential subjects you need to interview, and that is people can influence other people and their decision making.

FIGURE 2.2 Columbia, TN, Police Department's Soft Room

One option in a controlled environment is a soft room. A *soft room* is a room is a controlled environment, typically at the police department, children's services, or another location, such as a forensic interviewers office. Commonly used for children or victims of trauma, this room provides a more comfortable approach to interviews. Investigations can use a soft room with sexual assault victims to provide a safe place, where they may feel more comfortable as compared to the generic police interview room that is designed to make people feel uncomfortable. A soft room has the appearance of a home living room with a sofa, chairs, photographs on the walls, a lamp, kids toys, table, and so on (see Figure 2.2).

Uncontrolled Environment

An uncontrolled environment could be a field interview, as mentioned above. Other uncontrolled environments include initial investigative responses and active crime scenes. In an uncontrolled environment, you will not likely have the advantage of planning. Interviews, in any form, heavily rely upon gaining rapport with the subject being interviewed. In an uncontrolled environment, finding a connecting point with the interviewee is critical. Talking to the subject with respect can also help build rapport. Consider a stranger walking up to you and starting a conversation. If the stranger was nice and respectable, would you speak to them? Most likely, yes. If the stranger connected with you, maybe through a common interest, would you continue to talk or walk away? Use this same mindset to approach subjects that you want to interview, and you can be successful. In a field interview, an officer may approach a person who they reasonably believe may be involved in criminal activity or witnessed criminal activity. The way that officer approaches and talks to the subject may be the difference in obtaining information or not.

Strategies

It's important to make sure the interview room or area that you plan to conduct a controlled interview in is set up properly. Room setup strategies may differ depending on the type of interview you are conducting, be it a suspect, witness, or victim. The room should be a comfortable setting, even for the suspect at this stage. An example of a comfortable setting is a private room as opposed to an open office space. Some considerations in preparing the interview room include but are not limited to reducing physical barriers (e.g., tables or furniture) and seating arrangement. Below are examples of a seating arrangement for an interview, without and with a desk. Note there are no barriers or furniture. Also notice that the subject is close to the door and nothing is between the subject and the door. That is a key component to the arrangement.

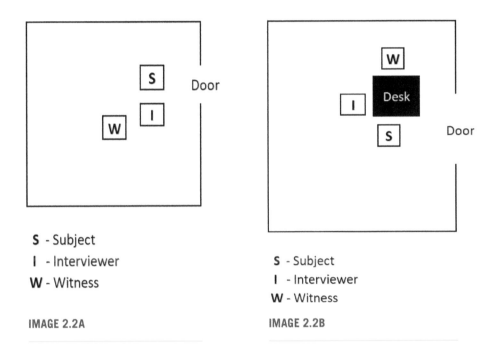

S - Subject
I - Interviewer
W - Witness

IMAGE 2.2A

S - Subject
I - Interviewer
W - Witness

IMAGE 2.2B

During an interview, a potential suspect (and even a crime victim or witness) is free to go at any time. While this setup may be more specific to a suspect interview, it is designed to ensure there is nothing preventing the suspect from "walking away." This helps if voluntariness of a suspect is being challenged in court. **Voluntariness** is the state of being free without constraint. A defense attorney may argue if a suspect provided a statement voluntarily or the suspect believed they weren't free to leave and forced to provide a statement.

There may be times when an interview turns into an interrogation. When the courts look at voluntary statements, they look at three primary area to determine the voluntariness of a statement or confession:

- methods used by law enforcement

- the suspect's degree of susceptibility

- the conditions under which the statement was received

The 14th Amendment of the U.S. Constitution provides due process protection to citizens as it relates to statements to law enforcement and voluntariness. Interrogations will be covered in other chapters and that's when a challenge of voluntariness is used most. A violation of the 14th Amendment is the most egregious of all violations and can subsequently taint all it touches in a criminal investigation.

Correctional interviews are a little different than interviews conducted on the street or in a specific criminal investigation. In some cases, you do not need to get permission from a supervisor or notify peers in advance that you are going into an interview. It could be that the interview is a routine expectation from your bosses, such as a classification interview in jail. It will still be documented on paper or via computer in case there is an issue later on. If it is a routine interview, you may not need to do anything—or little—to notify your peers. It is considered a professional courtesy to provide your interview list to your peers so they don't interview the same individual(s) for the same purpose.

MORALES

I can't tell you how many times this became an embarrassment, not to mention a waste of time, when an inmate never notified me that they were already classified during a previous interview. Several times after and when we were halfway through the entire process, they would finally let me know somebody already asked them the very same questions. The previous interview and classification record had not yet been entered into the system, so I did not know it was already conducted. Just a simple heads up and communication between peers can avoid this. Or you can ask at the beginning of an interview, "When was the last time you were interviewed by one of our staff?"

In more complex interviews, you may want a peer to sit in as a witness. If both of you are going to question the individual, not necessarily interrogate, then you will want to strategize on a game plan. You may also need to explain to the interviewee why your partner is sitting in, such as to translate or because there was a previous complaint of unfair treatment, also known as CYA (cover your a**).

Goals

One common goal of any interview is to seek facts. This is done by determining the five "W's" and the "H": Who? What? When? Where? Why? How? These questions should always be part of the goal of any interview.

- who: Who was involved (suspect, victim), and what are their identifiers (name, address, sex, age, etc.)? Who witnessed the crime(s)? Who could have benefited from the crime?

- what: What crime occurred? What did the interviewee eyewitness? What did they hear or learn by their senses (smell, sound, touch, taste, etc.)? What connection do they have to the scene, if any? What was damaged? What was moved? What is a possible motive?

- when: When was the crime committed? When did they last see or speak to the victim, another witness, offender, and so on? When did they hear, see, or learn of what they previously mentioned?

- where: Where did the crime occur? In there a secondary scene? Where did the victim(s)/offender(s) come from or go to?

- why: Why did the crime occur? Why was the interviewee present? Why did they leave? Why was an object damaged? Why was an object moved?

- how: How did the crime occur? How did the suspect, offender, victim, and so on arrive or leave? As a follow-up to the answers of any "W" questions, ask, "How?"

Personnel

Interviews may be conducted by a sole investigator/officer. If conducted by more than one, you should identify roles as explained in the Strategies section above. One should concentrate on questioning, and the other should take notes from the interview. If somebody outside of normal interview staff is brought in, such as a nurse or psychiatric staff, it should be explained why they are there to encourage cooperation.

Having too many people in an interview can be distracting to the interviewee and investigator/officer. No more than two are recommended. Some departments have a mirrored window or camera system so that others can monitor interviews in a controlled environment. This strategy can assist the interviewer(s) with monitoring body language of the interviewee, it provides an extra set of ears to listen to the conversation, and it helps with recording the interview. There are many different techniques that agencies use in these situations for the monitoring investigators to communicate with the interviewing investigators. Some simply use a messaging system and/or other applications may discuss their review or finding during a break in the interview process. Just remember that any form of communication, such as messaging or written communication, is discoverable in criminal cases.

Documentation

Whether you are just starting out in your career or you are a veteran, you'll always want to make sure you are prepared for an interview. If physically and legal able, you'll want to run a criminal rap sheet (criminal history) of the individual. This would include but is not limited to a National Crime Information Center (NCIC) crime history request, a departmental call history and/or incident reports, intelligence or information bulletins, or any agency documents related to the subject you are questioning. Of course, it would be best utilized before any interview, if available. You'll want to review other online and written records. This includes open-source records, databases, or third-party information that can help you know more about a subject. Sometimes state fusion centers or a Regional Information Sharing System (RISS NET) can provide much of the information about a subject upon request. You may also want to read past interviews to gauge behaviors, but keep an open mind for your new interview.

As an investigator, if you have time to gather information on a specific person who you plan to interview, then it is highly recommended to research that person. Do they have no criminal record or a long criminal record? Are they very young or old? This is when the criminal history and open-source record search can be helpful, especially if the interviewee is the suspect of a crime. This can make a big difference in their replies and in your approach. If you interview a person who you suspect is involved in a crime and they have served penitentiary time for a similar crime, what is the likelihood that they will be forthcoming?

Maybe not as much. That may be when you spend a lot more time on rapport building. Look for something you may have in common, like hobbies, interests, family, children, and so on. Just be careful here. It's not suggested to confide personal information about your family in this situation.

When you are conducting your initial interview and rapport-building session of the interview, you should establish some baselines. Ask question that you know the answers to, and determine the difference between truthful responses and deceptive responses, to include the body language associated with those responses. It could be the subject's eyes, looking to the right or left, up or down. Posture changes could also indicate truthfulness and deceptiveness. If you ask a question that has a deceptive response, the subject may use their hands to rub their face, mouth, or head. Maybe the subject wiggles their leg abruptly when being deceptive.

Documentation should also include taking notes from the interview. One should document verbatim (word for word) every response from the interview. Highlighting specifics and using bullet points on key information is suggested. Along with notes, many interviews are now audio and video recorded. However, it's not suggested to relay on electronic equipment to document your interview. Electronic equipment can fail, so being dependent solely on this type of equipment is not suggested.

Interviews can be structured or unstructured. The University of Illinois (n.d.) provides a resource for these interview approaches. While they are addressing job interviews, this information can apply to the criminal justice system as well. During structured interviews, the interviewer asks a set of prepared questions tailored to the interviewee, the investigation, and any other relevant circumstances. For instance, new inmates undergo a structured classification interview before being released to the facility's general population. Answers to structured questions can be easily recorded and compared to responses from other interviewees to identify patterns and flag crucial details. Unstructured interviews, on the other hand, are looser and unplanned. These are not scripted or necessarily asked in a predetermined manner. The danger with an unstructured approach is that the interviewer may end up asking generic questions that don't provide much detail.

Still, whether highly structured or more unstructured, the interviewer should know the key details of the interviewee and events surrounding the interview. Probe for more detailed answers than just a simple yes or no. For instance, if you ask if they are suicidal, they may answer, "No," but their body language and tone may indicate a "Maybe" or a "Yes." A true professional will pick up on these signals and dig deeper into the answer.

It's best not to script your follow-up questions. Also, you should give the interviewee time to think about their response. Just because they are pausing before answering does not necessarily mean they are trying to think of a lie to tell you.

On the other hand, if they are too quick to answer, they may not be forthcoming and may be just trying to get through your questioning as quickly as possible. Remember, this is an interview, not an interrogation. While some questioning may be the same or similar, they are usually done for different purposes. We will discuss the differences between an interview and an interrogation more in Part II of this book.

There are few occasions where you'll have to go into an interview blind, so do your homework. You may have to take some initial information from witnesses, such as their documenting their contacts, but the vast majority of the time, you will be able to get back to these individuals later for a more thorough interview.

References

Bandler, R., & Grinder, J. (1988). *Reframing: Neuro-linguistic programming and the transformation of meaning*. Real People Press.

Hochstetler, A., Williams, J. P., & Copes, H. (2010). "That's not who I am": How offenders commit violent acts and reject authentically violent selves. *Justice Quarterly, 27*(4), 492–516. Htttps://doi.org/10.1080/07418820903173344

Holmes, B. (2013, July 12). *Focusing on your interview technique: The cognitive interview process*. PInow. https://www.pinow.com/articles/1672/focusing-on-your-interview-technique-the-cognitive-interview-process

Katz v. United States, 389 U.S. 347 (1967). https://www.oyez.org/cases/1967/35

Lindegaard, M. R. (2010). *Method, actor and context triangulations: Knowing what happened during criminal events and the motivations for getting involved*. Office of Justice Programs. https://www.ojp.gov/ncjrs/virtual-library/abstracts/method-actor-and-context-triangulations-knowing-what-happened

McLeod, S. A. (2023, June 15). *Cognitive interview technique*. SimplyPsychology. http://www.simplypsychology.org/cognitive-interview.html

Merriam-Webster. (n.d.). Integrity. In *Merriam-Webster.com dictionary*. Retrieved November 4, 2022, from https://www.merriam-webster.com/dictionary/integrity

Oregon v. Mathiason, 429 U.S. 492 (1977). https://www.oyez.org/cases/1976/76-201

Terry v. Ohio, 392 U.S. 1 (1968). https://www.oyez.org/cases/1967/67

United States v. Russell, 411 U.S. 423 (1973). https://www.oyez.org/cases/1972/71-1585

University of Illinois. (n.d.). *Interview approaches*. https://www.hr.uillinois.edu/UserFiles/Servers/Server_4208/File/ERHR/Recruiting/InterviewApproaches.pdf

Wicklander, D. E., & Zulawski, D. E. (2007). *Interviewing and interrogation: Non-verbal cues*. Wicklander-Zulawski & Associates. https://www.w-z.com/wp-content/uploads/2012/10/LP-Mag-mar-apr-2007.pdf

CHAPTER 3

Conducting Interviews

Purpose

There are two sources of information an individual can offer an investigator during an interview. The first is investigative information (e.g., establishing a person's alibi, determining what a person was and heard, or finding out what really occurred in a crime). Investigative information primarily represents physical or circumstantial evidence, which establishes the facts used to identify the guilty in the court of criminal law. **Evidence** is any material (physical, court exhibit, or testimony) used to prove a crime was committed The second type of information that can be gathered in an interview is behavioral information. This includes things such as attitude, eye contact, posture, hands and leg movements, and verbal statement. When interviewing a subject, you should be objective rather than subjective. When we are subjective, we act upon preconceived notions or what we think are facts instead of taking things for what they actually are.

Building Rapport

One of the most important elements of communications is developing rapport between individuals involved in a discussion. Some people may think that entails liking or sympathizing with an individual. This is not the case. When interviewing a child molester or mass murderer, you will likely feel some negative emotional responses to the subject/interviewee when you learn of some of the ugly details of the crime they may have committed. But it is important to remember that everybody in the United States should be considered innocent until proven guilty in a court of law, and even then, you may find yourself having to reinterview the subject later in the future as an informant or to gather information on future cases. If the subject and you had poor communications and little rapport, that is likely to hinder your future investigations and interactions.

Building rapport takes work, and we will discuss what it takes to build common ground. This does not mean you trust or sympathize with an individual but that you understand the importance of good communications. You do not need to sympathize with somebody to empathize with them or to at least be cordial. Building rapport is strongly supported by most law enforcement and counseling professionals in their efforts to encourage voluntary statements and hopefully increase the accuracy of adult eyewitness reports and information obtained from suspects. Paraphrasing as Vallano and colleagues (2015) note, "Little data exists regarding how law enforcement interviewers actually define and build rapport in real-world investigations" (p. 371).

Common Ground

Developing **rapport** with the person being interviewed is the key to any successful interview. It is important that the interviewee gets the opportunity to talk about themselves. This allows the interviewer to determine what interests or common ground they have with the person being interviewed. The art of establishing rapport is nothing more than a strategic sales pitch. For example, an officer/investigator may start an interview like this:

Investigator: Hello John, my name is Korey. I'm an investigator with the State Police. Tell me a little bit about yourself.

John: I'm John Doe. I worked at _____. I'm married to Jane Doe. We have three kids.

Investigator: You have three kids ... boys or girls?

John: Two girls and one boy.

Investigator: How old?

John: The girls are twins, age 16. The boy is 12.

Investigator: Wow, two 16-year-old girls. I have a 18-year-old girl, so I know a little about what you are going through there. I also have a younger son. I couldn't imagine having twins.

During this brief conversation, the investigator started developing rapport by showing some common ground with them both having children. Additionally, the investigator laid the ground to continue the conversation by saying that they couldn't imagine having twins. This allows the interviewee the opportunity to openly talk about raising twins. The conversation should go back and forth. In our experience, as the conversation continues, the interviewee becomes more relaxed and comfortable with the interview.

To assist with developing rapport, an officer/investigator can use small talk. This is a conversation related to nonthreatening topics that have nothing to do with the purpose of the interview. It is a tactic to reduce nervousness of the subject. It can provide additional time to find common connections with the subject where their answers have no consequence. This can also establish a baseline of behavioral norms related to questions and answers.

The conversation should take some time. You should not rush through this process. This is a critical step. As you are developing rapport through conversation and common ground, you can also start to determine behavioral norms for the subject, such as in this example:

Investigator: John, I need to get some basic identifiers. Please spell your name out for me to make sure I have it right. I understand it's a common name, but some people spell it differently.

John: J-O-H-N D-O-E.

Investigator: What is your date of birth?

John: January 1, 2000.

Investigator: A New Year's baby, huh? And even a new century?

John: Yes, I ... (This should start some additional conversation.)

Investigator: Where are you employed?

John: ABC Electric.

Investigator: What do you do there?

John: I'm a lineman.

Investigator: What does that consist of? (This open-ended question allows for explanation.)

The conversation above continues the process of developing rapport. It also allows you to observation behavioral norms, verbal and nonverbal, to questions. These norms should be nondeceptive unless the subject is lying. That's where your background and interviewing planning, discussed in Chapter 2, help you with determining the norm. If you conducted a thorough background and interview plan, you should already know the answers to the questions that you are asking. Therefore, you should be able to see and measure what a normal nondeceptive reaction is.

A verbal norm may include tone or projection of voice, if long or short answers are common, the type of words the subject uses, and so on. Is the subject soft-spoken or loud? Does their voice project louder if they want to emphasize something? As the subject answers your open-ended questions, do they just answer the question or do they explain every detail? For example, the question above related to what a lineman does. If the answer is as simple as "I climb poles and fix broken lines," it basically explains a duty of the job. However, if the subject offers a 10-miunute detailed explanation of the job, then it can be determined that their norm is being a talker. To be fair, you should measure those type of questions with multiple questions/answers, but if you have someone who likes to talk, you will certainly know it with simple open-ended questions. That's important to note as a norm for that person. Another verbal norm is noting the types of words the subject uses. This can explain the education level of the subject or how the subject carries themselves. In my experience, I've interviewed people who mentioned words that I couldn't spell. Is that a norm or just someone trying to be impressive? Before I moved to the information-seeking phase, I would determine if it was a norm or not.

Nonverbal norms include body language, the uncontrolled movement of the eyes, head, hands, legs, feet, body, and so forth. While these nonverbal behavioral skills will be explained in detail later in this chapter, it is important to determine the norms of nondeceptive answers. Is it normal for the subject to sit straight up or slump over when they are talking comfortably? Some people have a chronic leg movement when they are sitting down, thinking, or recalling information. Others may display habits that are normal while carrying on a normal conversation, as opposed to nervousness related to deception. Sometimes nonverbal norms can be mistaken, so it is important to identify any nonverbal norms during the introduction or rapport-building stage of any interview.

Finding common ground with the subject being interviewed does not come without some critique. Many law enforcement personnel don't want to link their personal life with an offender or case being investigated. We get it. That is a personal choice. In a small jurisdiction where everyone knows the people in the area, you may weigh out talking about your own family or personal circumstances. At the same time, in a small area, the subject could be familiar with who you are talking about and may be able to better relate to you. In larger cities, this may never be a problem for the investigator to mention. There may be times when you can relate to what the subject is telling you, whether it is by personal experience or life experiences. The key is to make the interviewee feel a "connection" and talk to you. For example, the subject may keep speaking about their brother and how they do things. Just because I don't have a brother doesn't mean that I can't relate to their situation or feeling. I can respond by saying, "I understand" or "I know what you mean." I could even respond by saying, "Yeah, I know because my brother does that too." Is that wrong or illegal? No, but we always suggest being truthful with the person being interviewed.

Demeanor

Remember, interviews are not interrogations. Your interview should be an information-seeking mission. You should not be confrontational during the interview. Whether you are interviewing a victim, witness, or suspect, you should always show concern to obtain the facts. You should have the ability to act sympathetic, even when you may not be so. For example, you may have to sympathize with a suspect in an assault investigation by saying that you understand that "someone can push your buttons" (meaning that someone can get on your nerves). You are nonjudgmental, but the suspect may relate or assume that you understand their ideology. You may also simply nod your head in an up and down motion, commonly known as a signal of acknowledgment.

A good interviewer should control themselves and the direction that the interview goes. You must control your emotions. Some of the most difficult examples may be in child-involved cases. It will be more difficult to control your emotions in a child abuse case, especially if you also have children. But it is imperative that you prevent your emotions from getting involved in the direction of an interview. Your mission is to seek the truth of whatever you are investigating.

A good interviewer is a good listener. As the interviewee is speaking, you should listen to what they are saying and watch their body language or nonverbal communication. Maintain a professional demeanor and appearance. Failure to do so could redirect the interviewee and prevent them from talking. You should be patient and not forceful in an interview.

Sometimes initial responding officers tend to be too pushy in interviews when responding to more complex crimes. The officers want to get as much information as possible, which is great. However, they may use preconceived notions from outside factor that they shouldn't consider. For example, an officer may interview a complainant who is the significant other of the person whose death the officer was called to. The officer may believe that the incident was a homicide and that the significant other was involved. With this preconceived notion, the officer may ask questions that are more specific to their notion than the basic who, what, when, where, why, and how questions. By doing so, it could revictimize the significant other. The initial interview is not the place to be forceful. If the officer's preconceived notion is incorrect, what has their demeanor or attitude done to the complainant? It could jeopardize their trust and any follow-up interview that an investigator may need to do.

Privacy exists in the mind of the person being interviewed and is a function of the interviewer's demeanor. The officer/investigator must break down these barriers of privacy and get the interviewee to open up. You should remain objective, even-keeled, polite, sincere, interested, and understanding. This does not mean that the officer/investigator ignores professional standards and "befriends" the subject being interviewed. However, it does require the officer/investigator to not expose negative emotions and to allow the subject (victim, witness, or suspect) to provide information on their own. Be a good actor, and leave out all human biases.

Interpersonal Communication Skills

Interpersonal communication skills are behaviors that help you interact with others effectively. Maintaining rapport with an interviewee is an interpersonal communication skill. Your ability to interact with the interviewee and exchange information and meaning through verbal and nonverbal communication is a form of interpersonal communication. You must be able to accurately interpret people's emotions in order to maintain their rapport and interest in talking to you. An effective interview starts with building a rapport and involves multiple interpersonal communications skills used to seek the truth. It has been my experience that it takes less 5 minutes for someone to be accepted or rejected when a conversation is started with someone new. Keep this is mind as you are conducting your interviews. If their verbal and nonverbal behavior indicates rejection, your interview could be in jeopardy in terms of obtaining accurate information. It's important to be sincere and redirect any negativity or rejection.

Information Seeking

When gathering information during an interview, you are seeking details that can be connected to the investigation. Sometimes an interview develops details that can be corroborated as admissions. Other times, an interview may develop obvious lies that can be proven as such. Both are extremely important to the investigation. That's why it's important to document the first interview with a formal statement.

Admissions

Although interviews aren't specific to suspects, most people think of interviewing a suspect when discussing law enforcement interviews. When interviewing a suspect related to a criminal investigation, a Miranda warning is not always required. *Miranda v. Arizona* (1966) only applies when the interviewee is in **custody** or not free to go. If a suspect is being interviewed when in custody, it should be considered an interrogation. For the purposes of this section, we will discuss interviewing a suspect who is not under arrest or being deprived of their freedom of movement to the degree of feeling they are detained. The U.S. Supreme Court has resisted efforts to require officers to advise suspect of their rights outside of the three prongs set by Miranda: (a) questioning about a crime, (b) questioning by a law enforcement officer or someone who is asking questions on behalf of law enforcement in an adversarial process; and (c) questioning someone who is in police custody.

When interviewing a suspect, you ultimately want them to admit their part in the crime you are investigating if they are in fact involved. To prepare for this, you should first know the elements of the crime you are investigating. If you are investigating a robbery, the elements include knowing depriving one of property by force or a threat of force. During the interview, you want the suspect to acknowledge the taking of property. If that is accomplished, then you would work toward how the crime occurred. From your prior interviews of the victim and/or witnesses, you know the type of force that was used to deprive the victim. In the suspect interview, you may have to "downplay" the element of force, such as in the following example:

Investigator: You told me that you took the money from _____. How?

Suspect: I told him to give me the money.

Investigator: Did you show him a gun or knife?

Suspect: No.

Investigator: Was your hand in your pocket?

Suspect: Yes, but I didn't show or tell him I had a gun.

In this example, the suspect admitted to being present at the time of the reported crime. The suspect admitted they took the money from the victim. But did the suspect admit to using force? If your investigation or prior interviews indicate that the suspect threatened the victim with a gun in his pocket and there is video to corroborate the victim's statement, is the information the suspect provided an admission? Yes, because the element of force or a threat of force is how the victim interpreted the offender's action. Remember, the interview is information seeking and not adversarial. The point is not to confront the suspect about force or a threat of force. The statement above is an admission, not a confession. Confessions are obtained in an interrogation. There is a difference.

At what point does an interview become an interrogation? Once you decide to arrest the suspect or control their movements, custody applies. In the case above, if the suspect stopped the conversation or interview at that point and asked, "Am I under arrest?" or "Can I leave?" when does Miranda warning start to apply? If they are free to go, the admission was legally obtained. Miranda is not necessary at that point. If you decide to arrest the suspect, Miranda would be necessary at that point.

CASE STUDY 3.1: CRIPS SHOOTING

The following case study is from coauthor Korey Cooper and is related to a gang related shooting in 2009.

In 2009, a group of 87 Kitchen Crips conducted a drive-by shooting targeting 107 Hoover Crips in Columbia, TN, in retaliation for a previous shooting. The two gangs had been conflicting with one another and shooting at each other. A truck was used in the shooting, which had three shooters and a driver. As the 87 Kitchen Crips stopped at an intersection and started shooting at the 107 Hoover, one of their bullets struck an innocent neighbor in their own house. The results killed the innocent third party. An investigation ensued. During the investigation, the occupants of the truck were identified. Each of the suspected shooters were interviewed at different times over a long period of time. The driver was not interviewed until we had evidence to corroborate the investigative theory. Over a year after the crime occurred, we decided to go to the driver's house and talk to the driver. We knocked on his door, but no one answered. We left a business card to call an investigator.

Less than an hour after leaving the house, the driver called to inquire why we visited his house. He was familiar that we had interviewed the other suspects in the vehicle on different occasions, as well as targeted the gang with other criminal violations. We were honest with the driver and told him that we needed to talk to him about the shooting. The driver agreed to meet at the detective's office for an interview. Upon his arrival, he was taken to the interview room and interviewed. He sat closest to the door, and two investigators sat across a table from him. The driver was told that we appreciated him meeting with us and he was not under arrest. He asked if he would be arrested after the interview. We told him no. He seemed surprised. We explained that we were seeking the facts first and then presenting our finding to the prosecutor later. The driver was free to go at any time.

We started the interview with an introduction of the investigators and then asked the driver to tell us a little about himself. He did, which corroborated some of the information that we knew from our interview planning. This included family makeup, employment status, and lifestyle information. This was important because we were able to build some rapport with him. We were also able to see some emotional behavioral changes when we talked about the victim in the shooting. The victim in the shooting was well-known throughout the community. He had an intellectual disability, but was fully functionable and walked around the downtown area to go places. The victim also worked at a local elementary school part time. What we didn't know prior to the interview was the driver has an indirect family connection to the victim, which included the part-time job.

As we moved into the interview process, we explained the interview was related to the homicide. We told the driver that we believed we knew what happened, but we needed his side of the story. We told him that we didn't believe he was a bad person but was just put in a bad situation. He started to display more emotion but seemed reluctant to talk too much. He asked for reassurance that he was not going to be arrested that day. Again, we explained that we were just interviewing him to get his story and the case would be presented to the prosecutor days, maybe even weeks, later. He was not under arrest, nor would he be arrested that day.

The driver was asked what happened the day of the shooting. He started out by saying, "I was just driving." During the interview, he described what lead up to the shooting. There was a feud between the two gangs that included multiple shots fired back and forth. On the day in question, he described how all occupants of the truck got together and planned to seek out particular members of the rival gang. Once they saw a car that they knew was driven by members of the rival gang (which also was involved in a previous drive-by shooting), the driver was directed by another ranking gang member in the front seat of the truck to follow the vehicle. The vehicle went to a known gang hangout, so the occupants in the truck (driven by the person being interviewed) decided to shoot at the 107 Hoover Crip hangout. He said he was told to stop in a nearby intersection. That's when the other three occupants of the truck shot from inside the truck at the gang hangout. He said that he pulled away fast as soon as he was told to go.

At that point, he had admitted his involvement in the crime. He was very emotional and even sympathetic. We were able to get specific information about what led to the shooting and what occurred afterwards from the interview. This information was corroborated from information already developed in the investigation. This interview was a huge success and was a key component to linking missing pieces of the investigation. The driver was not arrested and was able to leave the detective's office.

At no time did we read the driver the Miranda warning. He was not in custody, detained, or arrested when the interview took place. He was free to leave at any time. But he didn't. He really wanted to talk and get the information "off his chest" (or off his conscience). He drove himself to the detective's office and drove himself away from the detective's office when the interview was complete. The investigation was a long-term investigation that led to indictments months later. The driver was indicted for his part of the crime and ultimately pled guilty for his part.

It should be noted that in *Vega v. Tekoh* (2022), the U.S. Supreme Court held that law enforcement cannot be sued for failing to advise Miranda warnings to a suspect. In this case, Deputy Vega, of the Los Angeles County police, questioned Tekoh at a hospital in reference to a sexual assault of a patient. Tekoh was not informed of his Miranda warning. Tekoh ultimately provided a statement and was prosecuted for a sexual offense. At trial, his statement was used against him. Tekoh was found not guilty by a jury. He filed a federal lawsuit against Deputy Vega for civil rights violation under 42 U.S.C. § 1983.

The Ninth Circuit court upheld the claim that the failure to Mirandize Tekoh was not only a Fifth Amendment violation but also supports a Section 1983 claim. The decision was appealed to the Supreme Court. In 2022, the Supreme Court reversed the lower court's decision, saying that a Miranda violation is not grounds for a Section 1983 claim. Furthermore, the Supreme Court required "additional procedural protections" to prevent self-incrimination. However, this is not to say that a Miranda violation and a Fifth Amendment violation are synonymous. While the Miranda rules have been described as "constitutionally based" with "constitutional underpinning," violating these rules is ultimately different from a violation of the Fifth Amendment right (*Vega v. Tekoh*, 2022).

Omissions

While it is good to obtain an admission from a suspect in a crime, omissions can be just as good. An **omission** is a statement given that can be proven to be a lie or something intentionally left out. For example, suppose a suspect says they were at home asleep at the time a crime occurred, but a surveillance video clearly shows the identifiable suspect in the store at the time of the robbery. That omission is great evidence. It discredits their statement.

Often, omissions are called "denials." A **denial** is any statement by the suspect that contradicts the truthfulness of an allegation relating to a specific crime. A denial is more common in an interrogation during the accusatory stage. Interviews are not meant to be accusatory; however, a denial can start in the interview. If that occurs, it's not suggested to challenge the suspect in the interview phase. If a denial in identified in an interview, the interviewer should start to direct questions that they know can be otherwise proven. For example, suppose you are interviewing the robbery suspect mentioned above and he says that he was home asleep at the time of the crime. This is one way to work that statement without confrontation:

Investigator: You were home asleep Monday night, right?

Suspect: Yes.

Investigator: What time did you go to sleep?

Suspect: 9:30.

Investigator: Was anyone else at home with you?

Suspect: No.

Investigator: What time did you wake up?

Suspect: 8:00 the next morning.

Investigator: What time did you get home that night?

Suspect: 6:00.

Investigator: Where were you prior to that?

Suspect: At my uncle's house, working on a car.

Investigator: Were you on Main Street at any time Monday or Tuesday?

Suspect: No.

Investigator: Did you go to Zip Mart? (the store that was robbed)

Suspect: No.

If the store was robbed at 10:00 p.m. and the suspect was identifiable on video as the robber, the suspect's cell phone was pinging off a tower nearest the store, and an eyewitness described the suspect and his vehicle as the get-away vehicle leaving Main Street just after the robbery occurred, then the suspect's statement above is an omission. As the interviewing officer/investigator, allow the suspect to continue painting a picture that he was nowhere near the crime when it occurred. The more of his statement that you can prove is false, the better evidence of his involvement by omission.

Even after a first statement has been taken, an investigator can work to prove the information in the statement is false. That's also an omission. Sometimes the offender/suspect being interviewed will change the story around. They may leave themselves out and replace themselves with someone else. There was a case where the shooter in a homicide was being interviewed. He denied being present during the shooting but said he heard from a friend (whom he identified) exactly what happened. He gave a full description of the event that only a subject involved or someone close to the involvement would know. It was practically a confession, but it was only "what someone told him" occurred. What he didn't know is that the other person had also been interviewed and had said what happened, and we could corroborate their story to exclude them as a suspect. This is a different type of omission, where the subject omits themselves from the event or crime.

Corroborating an omission of any type is important. You can corroborate these with statements from witnesses or with evidence. For example, a suspect says, "I was not (at the scene of the crime) because I was in (another city)," but the suspect's cellular phone tower ping clearly indicates the suspect was not only in the city of the crime but it's triangulated in the specific area of the crime. This is one way that evidence more likely than not corroborates that the suspect was not in another city but in the specific area of the crime.

Obviously, there should be more evidence to show that the suspect was in possession of the cellular phone at the time of crime. Asking questions about specific calls or messages during the time of crime can help prove the suspect possessed the phone at the time in question. One such way is to ask, "On (the day of the crime), did you talk to (specific identified caller) by phone?" If they answer "yes," then it's objectively reasonable that they possessed the cellular phone that day/time and their location was not in another city as the suspect mentioned.

Omissions are just as important in any investigations, and sometimes they are better than an admission. If the statement can be proven as a lie, especially with physical evidence, it tends to be more valuable at trial. Not only can it link evidence together, but it discredits the suspect/offender. Many investigators simply work for an admission. We suggest that you think outside the box and consider proving omissions too.

First Formal Statement

The **first formal statement (FFS)** is the first statement given by a person being interviewed. When you have a suspect or suspects of a crime, it's good to obtain their first formal statement as soon as possible. The first formal statement locks in their story. For instance, a suspect may create a false **alibi** during the interview to prevent law enforcement from linking them to the crime. If this statement is documented properly and the investigation proves otherwise, the suspect may feel that they must maintain their statement to support their innocence. This can benefit an investigation because evidence can prove the statement is false. In the previous section, we discussed omissions. The first formal statement best supports the investigator's ability to prove an omission. The first formal statement could be obtained by a first responding officer at the scene of a crime or an investigator assigned to a criminal investigation. Documentation is key.

When taking a statement related to a crime, it's always best to get a written statement. Whether it's from a victim, witness, or suspect, written statements are better than verbal statements. Without a recording device, a verbal statement could be documented more subjectively than a written statement. With today's technological advances (e.g., body cameras, in-car cameras, pocket recorders, cell phones, etc.), it is relatively easy to digitally document statements being taken. However, you should not totally rely on electronic devices to record or document statements. Technology can fail. By obtaining written statements, the statement is the subject's **formal written adopted statement (FWAS)**. You can still record the interview and statement, but the written statement is a formal statement in their own written words. It's suggested to do both. In the investigative stage, an investigator can analyze the subject's verbal statement from the interview and compare it to what they documented in the written statement. Was something left out? If so, why? Was it done purposely to cover something up, or was it just forgotten?

Establishing the Story

As you are interviewing a subject, you want to establish a story. Humans will provide cues through nonverbal communication or behavioral skills. By understanding these nonverbal communication behaviors, you may recognize deception and/or trauma. It should be noted that nonverbal communication identification is not always interpreted correctly. There are some factors that can be misinterpreted, such as cultural differences, which may influence the story. Identifying nonverbal behavioral skills is a science that must be practiced often. Misinterpreted nonverbal communication skills can be fatal to your investigation.

Evaluating Nonverbal Behavioral Skills

Recognizing nonverbal communication is important when conducting interviews. Being able to recognize nonverbal communication can assist any officer or investigator when conducting interviews. You can recognize deception, but you may also misread nervousness. A good interviewer should properly recognize the causes for changes in nonverbal behavior. You should also be familiar with the idea that different cultures may produce behavior that may be viewed as deception, but it's just their culture.

Body Language

When you are considering nonverbal behavior, you should monitor the entire body of the subject being interviewed. Body language is a nonverbal form of communication through conscious or unconscious gestures and movements. Although no single behavior, movement, or gesture should be considered an absolute form of deception, an accumulation of these should be considered when analyzing deception. Nonverbal presentation is responsible for approximately 55% of the communication process (Argyle, 1988). Most people will go to great lengths to protect what they are saying, but usually they fail to pay attention to the body language they display when they talk. Nonverbal behavior should complement verbal behavior. It's meaningless if isolated from verbal behavior.

When monitoring body language, you should determine if it matches the interviewee's truthfulness cues. This can be done during the introduction and rapport-building phase of an interview. This may include the subject's posture and personal movements. A subject's nondeceptive posture is usually straight up with their body squared forward. If you are conducting an interview when the subject is standing, look at their posture. How are they facing you? Are they in a defensive stance or comfortably standing? If they are sitting, what is their posture like during the basic rapport-building questions? That should establish a good baseline for their posture for truthfulness, if those response are in fact truthful.

You should look for a change in the body's movement as questions are asked, especially those questions that may relate to a crime or involvement in criminal activity. When a subject is deceptive or untruthful, they tend to be more fearful or concerned for detection of their untruthfulness. This is where their body language will show the difference between what they are saying versus what they know or believe. If you ask a question, they may indicate some defensive gestures, like crossing their arms, as they provide an answer. If you see that change in body language, it should be noted what the topic or discussion point was at the time. Body language can be divided into three categories: neutral, defensive, or aggressive. We will briefly describe some of the body language cues throughout the chapter.

Eyes

Most humans want to maintain some type of eye contact with the person they are talking to. However, you should be aware that some different cultures may not. As a general rule, most people of U.S. culture maintain eye contact during conversation between 30% and 60% of the time. In our experience, truthful people tend to look at you longer during interviews than deceptive people do. Emotionally disturbed or extremely shy people may have more limited eye contact. Deceptive people tend to focus on objects, look out a window, or just look away to reduce stress. It should also be noted that a gaze by a person being interviewed could also be a challenge. Criminals are familiar with or may educate themselves about interviews and nonverbal communication. They may try to keep direct eye contact with you during interviews to divert your attention to the deceptive verbal communication.

Neurolinguistics is the study of eye movement and how that movement relates to memory. For years the review of eye movement has been a controversial topic in law enforcement interviewing as it relates to the detection of truth and deception. Eye positioning corresponds to sensory-information processing

(Bandler & Grinder, 1975). When a person recalls information, the eyes will reflect the channel the information is being retrieved from. This information can be retrieved from our visual memory, our auditory memory, and our kinetic memory. Kamarul Ahmad (2013) summarizes Bandler and Grinder's findings:

> A person who is accessing a mental picture from [their] memory (visual recall) will be looking towards the top right (as seen by an observer). A person who is visualizing an imagined or constructed image not from memory (e.g., a six-legged cat) would look towards the top left. A person who is recalling a sound would look laterally towards the right (verbal recall) and a person who is imagining a new sound ... would look laterally towards the left (verbal construct). A person who is remembering the feeling of touching [something] (kinaesthetic) would look down and to the left. (p. 68)

If they were making a kinetic feeling up, they would look down and to the left. These eye directions are based on a person who is right-handed (Dilts, 1983). A left-handed person is just the opposite: Truth is toward the left, and deception is toward the right. There have been many different neurological research studies related to interviews and detecting truthfulness. While it has been our experience that the findings from these studies are generally true, you should only use those techniques as one of the many tools available to determine truthfulness.

Hands, Arms, Legs, and Feet

Some people communicate with the hands. In fact, very good speakers will incorporate hand and other body movement as part of their communication. When you are interviewing a subject, their hands are generally considered to be in a neutral position if their hands are open and relaxed. Their hand may be down to their side if standing or resting on a table if sitting. If so, they're neutral. A person who uses their hands to describe something may also be neutral. When a subject is consistently moving their fingers (like playing an invisible piano) or shifting their hands from a table to the lap back and forth, for example, they are demonstrating a defensive gesture. This could be a sign of deception. If the subject is clenching a fist or opening and closing their hands in a fist-type gesture, they are demonstrating aggression. While this may not always be a deceptive sign, it is certainly worth noting that the topic of discussion is causing an aggressive reaction.

Sometimes a person will pick lint off their clothes or start running their fingers through their hair. This movement is worth noting as well. If this occurs during an interview, it could be a sign of deception or a sign that the subject is trying to separate themselves from that part of the conversation by distracting themselves from what the interviewer is saying or asking. It could be a sign of the interviewee relieving stress. When talking, they may cover their mouth when providing a deceptive response.

Arms and hand coordination are practically the same. One arm gesture that can be worthy of noting is when the subject crosses their arms. That is a defensive gesture, which is forming a barrier between them and the interviewer. They could also cross their arms to hide muscle tension or shaking. If you have a subject who is crossing their arms, determine why. Is it to form a barrier, and is it related to muscle action? Muscle action could be related to a variety of reasons, including but not limited to nervousness, uncertainty, insecurity, guilt, or deception. Other indicators that occur in conjunction with these gestures can help direct your reading of this behavior. You may have to direct additional questions related to the topic you are discussing to help determine the likely reason for this behavior.

Legs and feet can also display defensiveness. Legs and feet can tell a lot about a person. If you are interviewing someone who is standing, the width of their legs may be an indicator. A position with the legs even with the shoulders or inward is more likely a neutral stance. A wider stance is more defensive. A person who has a wide stance and their body bladed to one side is most likely demonstrating an aggressive stance. A wide stance could also be a sign of power or dominance. This should be considered as dangerous, and an attack is possible.

If the subject is sitting down, a female subject will likely cross their legs in a neutral position. With male subjects, the crossed legs or ankles are similar to the arms and may indicate a barrier or some anxiety, especially if tucked under the chair. This may also create additional observed nonverbal behaviors in the arms and hands. The legs crossed at the knee could be a sign of defensiveness. If a leg is stuck out in a pointing type of manner, it may suggest interest in the discussion and should follow with upper-body movement toward the interviewer. If one leg is out and behind the interviewee or toward a door, it could indicate the thought of getting away from the conversation.

Some people have a habit of constant leg or feet movement, like a tremor. You should see that early in the interview—again, in the introductory phase. If so, you should not consider that movement as an indicator of nonverbal behavior. If not, a bouncing leg or foot may indicate impatience and defensiveness. If the movement becomes extreme, it may indicate agitation or aggressiveness.

Body

We have mentioned the eyes and limbs of the body, but we haven't discussed the head. The head can also indicate signs. The head and neck are generally the most animated parts of the body. Our facial expression can display a lot of emotion and feeling. With that being widely known, that is where most people who are trying to hide something or be deceptive tend to focus more on. Everyone wants to keep a poker face. If someone is trying to elicit some type of phony emotion, the face will be where that emotion starts.

The neutral position of the head is obvious. The head is normal, upright, and evenly balanced. A subject may lean back and create distance from the interviewer. If so, this is a sign of deception and displaying a defensive position. If a subject is leaning their head in toward the interviewer in what would make you think they are invading your space, that's a sign of aggression or intimidation. They many also lean in toward you to seek more information, but in this case, they'd likely not get into your personal space. If that's the case, that is more of a neutral position.

When reviewing language, the interviewer must be able to interpret what all of the body is saying and if it matches what the subject is verbally communicating. Fine motor coordination is generally not impaired when someone is being truthful. Not one sole nonverbal communication (or body language) could be considered alone. Body language is a combination of gestures throughout the body that indicate truthfulness or deception. Interpreting body language is a learned skill. You will not automatically become successful with interpreting body language during interviews. The more interviews you conduct, the more you will understand how the body reacts during conversation. There is a science to it. You should thoroughly document your interviews and the body language changes that you observe throughout the interview process. In time, the nonverbal behavior will become more obvious to you.

Identifying Verbal Cues

When conducting interviews, identifying verbal cues are important. Humans tend to minimize or downplay their involvement in criminal activity. Others may exaggerate or deny their involvement. You may hear a spontaneous utterance, or verbal slippage, while conducting interviews. That's why it's important to listen when you are interviewing someone.

Minimalization

Minimalization occurs when a suspect admits to crime but downplays it. One example of minimalization is when a suspect admits to stealing from a residence but minimizes it by saying that they didn't "break into the house." The suspect may give the appearance that it was "just a petty theft, not a burglary." Another way a subject would minimize is the type or class of an offense. The property value or list of items stolen could be minimized by the subject. For example, an element of felony theft may start at $1,000. The subject may say that the property was only worth $500. The subject's reasoning for minimizing the value in their mind is to downplay the offense as a misdemeanor. Another example may be in an assault investigation:

Investigator: What happened?

Suspect: I hit him.

Investigator: Where did you hit him?

Suspect: I hit him in the face once.

Investigator: Any more times?

Suspect: No.

Investigator: What did you use to hit him?

Suspect: Just my fist.

When a suspect minimizes during an interview, the officer/investigator should not stay focused on why the suspect is minimizing. The fact that the suspect is admitting an element of the crime is a good starting point. Most of the time whatever the suspect minimizes typically won't jeopardize the results of the investigation. Most likely, you will be able to work the statement into an omission. This is not the time to start confronting the suspect with contradicting information. That could "lock them up" or stop them from talking. If the investigation above indicated the victim was hit with a weapon multiple times, you might ask some additional questions related to the incident. Keep in mind that an interview is fact seeking and not confrontational.

Exaggeration

Sometimes people exaggerate what really happened during incidents. More often, an exaggeration will occur when you are working with informants. An informant may exaggerate about something to gain an investigator's attention or interest. Most informants are providing information to reduce their own charges or for monetary gain. Any information obtained from an informant must be corroborated and not just taken at face value. Sometimes an informant may exaggerate another's involvement to deflect their own involvement in criminal activity. You should always test your informants to ensure the information they provide is accurate.

There are times when a victim may exaggerate during an interview. If you find yourself in this situation, it's important to determine what their motive may be. For example, in 2019 actor Jussie Smollett reported that he was the victim of a racist and homophobic attack (Dasrath & Burke, 2022). Smollett, who is Black and gay, alleged that he had been brutally assaulted in a Chicago neighborhood. Two men were arrested for the attack. Further investigation indicated that Smollett had staged the phony incident and paid the two men who were arrested to attack him. Smollett's motive was to advance his career. He fabricated the incident and exaggerated the staged assault.

Direct Denials

When interviewing suspects, there will times when they deny everything. A direct denial is as simple as "I didn't do it." If you are interviewing a subject, the subject may consider the consequences for admitting their involvement in a crime. This can cause a direct denial. When you are interviewing someone who's been involved in the criminal justice system, they may also deny any involvement in criminal activity in fear of being arrested and/or jailed. During the interview process, direct denials can't prevent the interviewers from asking questions. The interview should document the denial and any other nonverbal behavior that may contradict the denial. If this occurs when you, as the interviewer, know and have proof that it's a lie, continue to ask questions that you know the answers to. If you can prove the suspect is lying, those omissions are just as beneficial when obtaining a formal statement. Direct denials with be detailed more in the interrogation process, where you will treat the denial differently.

Verbal Slips

A verbal slip may occur during an interview when the suspect inadvertently says something incriminating that they didn't intend to say. This is one of the reasons it's so important to be an active listener during interviews. Below is an example or a verbal slip:

Investigator: Did you stab (the victim)?

Suspect: Yes. I mean, no … I did not stab him.

Often, a verbal slip occurs when the suspect is thinking ahead of the question and trying to fabricate an answer to a question they are anticipating. If you see a suspect fabricating a story through eye movement or other nonverbal behavior during questioning, sometimes asking an off-the-wall close-ended question related to direct involvement may produce a verbal slip. If you receive a verbal slip, document it. However, if at all possible, do your best to act as if you never heard it.

Another verbal giveaway could be when you are speaking with a parent and you ask them to describe a little something about their child and the father or mother says, "She *was* a good kid" as they fight back tears. At this point, you may have been under the impression you were only investigating a missing child. But them using past tense in their description may indicate that they know the child is dead, and the parent may actually be a suspect.

SELECTION FROM "OUTCOMES OF MOTIVATIONAL INTERVIEWING TRAINING WITH PROBATION AND PAROLE OFFICERS: FINDINGS AND LESSONS LEARNED"

Melanie M. Iarussi

As Iarussi and Powers (2018) explain, correctional officers have the potential to be a positive force in clients' lives, in part by encouraging them to observe the terms of their probation or parole. They go on to summarize that motivational interviewing can be a good fit for corrections officers and even sometimes for police:

> Motivational interviewing (MI) is one evidence-based approach that appears to be a natural fit for delivering such services. MI promotes a working relationship between officer and client that is grounded in the belief that the client is capable of making positive changes. …
>
> Since William Miller originated it [motivational interviewing] in 1983, MI has been applied to a diverse range of helping professions, including mental health counseling, healthcare, and offender rehabilitation. … The method of MI involves the spirit of MI (partnership; acceptance of the person as a human being including expressions of empathy, autonomy, and affirmation; compassion; and evocation) and strategies to elicit and strengthen the client's movement toward positive change. Persuasion and pushing clients to see the officer's point (i.e., arguing) are avoided in MI; instead, the emphasis is on listening and drawing out motivations that are already within the client (Miller & Rollnick, 2013). …
>
> The historical approach to offender reform has been driven heavily by punishment and confrontation, often creating a culture of "us versus them" between officers and offenders, which can inhibit effective rehabilitation (Ginsburg, Mann, Rotgers, & Weekes, 2002). In contrast, compassion and respectful treatment are hallmarks of MI (Miller, 2013). … In this process of eliciting the client's motivation, the officer invites the client to share and then respectfully listens to the client's relevant experiences, perceptions, values, and goals. Such conversations allow clients to feel heard, valued, and engaged in their own process of change. …
>
> MI has shown strong evidence in reducing substance use, which tends to be prevalent amongst offender populations. (Iarussi & Powers, 2018, 28–29)

Debriefing Criminals

Once you become a veteran criminal justice worker, you may be assigned to a task force. These groups often consist of local, state, and federal law enforcement who combine resources in a better effort to apprehend criminals. These are usually not your run-of-the-mill criminals but are usually violent fugitives responsible for committing major crimes. Among these may be drug cartel members who belong to very sophisticated and dangerous organizations.

David Contreras is a veteran investigator who worked the border between San Diego, CA, and Tijuana, Mexico, for many years. He has some strong advice when interrogating individuals from drug cartels:

- Know your subject and their background.

- Get as much information as you can before you speak with them.

- Review all records and speak to other investigators who have knowledge of them.

- Listen carefully to everything they say.

- Realize they may talk in codes and slang they are familiar with.

- If you don't understand exactly what they are saying, ask to clarify.

- Always be respectful even if they have committed atrocious crimes.

    When debriefing an organized crime figure:

- Bring up a loved one of theirs to bring the humanity back to the person.

- Most cartel members have at least one loved one they have lost or miss.

- Get them to talk about this person or persons.

- Take them back to their childhood and their memories of that person.

- Talk and walk them to their present state and how things affected them and the loved one.

- It is OK to suggest possible solutions like, "How can you make this right?"

- Be consistent during your discussion and read their body language and tone.

- Everybody talks, given the right circumstances. Work on them, and don't give up!

In the California prison system—and in many other prison systems—criminals, including organized crime/cartel figures, prison gang members, and street gang members, often have to go through a debriefing process before they can come out of higher security and more restrictive housing.

When they go through this debriefing process, they are usually held in a "keep separate" area from members of their former gang or other individuals who may harm them. In this housing area may be members of other gangs, many times former enemies, and they are watched very carefully for any signs of being a "sleeper." In other words, whether they are just pretending they want to disassociate with their gang with the intention of striking at their enemies.

While they are going through this process, staff are reviewing their criminal and institutional records and looking for any supporting documentation, such as finding their names on various hitlists by their former gang. They will usually have a lengthy questionnaire whereby the "drop out" candidate writes in detail everything about their life—in particular, any criminal activities.

After this is completed, investigators will interrogate the individual verbally to see how close what they say matches up to what they wrote. They are often then placed in a step down program whereby they get more and more freedom and are monitored for any digress and given approval by program supervisors to be designated as an official ex-member or dropout of the gang.

EXHIBIT 3.1 PART OF AN ACTUAL DEBRIEF (NAMES/LOCATIONS OMITTED)

2001 Debrief by Former Controversial EME Member

Subject stated that he received the following information regarding how _____ became a member of the EME (Mexican Mafia). _____ was incorrectly validated as an EME associate and should be validated as an EME member.

According to Subject, _____ membership has been a controversial issue for several years throughout the prison system. This is due to the fact that it was discovered that _____ worked as a confidential informant in the late 1970s and is still recognized and allowed to participate with EME activities while on condemned row. Subject stated that there are copies of police reports that have been duplicated and distributed throughout the prison system. It should be noted that a copy of a nine-page document was discovered within _____ central file indicating his cooperation with law enforcement (refer to _____ County Drug Enforcement Unit reports dated April 14, 1977, and April 18, 1977). _____ has subsequently had his death sentence overturned and is currently serving a sentence of life without the possibility of parole at _____.

According to Subject, _____ was sponsored into the EME by _____ and _____ in 1992. Subject stated that while he was on the streets, he recalled _____ sending money to _____ on several occasions. Shortly after he learned of _____, _____ informed Subject he found out that there are documents being circulated around the prison system that indicate he worked for law enforcement. Subject said _____ contacted _____ and asked him if this was true about _____. _____ informed Subject that _____ vouched for _____ because he knew them for a very long time and that they would not sponsor anyone who they believed to be an informant. At that point Subject began to hear things about _____ and his cooperation with law enforcement.

References

Ahmad, K. (2013). Lying eyes: The truth about NLP eye patterns and their relationship with academic performance in business and management studies (MBA). *International Journal of Business and Management, 8*(23). https://doi.org/10.5539/ijbm.v8n23p67

Argyle, M. (1988). *Bodily communication* (2nd ed.). Methuen.

Bandler, R., & Grinder, J. (1975). *Reframing neuro-linguistic programming and the transformation of meaning.* Real People Press.

Dasrath, D., & Burke, M. (2022, February 26). *Jussie Smollett seeks new trial or not guilty verdict following conviction for falsely reporting hate crime.* NBC News. https://www.nbcnews.com/news/us-news/jussie-smollett-seeks-new-trial-not-guilty-verdict-conviction-falsely-rcna17810

Dilts, R. (1983). *Roots of neuro-linguistic programming.* Meta Publications.

Iarussi, M. M., & Powers, D. F., (2018). Outcomes of motivational interviewing training with probation and parole officers: Findings and lessons learned. *Federal Probation, 82*(3), 28–35.

Miranda v. Arizona 384 U.S. 436 (1966). https://www.oyez.org/cases/1965/759

Vallano, J. P., Evans, J. R., Schreiber Compo, N., & Kieckhaefer, J. M. (2015). Rapport-building during witness and suspect interviews: A survey of law enforcement. *Applied Cognitive Psychology, 29*(3), Pg. 371. https://doi.org/10.1002/acp.3115

Vega v. Tekoh, 597 U.S. ___ (2022). https://www.oyez.org/cases/2021/21-499

CHAPTER 4

The Statement

Purpose

Statements are commonly taken from victims, witnesses, and/or suspects. Most statements in criminal investigations are made in verbal or written form. While a written statement is always preferred, there are times when a documented verbal statement (also known as an oral statement) is the only option. A verbal statement taken from a victim early in the investigation (just prior to being transported to a hospital) is one example of a verbal statement. It's a good practice to obtain a statement from any victim or witness of a crime as soon as possible.

There are times when a person being interviewed does not want to provide a written statement after an interview. Their reluctance may be based upon several possible reasons. Many people are willing to tell law enforcement what they witnessed but don't want to "get involved." They feel a written statement would get them involved. However, the mere fact that they provided information during an interview got them involved. Others are unwilling to provide a written statement because they cannot read or write. That's why recording interviews can be advantageous. If an officer/investigator recognized this is the reason, other ways to document the statement are available.

In this section we will cover the importance of documentation, how to properly take and store notes, the use of audio and video recording of suspect and witness statements, ensuring that reports are thorough and complete, detecting deception, the importance of ensuring there is justice and eliminating personal bias, how having a professional and good attitude can lead to success and accuracy, confronting hurdles, and reminding yourself of your purpose.

Documentation

One of the most popular sayings in this business is "If it isn't in writing, it didn't happen." This is true for the most part, but be aware that people can sometimes give written statements that are not accurate or sometimes an outright lie, so it may not have happened the way they tell it. So, keep an open mind and always search for the truth. Remember that when people are in trouble, they often get defensive and may try to underplay their involvement and place blame on somebody or something else.

When documenting, you will probably construct your own system. Having clear and consistent short-hand writing is essential to fast note-taking that will be most helpful to you later. You can also jot down key questions and notes to yourself to help you remember certain things.

You will want to clearly identify who did what, who said or did what at a scene (where), and when they did it. We refer to this as the who, what, where, when, and some why and how (when important). One must be very careful with these last two, as they can lead to biased opinions that may taint a case or incident.

You may also want to draw diagrams such as a crime scene map or a diagram of the key elements involved (see Figure 4.1).

FIGURE 4.1 Elements of Crime

You will want to make sure you have the correct spelling of names; it is even better to have an official ID with numbers and date of birth. If not able, you may want to write a brief description of an unidentified possible witness or subject. You will want to note the gender, possible race, approximate height, approximate weight, hair and eye color, clothing, distinct tattoos, and so on. You will want to describe the true basis—or to the best of your ability—of what happened. You will want to be as specific as possible about where something happened (e.g., on the fifth floor of apartment #B511, in the bathroom or the second tier, in cell #211 near the inmate desk, etc.). You will want to get the most accurate time it occurred (e.g., on April 17, 2022, at approximately 0923 hours).

When a statement is taken, nothing should be erased, removed, or scratched out. If a mistake is made, whether it's the subject or the official taking the statement, only one line through the mistake should be used. This should be followed by the initials of the subject and the official taking the statement. A date can also be included to further document the change(s). This is done to show who made the changes and when the change(s) was made.

If there is additional information that could be extremely helpful of why or how something occurred, then you might include it, but still be careful to note it is not yet proven to be true, such as "The subject was known to be depressed in days prior to the incident, according to Witness A, which may have led to their suicide" or "It appears the subject hung themselves with a torn sheet made into a rope." You are just giving information that could be helpful but not stating that you are a certified coroner.

You will want to organize your notes on sequence, time, and environmental conditions in your routine style (Shults, 2019):

- Gather information.

- Record/remember.

- Organize/outline.

- Write/fill out required reports/records.

- Evaluate/edit (OK to add, but be careful if you change anything, as it may be subject to discovery and cause doubt about your honesty later).

In essence, you will want to be accurate, brief but clear, and complete.

Below is a sample of a witness statement form. In some states it's unlawful to provide a statement to law enforcement (see Figure 4.2). That is not the case in every state, so be sure to know the guidelines within

Statement Form

Page ___ of ___

Case Number:		Agency ID:			
Date of Statement:		Time of Statement:			
Location Given:		To Whom Given:			
Name:		DOB:	Sex:		Race:
Address:		City:	State:		Zip:
Phone#	Cell#	Work#		Other#	
1					
2					
3					
4					
5					
6					
7					
8					
9					
10					
11					
12					
13					
14					
15					
16					
17					
18					
19					
20					
21					
22					
23					
24					
25					
26					
27					
28					
29					
30					
Statement Received By:		ID#			

_____
Signature

FIGURE 4.2 Sample Witness Statement Form

your state. If your state does have a law against providing false information to law enforcement, your statement form should include an acknowledgment of understanding that the subject knows and understands that providing false information is unlawful and they can be prosecuted for providing false information.

One of the most important interviews that an officer/investigator may document is a **dying declaration**. This is the last words of a person who is dying or thinks they are dying. They must make the statement, based on their actual knowledge, that relates in some way to the manor or circumstances of their death. When considering a dying declaration, the statement must be in the victim's own words, not paraphrased but verbatim. Therefore, documenting the declaration is extremely important to ensure the statement is admissible in court. Otherwise, the statement is just a lead to investigate and a jury will never know the source was the victim.

There are times when a subject (victim, witness, or suspect) either doesn't want to physically write a statement or cannot read or write. They may request the investigator write their statement out for them to adopt. If this happens, an investigator should be careful. While it's certainly understood that there are circumstances that lead to this, investigators should follow some guidelines:

1. Take one sentence at a time, and write it verbatim as they say what they want in their statement.

   - Take your time and document their statement with their emotion or wording.

   - Don't cut corners or change words.

      - For example: The witness says, "does not" and you document "doesn't" or "don't."

2. Use their words, not yours.

   - Document the statement with the words that the subject says, not what you think they meant to say.

   - For example: The witness says, "She told me to ..." but you document "She advised me to ..."

      - The word "advised" is more common used by law enforcement.

3. Avoid trying to be chronologic if the interviewee isn't.

   - Most witness will remember things outside of the order that they occurred.

      - Don't document their statement outside of the sequence of event as they tell you.

4. Create one or more purposeful mistakes that you and the interviewee can mark through, and initial the correction(s).

   - This is a method that helps ensure the subject understands the statement they are adopting.

   - For example, a statement may look like this: "The car van was green."

      - By marking through "car" because the subject said "van," the investigator and the subject will add their initials over the correction. This indicates the subject understands and agrees to the statement modification. With a subject who can read, it also shows the subject read the statement before signing and adopting it (see Figure 4.3).

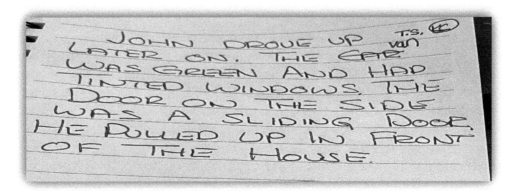

FIGURE 4.3 Initialing Corrections

Taking Notes

When you are in the field, you will often want to take notes. Even the best minds can forget details that may be important to a case or incident. Keep in mind that these notes may be subject to discovery, so you'll want them to be brief but also helpful to your official reports and documentation later. This is considered **Brady material** (*Brady v. Maryland*, 1963).

PERSONAL EXPERIENCES

Morales

I would always carry a little notepad in my pocket to take notes on important matters and to detail key statements or critical information.

Cooper

As a patrol officer, I always kept a small notebook or notepad in my shirt pocket. At every roll call, I would write the date and my zone assignment on the first available page and draw a line. During roll call, I would add important information, such as BOLOs (be on the lookout for), alerts, and so on. As I answered calls on shift, I would use the notebook to note field interviews and any information that needed to be documented on shift. Once the notebook was filled up, I would safely store it in a box in my home office (or closet) in chronological order. As mentioned before, you should understand that all notes related to a criminal case are subject to discovery in a criminal proceeding. Just throwing the notes away after you are done or when the notebook is full is not suggested.

Our courts have held that law enforcement officers "may not destroy contemporaneous notes of interviews and observations ... after producing their final reports" (*State v. W.B.*, 2011). In *State of New Jersey v. Cook* (2004), the court disapproved of the destruction of interview notes, specifically mentioning that "once each officer prepared his report, he destroyed his note from the interrogation sessions, a practice that is apparently common, but one that we disapprove of." The retention of field notes will vary from state to state; however, we believe it is best practice to retain your field notes for potential discovery. Some states have added a retention period, as little as 30 days. Other agencies have departmental policies to retain field notes for a year or more. It's important to know what your jurisdiction requires.

Some courts have ruled that it was permissible to throw away field notes when (a) they were incorporated into a formal report and the report reflects what the officer(s) remembered; (b) they were destroyed in good faith; and (c) the discovery in a criminal case included the formal report that has documented what the notes would have said is permissible. You should first follow departmental policy and then communicate with your local prosecutor's office. By communicating with the prosecutor's office and asking important questions about things like field note retention, you will be better prepared.

While taking notes, you'll want to conduct a LEAPS assessment:

- **L**isten carefully.

- **E**mphasize important details.

- **A**sk for clarification.

- **P**araphrase to validate you have it right (e.g., "Let me make sure I understand correctly. You're saying he …").

- **S**ummarize information as a final recap.

Be sure not to rush. Pace yourself, because as you're thinking about what to write, they are probably thinking about what to say. If they are being truthful, you won't want to hurry them. It is OK to pause, as they will want to make sure they are relaying correct information. If they are being untruthful, they will be thinking about not self-incriminating themselves or incriminating others they are trying to protect and they will pause a lot, say "Uh," and display other body language and tone changes.

If you are conducting a more formal interview, one in an office or interview room, there are some techniques to consider. If multiple law enforcement officers are involved in the interview, one should conduct all the talking while another takes notes. Typically, no more than two officers/investigators should be involved in an interview. It is important to document who is present during an interview. If only one officer is involved with the interview, you should still take notes. Watch how the subject reacts to note-taking. Are they watching want you are writing? Maybe they are nosy, or it may be to see what you believe is important versus what you don't document. Therefore, document everything. If you document everything, they can't tell what you believe is more important versus what you are simply noting about the interview. Most people expect an officer/investigator to take notes from what they have seen on television or the movies. So, it's not odd if you are documenting the interview.

One of the primary purposes of using two officers in the interview is for one to focus on the questioning and listening to the answers. The other one should take notes, including what the subject is saying and documenting body language changes. Listen for the use of verbs and any changes in their tense, such as a change from "is" to "was" (present tense to past tense). Consider if you were interviewing a suspect who you believe killed his wife and during the interview he said, "She was my best friend." The tense of the verb "was" is noteworthy because "was" is in the past. If they are still married, why use the past tense? Listening carefully for slippages like this is important. It's certainly important to document such instances.

There may be times when you don't take notes. When the subject that you are interviewing is focused on what you are writing or noting, it could be best to stop writing. If they are watching what you are writing, it could prohibit you from getting information in the interview. Maybe they are scared to tell you something because you are documenting everything. Sometimes witnesses want to tell you what happened, but they don't want to testify in court or "get involved in the investigation." If that's the case, they may stop providing you information if you are documenting everything they say. If you notice the interviewee looking at what you are writing, stop writing for a bit and see if there is a change in their demeanor. Try to determine what their motive may be for the demeanor change. If you are recording the interview by audio and/or video, not taking notes should not be a problem because you will have a "back up" to the documentation with the recording.

Audio/Video

Audio and video recording have been used for decades now. The advancement of technology has improved audio and video quality and should be used as a tool where appropriate. Depending on the situation, you may be under legal obligation to notify subjects they are being recorded. For instance, when prisoners are on the phone in jail and prison, the recorded call often starts out with, "This phone call may be recorded." This lets them know that it is very likely being recorded, barring technical problems. Today's technology can let investigators know the exact time a call was made and ended as well as where the call was made from and if calls are frequently coming from specific numbers, which can be used on tracking charts with photos and diagrams.

Always record the interview for your protection. How or when the recording is used is up to you. You are conducting these interviews for the safety and security of the facility. Any other information is secondary and not the original intent. Consider these pointers during the interview (Moreno & Morales, n.d.):

- Choose the right/best location possible.

- Covertly record if possible.

- Avoid having too many people in the room.

- Avoid taking too many notes.

- Show mutual respect; be firm but fair.

- Avoid rushing.

- Be prepared to call their bluff.

- You control the interview and the course of it.

- Be patient! You can always interview again.

- Know the cultural background of suspect/inmate, gang relevant information, and so on.

- Know case details, but do not introduce case details initially. If they insist on talking about the case in detail, remind them of their inmate rights.

If the inmate starts to talk about criminal activities they are involved in but you did not ask the question, let them run at the mouth. Stay away from follow-up questions in this area so that it cannot be construed you solicited the information. Return to your general gang questions.

Take the questioning as far as you need to, and don't let them be vague. For example:

Investigator: Where are you from?

Suspect: Arizona.

Investigator: Where at in Arizona?

Suspect: Tucson.

Investigator: Where in Tucson? (Tucson is a BIG place!)

Suspect: The West Side.

Investigator: What barrio, hood, or set? (Ask according to suspected gang lingo.)

Suspect: Hollywood.

Investigator: What clique?

Suspect: Crazy Cats. (Look for tattoos of University of Arizona logo, West Side, Hollywood, etc.)

Investigator: What do they call you? (i.e., moniker)

Suspect: Lil Loco.

Investigator: Why "Lil Loco"?

Suspect: My father is Big Loco.

Continue as long as you can to back up the information. If and when an inmate requests to talk, always remind them their attorney would not want them talking to you. In my experience the inmate usually informs me they do not care what their attorney thinks. Remind them the interview is taking place at their request. Remind them not to talk about the current case.

This information is solely intended for training and educational purposes and shall not be considered as legal advice. If you decide to use any concepts from this material, you should consult your department's legal counsel to determine how the laws of your jurisdiction affect the application of this information to your individual department (Stewart, 2017).

Many law enforcement agencies in the United States use in-car video cameras and officer-worn body cameras. Some have chosen to utilize these cameras to reduce liability and become more transparent for the community. Others use the cameras more for evidentiary purposes. As departments become more transparent, footage of law enforcement cameras is becoming more and more available for the public to review immediately after critical incidents.

In-car video cameras were first used to document activity of law enforcement on the beat. These cameras were used more for documenting traffic stops and arrests near the patrol car. An in-car video camera can also document custodial interviews or interrogations when the suspect is under arrest and in the rear seat of the patrol car. In-car cameras have also been valuable in cases where a suspect was in custody in the back seat of the patrol car and the officer was not inside the car. Suspects tend to talk to themselves and seemingly incriminate themselves at the same time. Courts have ruled that there is no expectation of privacy in the back seat of a patrol car (*United States v. Paxton*, 2017). If you are conducting an interview with a subject in the backseat of a patrol car, they are most likely in custody, and that would constitute an interrogation. Interrogations will be discussed in Part II of the textbook.

Officer-worn body cameras are very popular amongst U.S. law enforcement agencies. These cameras can be attached to the uniform of an officer and record activity from the officer's point of view. These digital cameras can be activated by the officer manually or programmed to record at intervals when not manually activated. For interviewing purposes, these cameras are helpful to document encounters such as field interviews or investigations. Officers initially responding to a crime may interview victims and witnesses. A verbal statement can be taken during the initial investigation. A written statement should also be taken from each victim/witness while on scene. When the initial statement is taken by an officer with a body-worn camera, the recording of the interview should also be logged as evidence. The two statements can be compared for more details. Oftentimes, a victim/witness will unintentionally leave out important information in their written statement. They may not do this to hinder the investigation but just to summarize what they think is important. Officer-worn cameras are valuable to document interviews and statements to get as much information as possible. It's highly recommended that you always review recordings when documenting the interview in your own report. Details that you may fail to take note of or simply missed could be found while reviewing the recordings.

There will be times when a subject will give a verbal statement but is reluctant to or refuses to give a written statement. In those cases, it's important to document their statement as soon as possible, even if it's recorded in some way. If their interview was not audio or video recorded, your notes will be very important to document what they said, and your written documentation is critical. Therefore, documenting their interview soon thereafter is a must. You shouldn't wait for days to document their statement(s).

Most law enforcement agencies have access to rooms specifically designed for interviewing, which include audio/video recording capabilities. Some investigative units have rooms with two-way mirrors for additional officers/investigators to watch the interview without the subject seeing them. Some agencies have also utilized computer electronics in their interview rooms for investigators to communicate via tablets through messaging applications as an interview is being conducted. If these applications are used, keep in mind that any conversation should be considered discoverable for criminal court purposes. In these cases, the conversations should be documented accordingly.

There will always be pros and cons to documentation. Electronic devices make documenting interviews easy. But remember, if you are using electronic device to document your interviews; anything can happen! Recording devices can damage the recording. Perhaps you forgot to press the "record" button and the interview was not recorded. Don't solely depend on electronic devices to record your documentation of an investigation.

There are pros to using electronic devices:

- Electronic devices supplement documenting exactly what occurred in an interview.

- You can use the recording to review and document the interview in written form.

- You can look at demeanor and/or body language of the interviewee (that you have missed).

- The recording can be played for the court.

  There are also some cons:

- The device can malfunction, meaning it didn't record.

- Damage to the media used in the recording.

- Officers/investigators become dependent on electronic devices and fail to physically document well.

- Interview technique can be misinterpreted.

You have options for recording devices. Besides those previously mentioned, you could also use a cellular phone with a recording application (app) to record interviews. Keep in mind, though, that the device used could be considered a part of discovery. While there is not yet a definitive case to reference when an officer's personal cellular phone and its content is or isn't considered discoverable, there is a case in New Mexico where a criminal case was dismissed because the prosecutor did not provide contents from an officer's personal phone. In *State v. Ortiz* (2009), Officer Boerth arrested Ortiz for driving while intoxicated. During retrial arguments, Ortiz argued that Officer Boerth's "personal cellular phone records were potentially material to the defense," given that they might contain information indicating why the officer stopped Ortiz.

The prosecutor in *State v. Ortiz* (2009) refused to provide contents from the officer's phone. The trial court dismissed the criminal case against Ortiz. The state appealed the decision to the New Mexico Court of Appeals, which upheld the district (trial) court's decision.

Since there is not precedent case to follow, it will be a local court decision to allow (or not allow) contents from law enforcement personnel's personal cellular phone if it's used for investigative purposes. While it may be reasonable for a court to limit the scope of forensic analysis of an officer's personal cellular phone, it's not a given that a limited scope will be granted. With that said, there is some concern for officer safety reasons, and it's not suggested to use a personal device to document crime scenes or criminal evidence in any investigation.

To minimize the potential of sharing materials from other investigations like photos or videos with friends, family, or even on social media, some agencies forbid their officers from using personal devices such as cellular phones and tablets (Welty, 2017). Of course, sharing information like this is not recommended, and using any personal device is highly discouraged.

Any audio and/or video media used for investigative purposes should be treated as evidence and logged in with the agency evidence custodian. Original recordings should never be left in the investigative file. If a recording is needed in the file, a **working copy** should be created. A working copy is a copy of digital media, such as a video, audio, or photographs, that is used for review and may be modified or enhanced for investigative purposes. The working copy may be kept in the investigative file. The original copy should never be modified in any way and should be preserved in the evidence room.

Thorough Reports

Documenting and reporting in the interview phase are two of the most important tasks for any investigation. The first responding officer's thoroughness in reporting will provide an investigator information to follow up on and may develop additional leads to solve crimes. Referencing your notes or video recordings when creating your reports is also important, but these shouldn't be solely relied upon.

As a first responder to a reported crime, the initial incident report can provide an investigator some of the best information. For example, at a reported burglary, documenting and reporting "the residence was ransacked" is subjective and may not provide necessary details to help solve the crime. Compare that to this report: "The residence had furniture overturned, all of which contained storage areas such as drawers, consoles, boxes, and so on. A jewelry box in the master bedroom was lying on the floor and its contents were missing." This example is more thorough and provided details than simply "ransacked." A reasonable conclusion could be drawn the offender was looking for some specific material (e.g., money, jewelry, drugs, etc.). If the reporting officer continued with "The jewelry box had contained $500 cash prior to the reported incident," then one may conclude the offender's motive and intent was to steal money. That could also lead the responding officer to ask the complainant to look at other known areas where money is stored and determine if more cash was taken. This is just one simple example of how a thorough report can provide more details, which can develop additional leads for the investigative phase.

When documenting information provided from witnesses, you must report what is provided. Don't just report what you believe is important at the time. What you feel may not serve any purpose, but it may be valuable to a follow-up investigation. This information may include but is not limited to detailed descriptions of people, vehicles, clothing, items, materials, merchandise, and so on. You could include information such as "a White male subject, approximately 5'9" tall, 185 pounds, medium complexion, short brown hair, blue eyes, wearing a black polo short-sleeve shirt with tan cargo pants, and in black tennis shoes." Compare this description to a less descriptive "short White male with dark hair." You should see how the more thorough reporting can provide an investigator with details to assist. These details can help investigators develop suspects from the information provided. They also may provide descriptors that can reduce the number of possible subjects or suspects to be used in a photographic or in-person lineup.

Documenting witness interviews is similar to documenting victim interviews. Eyewitness information is important because, many times, witnesses are less trauma-influenced than victims. Keep in mind different witnesses may see different things. This may be caused by different angles or views, a difference in perception, a sensory failure or overload, and much more. One witness could be more visual and may provide a better visual description versus another witness who is more auditory and may provide a better description from sounds (e.g., voice, music, crying, etc.). It doesn't mean that one is better than the other, but a combination of multiple witnesses can more likely provide a better overview of the situation that was witnessed.

When a possible suspect of a crime is interviewed, it is extremely important to thoroughly document the conversation. Typically, this is the first formal statement of the suspect in the early stages of an investigation. This interview is important because it sets a timeline and a foundation of a statement. This information can be corroborated to better assess their involvement. It can also be used to compare to evidence in the investigation that can later be used in an interrogation, if the suspect is later arrested for the crime. A thoroughly documented interview of a possible suspect will be valuable to an investigator preparing for an interrogation. You may be able to disprove information gathered from the interview, which may add to a motive or evidence linking the suspect to the crime.

Your primary job will be to record the facts: the who, what, where, and when. At times, it may be appropriate to add the how and why, but you will need to back that up with facts, not opinions. Thoroughly reporting the information you obtain during any form of the interview process will be very valuable in the other processes of interrogation, investigation, and intelligence. It all starts with your documentation of interviews.

Detecting Deception

As we stated previously, people may be misleading by accident due to forgetting or on purpose to be deceptive. It is your job to bring out the truth by your questioning and review of verbal, written, and recorded statements. Matsumoto et al. (2011) shared the following:

> While interviewing the suspect who claims ignorance about an incident, the witness who saw it happen, or the informant who identified the perpetrator, the detective asks a question that will eviscerate the perpetrator's story. As the suspect prepares to answer, he looks up and to the left, purses his lips, tenses his eyelids, and brings his eyebrows down. (p. 1)

Matsumoto et al. (2011) go on to explain that many investigators who are trained in behavioral deception are aware that shifty eyes from a subject can mean deception. But this is not always the case. In some cultures, it is considered disrespectful to look directly into an elder's or person of authority's eyes. If they are looking up and to the left when answering uncomfortable questions, it can mean they are exhibiting signs of lying. This is what is taught in many interview and interrogation classes and is based on studies of truthfulness. But there are always reasons for exceptions. Other things, like being under the influence, can affect the accuracy of statements and taint an interview.

Often, a suspect can be more hesitant to be involved in the interview, as opposed to being directly deceptive. For example, a suspect may have been present and witnessed the crime being committed by someone they are acquainted with but doesn't want to be a "snitch." That suspect will most likely provide the same body language and "eye movement" that the offender who committed the crime would display. The investigator may assume the suspect's behavior suggests they are the offender, which may induce a higher level of questioning in the interview.

> Unfortunately, this investigator likely would be wrong. Twenty-three out of 24 peer-reviewed studies published in scientific journals reporting experiments on eye behavior as an indicator of lying have rejected this hypothesis. No scientific evidence exists to suggest that eye behavior or gaze aversion can gauge truthfulness reliably
>
> Some people say that gaze aversion is the sure sign of lying, others that fidgety feet or hands are the key indicators. Still others believe that analysis of voice stress or body posture provides benchmarks. Research has tested all of these indicators and found them only weakly associated with deception.
>
> Relying on false clues, or signs, about lying can have dire consequences. It can lead to inaccurate [interpretations about] witnesses, suspects, or informants. (Matsumoto et al., 2011, pp. 1–2)

One may assume they are lying when they are not or that they are telling the truth when they are not being totally forthcoming.

In the last chapter, we discussed nonverbal body language cues to detect deception. Understand that some practitioners and professional trainers like the John E. Reid & Associates or Wicklander-Zulawski & Associates use techniques to train law enforcement how to utilize these techniques effectively. We

David Matsumoto et al., Selection from "Evaluating Truthfulness and Detecting Deception." leb.fbi.gov, Federal Bureau of Investigation, 2011.

have and still do utilize these techniques from time to time. However, some scientific, nonpractitioner, evidence-based data suggests it's not as accurate as some assume. These techniques have recently come under fire, with suggestions made that false confessions come from investigators using these techniques. A **false confession** is a claim that someone was responsible for a crime they did not commit. We believe nothing is 100% accurate. Factors such as cultural considerations, alcohol or drug influence, mental incapacities, and so on should be considered. More specifically, continuous training and experience by recognized professional services, as mentioned above, is highly suggested. These are techniques that should be corroborated by evidence and not based solely on the opinion of an investigator, especially those who lack specialized training in using the techniques.

Importance

The general public rely on law enforcement to detect the difference between the trust and a lie, especially related to criminal investigations. As Docan-Morgan (2007), paraphrasing several studies, explains, "Research suggests that most law enforcement officers are not able to detect deception better than chance" (p. 144). It's important for any investigator to seek training and gain experience with interviews, including in the area of detecting deception. The art of body language and deception continuously evolve—hence the reason investigators must stay abreast of best practices and research related to techniques in detecting deception. Otherwise, investigators may mistake nervousness and anxiety as lying and culpability.

Best practices for investigators should include corroborating evidence to support an investigative hypothesis. Investigators should not rely solely on an interviewee's potential sign of deception, whether it's body language or other nonverbal indicators, to determine if the subject is lying or not. You must consider physical evidence and corroborating circumstances when detecting deception. This is another reason it's important to prepare for your interviews. In Chapters 2 and 3, we discussed the processes to prepare for an interview. You cannot skip a process and be successful. Each process has a purpose.

Attitude

The attitude that you take into an interview can set the stage for failure or success. It is often said, "Attitude is everything," and we agree. In this business, it is easy to get cynical and have a poor attitude. This will, no doubt, tarnish the quality of your work and possibly ruin a case.

In Chapter 3, we emphasized the importance of rapport, making a good and professional first impression, and building appropriate relationships as the process goes along. You know what you need to do and possibly say, but how are you coming off to your subject?

To put yourself in the other person's position and to keep and even improve your attitude, try to recall a recent group meeting you've attended:

1. Could you tell who was paying attention and who appeared bored and wanted to leave?

2. Could you tell who was nervous and maybe guess why?

3. Could you sense when somebody was dishonest or being deceptive?

How did the person in the situation in Question 1 come off? How was the person in Question 2 distracted and distracting? How did the person in Question 3 give off a negative reaction?

When you are taking a statement, keep a positive attitude, even in negative situations. We understand that is sometimes easier said than done. Some part of law enforcement is acting. Sometimes you will need to use your car salesman acting skills. One example is investigating a child abuse case. Most law enforcement officers and investigators will agree child abuse cases are difficult to work. When you are dealing with a known suspect, it may be difficult to maintain yourself. In these cases, your attitude can make or break the case.

If you are tasked to interview the suspect, you may have a whirlwind of emotions. If you go into the interview with the attitude or mindset that the subject is worthless and should be put under the jail, you will exit the interview without any purposeful information. Why? Because your negative attitude will prohibit you from taking the time to follow the procedures to a successful interview. You may feel the subject is sick and therefore talk down to them. If so, the subject will deny everything and seek to end the encounter.

PERSONAL EXPERIENCE

Cooper

I was once assigned a child sex abuse case. It involved twins who were allegedly sexually abused by their father. A forensic interview of the children reveals the likelihood of sexual conduct. As the children were being evaluated by medical personnel, I interviewed the suspect (father). He voluntarily agreed to meet at the detective's office to discuss the allegations. It should be noted that the father had been investigated by another local agency for similar allegations and those cases were unfounded. When I spoke to the father on the phone, he mentioned those incidents. I believe he was comfortable with those prior dispositions and that's why he agreed to come in for the interview.

I must say that the allegations bothered me. I was sickened. But my job was to seek the truth. Another detective and I met and discussed the case and updates. I had conducted my preliminary research and information gathering on the father, as well as the family. The father arrived, and we conducted an interview with him. It was hard to keep composure when sitting face to face with the father. But I did, and it paid off.

I conducted the interview with an open mind. The purpose of the interview was not to arrest the father at the time but to simply seek facts. While talking to the father, I noticed a pattern of him blaming the children for everything. He seemed to be confident in his fathering skills. So, I used that direction for my questioning. I used a theme of preparing the children for the future (teen and adulthood). As I mentioned this, I saw the subject's face and body language change. He started nodding his head forward in an affirmative manner. I had his attention. We just continued talking about life and the "crazy world." Before long, he started talking about the kids acting out sexually on him (an admission to one element of the crime) without me asking a specific question. He described in detail how he was preparing (i.e., grooming) the children for life. The interview continued and ended very successfully, from an investigative standpoint.

The point in explaining this interview is all about attitude. The success in the interview was attitude. Had the interview been conducted with a negative or confronting attitude, the father would have more than likely just clammed up and denied everything. But by gaining rapport, the subject felt comfortable telling investigators about what he had done because the investigators went in with an open mind and good attitude. The investigators didn't let feelings affect their attitude. The statements gathered in this case lead to a confession and eventually a guilty plea to multiple counts of child sex abuse charges.

The attitude of the subject being interviewed is also important. During the rapport-building process, you may discover the subject's attitude is noticeably different than you would expect a reasonable person (in the same circumstances) would be. Be careful not to solely focus on one characteristic or circumstance, such as attitude. Consider what may cause the attitude that you are observing. For example, the parent of a missing child may seem less interested in answering some of your questions, which may seem unusual. It is certainly worth noting as a "red flag," but think what may be influencing the different attitude. Is it shock, confusion, stress, or something else? It could be anything. And it's also possible that the parent is involved in foul play. Stay focused on facts.

It is also worth noting that the parent may possess a feeling of guilt that the child was missing without that guilt being criminal in nature. For example, if the parent allowed the young child to play in a fenced back yard and the parent was only away for less than a few minutes but during that time, the child was abducted by a stranger, might the parent feel responsible? Yes. What if there was no foul play involving the parent and the abductor but the officer/investigator detects the attitude of the parent as suspect? Could that lead the officers/investigators to focus in the wrong direction? Absolutely, and that's why keeping an open mind is so important. Acknowledge the red flag, but don't solely focus on it to direct your response or investigation. Victims and witnesses will vary in their attitude or reactions to different situations depending on specific circumstances (e.g., stress, violence, etc.). Recognize it, and don't dismiss it, but don't assume it's more than what the facts provide.

Confronting

You will be doing many of the tasks covered in this book over and over. It can be very easy as time goes along to get complacent, and we have seen some of our peers just not care anymore, a phenomenon commonly known as "burnout." This does not serve justice and may even result in injustice.

Being confrontational has its place from time to time to produce stress, such as at certain points in interrogations, but it is not always the best practice. Being confrontational during a cooperative interview process is not effective when gathering statements. If someone was yelling at you, would you talk to them? Probably not. Remember, interviews are designed to be fact seeking. If you are confrontational, you will not achieve your goals for the interview.

If you follow the steps we have described above, you are more likely to have success in your job.

References

Brady v. Maryland, 373 U.S. 83 (1963). https://www.oyez.org/cases/1962/490

Docan-Morgan, T. (2007). Training law enforcement officers to detect deception: A critique of previous research and framework for the future. *Applied Psychology in Criminal Justice, 3*(2), 143–171.

Matsumoto, D., Hwang, H.-S., Skinner, L., & Frank, M. (2011). Evaluating truthfulness and detecting deception. *FBI Law Enforcement Bulletin, 80*(6), 1–8.

Shults, J. F. (2019, June 13). *5 keys to great report writing.* Police1. https://www.police1.com/investigations/articles/5-keys-to-great-report-writing-g3a3fvJ3Xwyi79ZD/

State of New Jersey v. Cook, 179 N.J. 533 (N.J. 2004). https://law.justia.com/cases/new-jersey/appellate-division-unpublished/2012/a3740-10.html

State v. Ortiz, 215 P.3d 811 (N.M. Ct. App. 2009). https://law.justia.com/cases/new-mexico/court-of-appeals/2009/f580-118d6-12616.html

State v. W.B. (A-80-09) (2011). https://law.justia.com/cases/new-jersey/supreme-court/2011/a-80-09-opn.html

Stewart, S. T. (2017, October 10). *How to interview gang members*. Corrections1. https://www.corrections1.com/corrections-training/articles/how-to-interview-gang-members-5JMY65NEC1DLiw97/

United States v. Paxton, No. 14-2913 (7th Circuit 2017). https://law.justia.com/cases/federal/appellate-courts/ca7/14-2913/14-2913-2017-02-17.html

Welty, J. (2017, October 9). *Should an officer use his or her personal cell phone to take work-related photographs?* North Carolina Criminal Law. https://nccriminallaw.sog.unc.edu/officer-use-personal-cell-phone-take-work-related-photographs/

Part II

Interrogation

CHAPTER 5

Legal Aspects

Purpose

Interrogations are detailed interviews commonly conducted by law enforcement when the subject is in custody and is suspected to have committed a crime in which the interview is directed toward. An interrogation is led by the law enforcement officer/investigator where **closed-ended questions** are commonly used to initiate the questioning. Interrogations are more accusatory than interviews. Typically, the interrogation is controlled by the interviewer. The goal of any interrogation is a confession. That is the reason why closed-ended questions are used to start the interrogation process.

Courts throughout the United States are always examining the processes and procedures law enforcement use when obtaining a confession through an interview or interrogation. The U.S. Constitution protects citizens in the United States as it relates to interviews and interrogations through the Fifth and Fourteenth Amendments.

As you could imagine, interrogations involve many different legal aspects. Since interrogations involve accusations of criminal activity in which the subject is being interviewed about and it commonly involves self-incriminating statements, there are many legal decisions that relate to interrogations. We will discuss a few of the more common decisions that govern police interrogations.

Miranda Rights

In *Miranda v. Arizona* (1966), the Supreme Court created a three-prong requirement for a warning to apply. The three-prong test must be met:

- law enforcement: The courts have required that in order for Miranda to apply, questioning must be by law enforcement or someone who is asking questions on behalf of law enforcement, in an adversarial process.

- questioning: The courts have held that law enforcement must ask the subject questions. Miranda does not apply to unsolicited statements the subject may make. The courts have also ruled that questioning can be made by actions intended to elicit a response from a subject; it is not restricted to verbal questioning.

- custody: This area has created some problems with the courts throughout the years. The court in this case acknowledged the "focus test" in their decision. The focus test involves timing. Is the subject being interviewed the focus of the investigation? Are they the primary suspect?

The court also defined procedural safeguards as a requirement that the suspects be advised of the following rights prior to questioning:

- Right to remain silent

- Right to consult with an attorney

- Right to have an attorney present during questioning

- Right to have a court appointed attorney, if (they) cannot afford an attorney

These warnings are not required to be read in any specific order or verbatim (like you may have seen on television or in the movies). However, it is best practice to read the Miranda warning verbatim or use a card to read the warning in the exact manner every time. It's a good practice because you'll be able to testify in court exactly how you advise the Miranda warning every single time. Additionally, this procedure helps you avoid forgetting anything, creates consistency in your investigations, and helps bolster your testimony.

The first two requirements are rather forthcoming and easily understood. However, let's discuss when someone is acting on behalf of law enforcement. When a law enforcement officer is acting in an undercover capacity, Miranda does not apply to a conversation with the undercover officer because the suspect does not believe the person acting in a undercover capacity is law enforcement. In *Illinois v. Perkins* (1990), the court held that Miranda was not required. Perkins had no reason to believe that the person he was speaking to could exercise any official authority over him or could use officially sanctioned force to compel him to speak against his wishes. An undercover officer was acting as a prisoner and was housed in the same cell as Perkins.

Miranda is not required when:

- public safety questions are asked

- asking routine booking questions

- the person being interrogated has a lawyer with them

- a statement is made by suspect without being questioned

Citizen (nongovernment/law enforcement) interrogations may also occur. You should understand that citizen interrogations differ from law enforcement/government interrogation. Custody is an issue for law enforcement, but that is not a requirement for citizen interrogation. As a matter of fact, a citizen interrogation is actually an interview in our opinion. While the types of questions may make the subject feel that are being interrogated, we don't believe it's a true interrogation. However, it is worth mentioning.

On example could be a shoplifting incident. The business's loss-prevention officer could question an offender outside of law enforcement presence. Another case where a citizen interrogation may occur is when an employer is questioning an employee about wrongdoing or accusations of misconduct.

Custodial Interrogation by Police

We have discussed that most interviews should not require the Miranda warning because interviews are nonaccusatory. However, some interviews are custodial in nature, like those conducted in jails or prisons. Law enforcement officials are sometimes confused as to whether or not they are required to advise a suspect their Miranda rights. Throughout the years, courts have inconsistently ruled as to when custody applies.

The case *Thompson v. Keohane* (1995) is often referenced to define custody. In *Thompson*, the court said that *custody* generally means being formally arrested or being restrained, which prohibits one's "freedom of movement to the degree associated with a formal arrest." Would a reasonable person believe they were "free to leave"? Some additional factors that may apply to whether one feels that they are in custody include location of the interview, whether they are handcuffed or not, length of time, the number of law enforcement present, and the demeanor or nature of questioning. That's why a nonaccusatory interview is so important.

To better determine custody, courts will use the objective reasonable test, also known as ORT. Custody is based on the totality of the circumstances. Would a reasonable person think they are in custody or not? The officer's subjective intent or views are not relevant. Some factors to determine custody include:

- prolonged interrogation

- time and location of interrogation

- duration and character of the questioning

- mode of transportation to place of interrogation

- number of officers (law enforcement) present

- display of weapons

- physical contact

- hostile demeanor or tone of voice

- restriction of movement

- accusations

- the extent to which the subject is made aware that they do not have to talk and can end the interrogation at any time

In *Berkemer v. McCarty* (1984), the U.S. Supreme Court ruled that Miranda rights should be administered whenever a person is subject to custodial interrogation, regardless of the seriousness, to include a misdemeanor traffic offenses. However, roadside questioning of a motorist stopped for a routine traffic violation does not constitute a custodial interrogation for the purposes of Miranda. The court further explained the difference between roadside questioning and custodial interrogation. A good rule of thumb in determining the difference would be if the questioning was specifically related to a crime or if it was the circumstance of the traffic stop.

When a subject has waived their rights under Miranda, the court has required the waiver be in writing. In *North Carolina v. Butler* (1979), the court even mentioned that the waiver could be implied "through the defendant's silence, coupled with an understanding of his rights, and a course of conduct indicating waiver." The Miranda waiver need not be "expressed," but "conduct" such as a head-nodding gesture of acknowledgement is acceptable. Although the court does not require a written waiver, it is best practice to obtain a written waiver when it's feasible.

There are some additional criteria to review in regard to the Miranda warning and juveniles. *State of Tennessee v. Callahan* (1998) stated that juvenile waivers shall be analyzed under a totality of circumstances test as well. The court considers the following factors:

- All circumstances surrounding the interrogation, including the juvenile's age, experience of criminality, education, and intelligence

- The juvenile's capacity to understand the Miranda warnings and the consequences of the waiver

- The juvenile's familiarity with Miranda warnings or their ability to read and write in the language used to give the warning

- Any intoxication

- Any mental disease, disorder, or intellectual disabilities

- The presence of a parent, guardian, or interested party

Tennessee v. Callahan (1998) goes on to cite *Colorado v. Connelly* (1986): "While courts shall exercise special care in scrutinizing purported Miranda waivers by juvenile suspects, no single factor such as mental condition or education should by itself render a confession unconstitutional absent coercive police activity."

Let's look at cases where a subject invoked their Miranda warning. In *Michigan v. Mosley* (1975), the court found that an investigator may re-Mirandize a suspect to question them about a new case without violating their Fifth Amendment rights, even if the suspect has invoked the right to remain silent. Mosley was arrested and subsequently questioned about some robberies he was suspected to have committed. He initially invoked his right to remain silent. Questioning related to the robberies stopped. A few hours later, a different investigator approached Mosley while he was still being held to question him around a homicide. The investigator read Mosley his Miranda warning. Mosley made a statement that incriminated him. Mosley was convicted, and he appealed. Even though investigators questioned Mosley about a second crime, this did not violate his right to remain silent because they re-read his Miranda rights.

If you forget to advise the Miranda warning when required, can you later correct the mistake? Yes, but only if the mistake was made in good faith. The unwarned part of the interrogation is inadmissible, but everything after the warning was given will be admissible (*Oregon v. Elstad*, 1985). If you forgot Miranda on purpose, as a tactic, you cannot correct it by a second confession under Miranda (*Missouri v. Seibert*, 2004). The U.S. Supreme Court expressed skepticism if a warning given after someone has already started talking has a legitimate effect. Below is a test to help determine if warnings were effective:

- completeness and details of unwarned statement

- overlapping content of two statements

- timing and setting of the first and second interrogations

- continuity of police personnel

- degree to which the second interrogation was treated as a continuation of the first interrogation

The burden will be on the prosecution to prove the failure to advise Miranda was an honest mistake.

In-Custody Interrogations by Corrections

It is important to understand that people who are already incarcerated may have different motivations for cooperating or not cooperating than predetention suspects. Most major jails and prisons have a classification officer or even a section of several staff who do assessments on offenders. This can happen at booking intake after law enforcement arrests them and/or transfers them into custody of a jail or prison or can occur after they are placed in a receiving unit.

These classification officers (a) look at the offense committed, legal holds from other agencies, incarceration experience, and what custody level they were placed in; (b) check for any escapes and assaults on staff or others; and (c) do a criminal background and behavior check of prior placements in custody. It can be to your benefit to check this information if you have access or to call if legally authorized to do so by your department policy.

People convicted of felonies can often be very manipulative of the system. The may volunteer "false information" on somebody else in order to take the heat off of them. They may be looking for a better deal on their case in the hopes that the officer will provide information to the courts that makes them look better as a cooperating witness to major crime(s).

Informants in and out of jail and prison are often referred to as being "snitches," and there is a frequent saying, "Snitches get stitches." In other words, the threat of violence upon them in or out of custody is a very real consideration.

If you are working within corrections, you will quickly get to know these dynamics.

Always remember, experienced detainees in jail and prison often will try to gain information for their personal gain from staff during interviews and interrogations, so you will want to be professional and cordial but also direct and focused. Avoid giving away any clues to your case by extremely differing tone and very revealing body language. For example, your eyebrows may go up when they say something shocking to the conscience. They may be testing you to see what you know or don't know. You can almost be assured they are going to run back to the institution-provided phone and let people involved know what they found out from you. This can also be an advantage sometimes if you have somebody on alert and screening for outgoing letters or phone calls.

Some people not familiar with the criminal justice system may not be aware, but phone calls in most major jails and prisons are recorded. They will even have a warning at the beginning and often at periodic times during the call that it is being recorded. But guess what? Inmates still often make incriminating statements about crimes that have been committed in the past or may be committed in the future. These calls can even be tracked by data that may show triangulation between callers and receivers that can provide good intelligence and evidence for investigators.

The questioning of a person already in custody does not always involve the "shock associated with arrest," and a prisoner is not inclined to be lured into speaking for a prompt release, which was discussed in *Howes v. Fields* (2021). In this case, Fields was already in jail. Investigators who were not associated with the correctional facility interviewed Fields in a conference room of the facility. Fields was not handcuffed or restrained as he was questioned. Fields was questioned about sexual conduct with a minor. Fields provided a statement that was later used against him in court. Fields argued to the court that he did not believe he could freely leave. Fields claimed that his statement violated his due process rights by the lower court admitting his incriminating statement.

In *Howes v. Fields* (2021), the court upheld the lower court's decision and found there was no Miranda violation because Fields was told by the investigators he was free to leave at any time. They were in a well-lit room, he had on no restraints, he was offered food and water, the door was left open, and the interrogation time was not unreasonable. The court mentioned that "a reasonable person would have felt free to terminate the interview and leave" (*Howes v. Fields*, 2021).

The courts will look at the surrounding circumstance of the interrogation when a person is in custody for a while and jail is their "new home."

Voluntariness

The courts require a confession be voluntary in nature. The Fifth Amendment of the U.S. Constitution provides that no person "shall be compelled in any criminal case to be a witness against himself" (U.S. Const., amend. V). The Fifth Amendment also guarantees that the accused have legal representation in criminal proceedings to support their defense.

In *Oregon v. McCarthy* (2003), the court stated that "a confession is admissible in evidence only if it was given voluntarily, and the State has the burden to prove voluntariness beyond a reasonable doubt" (as summarized in *State v. Wiley*, 2013). In *Maine v. Mikulewicz* (1983), the court said, "A confession is voluntary if it results from the free choice of a rational mind, if it is not a product of coercive police conduct, and if under all of the circumstances its admission would be fundamentally fair." Law enforcement can't provoke the confession by mental torture.

In *Brown v. Mississippi* (1936), the Supreme Court ruled that the use of police violence to obtain a confession infringes on the Due Process Clause of the 14th Amendment, and these confessions cannot be entered as evidence in a trial. Torture created the unlikelihood a confession is untrue. The courts will base voluntariness on the totality of the circumstances approach, meaning that no one factor or lack of will kill a determination of voluntariness; rather, the courts will look at all factors to decide.

There are many factors the court will use to determine voluntariness:

- subject's mental health ability to resist police coercion (e.g., age, education level, criminal history, mental capacity, etc.)

- setting/location of interview/interrogation

- duration and manner of interview/interrogation

- number of officers and attire (e.g., uniform, weapons, etc.)

- brutality/threats of brutality

- false promises of leniency that the subject relies on in confessing

- lack of access to outside world

  - This developed into the right to counsel but started as the right to see family, friends, and so on (*Ashcraft v. Tennessee*, 1944).

- relentless interrogation (*Ashcraft v. Tennessee*, 1944)

- coercive threats to interfere with family

- trickery

  - What constitutes trickery depends on many factors, as will be described below.

In *New York v. Quarles* (1984), the court found "a situation where concern for public safety must be paramount to adherence to the literal language of the prophylactic rules enunciated in Miranda." Quarles was arrested as a rape suspect. The officers thought he was carrying a firearm. They found an empty shoulder holster on Quarles's person. The arrest occurred in a public place, a grocery store. The officers, fearing danger to the public, asked Quarles where the gun was at. Quarles nodded in the direction of some nearby empty boxes and said, "The gun is over there." A gun was recovered. Quarles was not prosecuted for the rape. He was prosecuted for the weapons possession. Quarles argued that he could not be convicted of the weapon possession because he had not been given the Miranda warning prior to being questioned about the gun. However, the court ruled the public safety exception applied to the normal Fifth Amendment requirement of Miranda.

Edwards v. Arizona (1981) held questioning must cease once the suspect invokes their right to counsel. Interrogation may continue once the suspect has been either been provided counsel, obtained counsel, or further initiated communication or conversation with law enforcement. If a suspect is released after questioning, police may initiate questioning after a break in custody lasting at least 14 days, per *Maryland v. Shatzerm* (2010). The court stated that "14 days provides plenty of time for the suspect to get reacclimated to his normal life, to consult with friends and counsel, and to shake off any residual coercive effects of his prior custody."

Another measurement that the courts look at related to voluntariness is if or when a subject requests an attorney to be present during questioning, which is mentioned in Miranda. When a suspect being interrogated requests an attorney, all questioning must stop until the suspect has their attorney present. If the suspect doesn't have an attorney, questioning must end until the court appoints them an attorney. Oftentimes, an attorney will prohibit the suspect from incriminating themselves and advise them to refuse to continue answering questions.

There are times when someone who is represented by an attorney allows questioning. One example is a **proffer**. The prosecutor and defense attorney can agree to a legally binding contract to interrogate an accused defendant about the crime of which they have been charged, as well as any other criminal activity. The agreement generally states that the accused must be truthful during the questioning. If the prosecutor can prove the accused subject was not truthful, then everything (including incriminating statements) can be used against the accused. However, if the accused is truthful in questioning, they may qualify for a reduction at sentencing or limited immunity. Proffers are not open court record and are kept secret.

All confessions must be voluntary to be admissible in court. When in doubt, always err on the side of caution.

Tactics

The courts have upheld different law enforcement tactics during the interrogation process. Some tactics include the use of deception or trickery. While it's not always the best practice, these processes (when properly used) can be used during an interrogation. However, under no circumstances can you coerce someone into providing a statement.

Use of Deception

Law enforcement can lie to a subject during questioning under certain circumstances, but lying can be judged as coercive. It is best to seek legal advice from your department before proceeding on this path as a tactic. Trickery will be analyzed by the court on the basis of whether or not the trick or deception would likely induce an innocent person to confess out of fear of a frame-up or police misconduct. Deception related to the subject's connection to the crime is generally OK. Lying about witnesses or fingerprints is OK because an innocent person would know that you were lying. Creating a false lab report is not an acceptable trick to use.

Deception unrelated to the subject's connection to the crime is generally not OK. For example, if police threatened a female subject with the loss of welfare and custody of her children but offered to recommend leniency if she would confess, that is not acceptable. Another unacceptable tactic is if the police told a subject they could "either lawyer up or cooperate with the government, but not both."

In *Rowe v. State* (1979), detectives approached a murder suspect (defendant) and said that the victim was a "no good (person) who deserved to die" and that he (the detective) would like to shake the hand of the man who murdered him. The defendant then stood and extended his hand. The court allowed this tactic.

In *State v. Chambers* (1988), an investigator lied and told a rape defendant that the victim's butt prints were found on the hood of the car, which was not true. During the interrogation, Rowe stated that he and the victim were sitting on the hood of the car. Detective Gosnell asked if they were clothed, and Rowe stated they were. The detective then said, "If you were clothed, then when I process the car for fingerprints, there is no reason I would find (her butt print) on the car, is there?" Rowe responded, " Maybe." This lead to Rowe providing more details and confessing. The court permitted this form of deception to deceive the rape suspect (defendant).

As stated previously in the In-Custody Interrogations by Corrections section, you should also be aware that some very experienced criminals have huge egos. As Dr. George Cartwright (2021) writes:

> Some experienced criminals or persons who have committed well-planned crimes believe that they can offer an alternate explanation for their involvement in the criminal event that will exonerate them as a suspect. An investigator may draw answers from this type of suspect by offering the same proposition that is offered for exoneration. This is the opportunity for a suspect to offer an alibi or a denial of the crime and an alternate explanation or exonerating evidence. It can be very difficult for a suspect to properly explain away all the evidence. Looking at the progression of the event, an interrogator can sometimes ask for additional details that the suspect cannot explain. The truth is easier to tell because it happened, and the facts will line up. In contrast, a lie frequently requires additional lies to support the untrue statement. Examining a statement that is believed to be untrue, an interrogator can sometimes ask questions that expose the lies behind the original lie. (Exoneration section)

This is known as "conning," named after the word "convict." When an interrogator asks for details that catch the suspect off guard, they may feel that it is easier to come clean and tell the real version of their story because it actually happened and collaborating facts will line up.

Seasoned investigators will explain that many criminals genuinely regret their actions, particularly first-time offenders who have committed a terrible crime against another person. It just shows that these people still have a conscience. It is fine to show some empathy toward the suspect or interrogatee in these types of cases. That does not mean you sympathize with them or will withdraw your information against them.

By the same token, you may encounter individuals who have no remorse for their horrible crimes and show no conscience at all. You may feel disgust for these individuals and may feel the urge to lash out at them verbally or even physically. Do not! It is important to remain professional at all times and not jeopardize a case or diminish your reputation as a fair, firm, and consistent investigator.

Also, never forget, inmates can and will sue in civil court for staff misconduct or deprivation of their rights. Many have nothing better to do than think of ways they can go after you or your department in court or make life as miserable for you as they can, so do not become an easy target. Lying can be judged as coercive. Law enforcement officers *can* lie to a suspect to obtain a confession. For example, police can lie to a suspect in telling them that a codefendant had already confessed to the crime (*Frazier v. Cupp*, 1969). Such lies by law enforcement officers are controversial because they may detract from the reliability of criminal proceedings. Although accepted by the courts, lying can be viewed by a jury as untrustworthy behavior.

Coercion

Coercion is the practice of persuading someone to do something by using force, threats, or promises. You cannot coerce a subject to give a statement to law enforcement. The 14th Amendment of the U.S. Constitution prohibits coercive questioning by law enforcement. Law enforcement is prohibited from using threatening language to get a subject to answer questions. Review the following examples of law enforcement coercion during an interview:

- "If you don't tell me where it happened, we will arrest your wife."

- A law enforcement officer pointing a gun at the subject and saying, "Tell me what happened or I'll blow your head off."

- Threatening longer sentence: "You will serve a life sentence if you don't tell me."

Many think of force and threats as they relate to coercion. However, promises are also coercive. Promises of leniency can also lead to coercion. The courts tend to review what would make a statement involuntary. Was the subject provided so much hope for leniency that they were not able to choose freely and rationally amongst other options available to them? Leniency must be clearly understood as a specific guarantee. For example, consider the statement "If you admit to (information sought), I promise you will not serve a day in jail." A statement would be rendered involuntary if the conduct of an officer/investigator was such as to overbear the willingness of the subject to resist the "offer" and resulted in an admission that was not freely self-determined.

In *Chambers v. Florida* (1940), the court found that 5 days of continuous interrogation was coercive. The court has also ruled about the amount of time an interrogation can last. In *Ashcraft v. Tennessee* (1944), the court ruled that 36 hours of continuous interrogation is considered coercive. While the court has yet set a specific time limit to an interrogation, there are circumstances that are considered when the amount of time of an interrogation is challenged, including breaks (to use the bathroom and eat), type of crime, and so on.

The use of force and threats relating to coercion could taint your case and investigation and could eventually bring criminal charges against yourself or lead to your possible dismissal. However, promises are also coercive.

Open-Ended Versus Closed-Ended Questioning

It should be the interrogator's preference when to use open- versus closed-ended questioning. Closed-ended questions are more often used during an interrogation because the interrogation is more accusatory. The purpose when initiating an interrogation is to overcome the subject's ability to develop resistance to an admission. Once the subject admits to the crime, then open-ended questions can be used.

There may be some concern when conducting interrogation related to false confessions. That's why it's important to be prepared for interrogations. You should have reasonable and articulatable facts that can establish probable cause that the subject you are interrogating, whom is in custody, committed the crime for which you are interrogating them. If not, you subject yourself to fundamental errors that may induce a false confession.

A good investigator will not conduct a custodial interrogation without facts that can be tested against a subject's statement, confession, or story. Those facts should come from the crime scene and the subsequent investigation that led to the interrogation.

Oftentimes, once a subject has admitted to their involvement in a crime, they will open up more. It's like they remove an elephant that's been standing on their chest. At this point, open-ended questioning is important to obtain details. These details can also be compared to the facts of the investigation. The confession should start to **corroborate**, confirm or given support to, the investigation if the subject is truthful. If you cannot corroborate the confession to the crime scene or investigation, that should be considered a "red flag," and you need to determine why.

Difference Between an Interview and an Interrogation

Interviews and interrogations serve different purposes, as outlined by Moreno and Morales (n.d.). In an interview, your main purpose is to get information, meaning:

- Note-taking is OK.
- Interviewee talks the most.
- Be supportive ("good cop").
- You both sit. Be relaxed but structured.

In an interrogation, your main purpose is to get the truth/a confession, meaning:

- Show no notes of the case.
- The interrogation can be secretly recorded.
- You talk the most via direct questioning.
- You are accusatory ("bad cop").
- They sit, and you stand if needed, but it is OK to sit when they are more cooperative in your questioning.

When preparing to interview a gang member, follow these guidelines:

- Never go into an interview with a hard-core criminal unprepared.
- Do your homework: They have done theirs!
- Review the current charge/PC, NCIC/rap sheet, past police reports/gang files.
- Review presentence reports/PC.
- Review parole and probation files.
- Check their prison and jail files.

Prior to an interview with an inmate, prepare yourself appropriately. This can include researching the inmate's charges and pending sentences, consulting with prosecutors, and confirming policies for interviewing charged suspects (Stewart, 2017). This aligns with the five P's principle: Proper preparation prevents poor performance (Stewart, 2017). Having some background information—even a small piece of information—may influence an inmate to provide more information. For example, a gang member may talk more freely if they think you already know about the situation (Stewart, 2017).

References

Ashcraft v. Tennessee, 322 U.S. 143 (1944). https://supreme.justia.com/cases/federal/us/322/143/

Berkemer v. McCarty, 468 U.S. 420 (1984). https://www.oyez.org/cases/1983/83-710

Brown v. Mississippi 297 U.S. 278 (1936). https://supreme.justia.com/cases/federal/us/297/278/

Cartwright, G. (2021, January 20). *10.1: Interrogations*. LibreTexts. https://biz.libretexts.org/Courses/Reedley_College/Criminology_1__Introduction_to_Criminology_(Cartwright)/10%3A_Interrogations_and_Police_Searches/10.01%3A_Interrogations

Chambers v. Florida, 309 U.S. 277 (1940). https://supreme.justia.com/cases/federal/us/309/227/

Colorado v. Connelly, 479 U.S. 157, 167, 107 S. Ct., 93 L. Ed. 2d 473 (1986). https://www.oyez.org/cases/1986/85-660

Edwards v. Arizona, 451 U.S. 477 (1981). https://www.oyez.org/cases/1980/79-5269

Frazier v. Cupp, 394 U.S. 731 (1969). https://supreme.justia.com/cases/federal/us/394/731/

Howes v. Fields, 132 S.Ct. 1181 (2021). https://www.oyez.org/cases/2011/10-680

Illinois v. Perkins, 496 U.S. 292 (1990). https://www.oyez.org/cases/1989/88-1972

Maine v. Mikulewicz, 462 A.2nd 497 (1983). https://casetext.com/case/state-v-mikulewicz

Maryland v. Shatzerm 559 U.S. 98 (2010). https://www.oyez.org/cases/2009/08-680

Michigan v. Mosley, 423 U.S. 96 (1975). https://www.oyez.org/cases/1975/74-653

Miranda v. Arizona 384 U.S. 436 (1966). https://www.oyez.org/cases/1965/759

Missouri v. Seibert, 541 U.S. 600 (2004). https://www.oyez.org/cases/2003/02-1371

Moreno, T., & Morales, G. (2005d.). *Interviewing techniques for corrections and law enforcement. PPT.*

New York v. Quarles, 467 U.S. 649 (1984). https://www.oyez.org/cases/1983/82-1213

North Carolina v. Butler, 441 U.S. 369 (1979). https://www.oyez.org/cases/1978/78-354

Oregon v. Elstad, 470 U.S. 298 (1985). https://www.oyez.org/cases/1984/83-773

Oregon v. McCarthy (2003).

Rowe v. State Md. App. 641 (1979). https://casetext.com/case/rowe-v-state-120?resultsNav=false

State of Tennessee v. Callahan, 9797 S.W.2d 577 (Tenn. 1998). https://casetext.com/case/state-v-callahan-39

State v. Chambers, 92 N.C. App. 230 (1988). https://casetext.com/case/state-v-chambers-171

State v. Wiley (2013). https://law.justia.com/cases/maine/supreme-court/2013/2013-me-30.html

Stewart, S. (2017, October 10). *How to interview gang members*. Corrections1. https://www.corrections1.com/corrections-training/articles/how-to-interview-gang-members-5JMY65NEC1DLiw97/

Thompson v. Keohane, 516 U.S. 99 (1995). https://www.oyez.org/cases/1995/94-6615

U.S. Const., amend. V.

CHAPTER 6

Effective Interrogations

Use of Interviews

Most interrogations are not conducted without a previous interview; thus, many times some of the questioning will be similar in nature. Of course, there also may be times when you conduct an interrogation based on evidence alone and the first contact with the suspect is custodial. Ideally, a criminal investigation will include an interview with the suspect prior to arrest. In those cases, it is important to review the interview notes and recordings (if used) before conducting the interrogation. When you review the interview, you may recognize or connect some responses to evidence in the investigation. If reviewing a video of the interview, you may recognize a change in body language during questions. Look for admissions and/ or omissions that you can prove or disprove. Note all of these while preparing for the interrogation. Use of the interview is certainly important to conduct effective interrogations.

Depending on the culture of your agency, department policies, smaller agencies, and so on, you may have a lot of leeway in how you proceed. In other agencies that are politically charged, have more strict policies, are larger agencies, and so on, you may be in communication with superiors and peers before you proceed.

You may need to "deconflict" with these people concerning the individual/suspect, as they may be undergoing far larger investigations involving more serious crimes and they may not want to put an informant in jeopardy or jeopardize a case. At first, this may sound like you are letting guys off the hook, thereby allowing crime to happen. Veteran officers and investigators know this can by a tricky situation, and outsiders often accuse corrections officers and police of not having enough supervision over confidential informants' activities while working for them. It is sometimes the case of letting the small fish go to get the bigger fish, and as long as there are no major law violations occurring, this is usually OK. However, you will very likely want to keep those with a need to know in the loop, and it will need to be carefully documented, as—be assured—defense attorneys will bring it up later.

Applying Similar Concepts

Interviews are the foundation to any criminal investigation. Interviews help investigators develop motive and assess similarities and differences in the investigation. There may be times where multiple follow-up interviews are conducted on the same person. New information may arise, which can develop the need to interview a victim or witness multiple times. Suspects may also need to be interviewed multiple times. However, our experience suggests limiting multiple interviews with a potential suspect. It could make the suspect feel the focus is directed toward them and could jeopardize a successful interview.

All the interviews in a criminal investigation can be compared to one another to identify similarities, differences, motives, and investigative needs. When reviewing details from interviews and similarities are found, consider their likeness and inconsistencies. Was the information connecting information that is common or public knowledge, or could only a person present at the time of the event know what information was disclosed? That's important. Information from different sources may match because the information is public knowledge. In that case, the information may not be as corroborating as information that only on eyewitness would know. On the other hand, if the person being interviewed or interrogated provides information that could only be known to somebody actually involved, that is also very important to note.

If witness statements are different compared to the victim's statement, the officer/investigator must establish why. It could be a difference in perspective, a different angle, or that they simply saw something differently. That's normal. As a matter of fact, if statements are the same or verbatim, our experience is that is more suspicious than when there are some differences. It can suggest collusion. When examining the differences, you must determine why the differences are there. Could the victim's statement be trauma induced? Was information left out? Was it intentional? Differences occur. If you have multiple conflicting statements, you must dissect each. Corroborating each statement with facts and evidence from the case will help you decipher the truth. Remember that people interpret what they see differently. Also, victims or witnesses may see or hear things differently because of different angles or distances or biases.

Interviews can help investigators develop a **motive** in an investigation. You don't have to prove a motive for every crime, but establishing a motive can help an investigation. While conducting interviews or comparing interviews afterwards, an investigator may identify a motive after everything is laid out.

Motives can help a jury understand the facts of the case better. For example, a jury may better understand why one subject shot another if it were related to an argument or gang violence. Gangs often demand respect, and if a gang member is disrespected in front of their fellow gang members, then the gang member who was disrespected must retaliate for being disrespected. Therefore, the gang member may shoot the person who disrespected them to prove themselves or show allegiance to their gang. Simple disrespect in this case is the motive for the shooting.

In these types of situations, you may need to bring in a gang expert (preferably from your own agency). But even better, keep yourself up to date and attend as many law enforcement–endorsed classes as you can. Contact your local gang investigator association, homicide investigator associations, and the like for training events. Also, you can read books on specific subjects pertaining to your profession. A judge will determine whether or not you or another agency source or outside source is an expert and whether to allow this testimony in court.

By conducting several interviews and an investigation, a timeline can be created to determine what happened and when it happened. Timelines are critical with any investigation. Timelines are used as a reference and may provide visual aid to identify connections between people, places, and things. This may provide information to develop a link analysis for the intelligence process to be covered in detail later in this book. Not only might this connect people, places, and things to one another but it can also provide additional leads or motives to further investigate. Timelines are useful for helping a jury to understand the chronological events in a criminal investigation.

Interviews will develop investigative needs as well. Since so much information can be developed from interviews, investigators are encouraged to create a "to-do list." After comparing interviews and evidence, investigator will see potential loose ends that need to be tied up in their case. That's why it's also important to prepare and review the case, specifically any other crucial interviews documented prior to conducting a new interview. As the case develops, it may become more important to prove or disprove another statement with facts or additional interview statements. You will not want to be intimidated by the fact that defense attorneys will later question everything you did during your investigation, but you will also want to be careful and proactive to not commit any major blunders. This can save you and your department a lot of embarrassment. Most supervisors are understanding that minor mistakes can and will be made, but commit major ones and you may find yourself working another position. In other words, if you like your job and reputation, don't do sloppy work.

Additional resources that may be needed for the investigation can also be identified through interviews. For example, an interview may produce a lead that suggests a local businesses surveillance camera may have captured a suspect fleeing from the crime. This information would provide an additional resource that may assist in developing a suspect description, timeline, and/or other information for the case.

Officers/investigators must keep in mind that interviews are fact-seeking missions. In the end, it's great if an interview of a suspect in a crime gains an admission. Unfortunately, that's not always the result. As previously discussed, interviews can also provide omissions. The interview is used to gather information that can later be used for connecting evidence, corroborating other facts or statements, and so forth. Disproving a suspect's statement is just as critical. Think outside the box, and don't forget the omissions. Sometimes people can tell you more with what they don't say or should have said, given information already known to you, than with what they actually say. With a suspect's interview, keep in mind that your interview is also preparing for the interrogation after arrest. That's when the interview is often more confrontational and controlled by the investigator/officer. Sometimes we get caught up with needing an admission from the suspect or getting one early to complete the case. While helpful, it's certainly not required. Hard work and good interview and interrogation tactics will and should prove what really happened in court.

To quote a well-known line by Denzel Washington from the movie *Training Day*, "It's not what you know. It's what you can prove" (Fuqua, 2001).

Confessions

Admissions are more directed toward suspects in a crime, rather than victims or witnesses. An **admission** is a statement or acknowledgment, typically from a suspect, that can be proven as factual. The proof may be corroborated by evidence in the investigation, other interviews, and the like. An admission may include an element of a crime, but it's not to be confused with a confession. A **confession** is an acknowledgment of guilt of a crime. Confessions are typically obtained in interrogations, not interviews.

Interrogations are more controlled by the interviewer than interviews. What do we mean?

In interviews, we are seeking facts from the person being interviewed. Therefore, we allow them to speak rather freely, and we (investigators/officers) speak less. During an interrogation, the investigator/officer speaks more and uses more closed-ended questions that require a simple yes-or-no answer. This process can produce stress on the suspect. It is well known that a liar with have to pause and think about the lie they just told before they answer the next question or try to explain their way out of a lie and cover themselves. You will want to control this by cutting them off and going to the next question before getting sidetracked. Somebody who has nothing to hide should not need long to think about it; they will answer yes or no relatively quickly. If they ask you to repeat a question, that may not mean they are lying; they just need to understand and process what is being asked of them. Somebody being manipulative and untruthful will ask you to repeat a question so they can have more time to try and think about how to get out of a predicament. It usually becomes clear early on in the interrogation if they are being truthful or deceptive.

Confessions should include an admission from the suspect to involvement in the crime that can also be corroborated by evidence from the investigation. Connecting evidence such as physical evidence (e.g., fingerprints, DNA, video recordings, etc.) or witness statements to a suspect's confession is always suggested.

Corroborating Evidence

When conducting interviews of suspect, you want to link the subject to the crime or crime scene. You also want to prove elements of the crime and how the suspect is connected. What are elements of a crime? Elements of a crime may include:

- intent: Also known as *mens rea* (a Latin term), this shows a person has the mental capacity or knows that they are committing a crime, which may include planning.

  - An example would be a suspect of a theft walking past a cashier without paying for merchandise.

- knowledge: Also known as *actus reus* (a Latin term) that includes that act or intent but also acknowledges a criminal offense.

  - In a theft, the suspect conceals merchandise in their pocket to deprive a store owner of the merchandise without paying for it.

- harm: Injury to a victim, such as bodily injury or death in violent offenses.

  - An example in an assault may include a victim being treated for a broken nose sustained by an offender/suspect striking them in the face.

  - Harm can also be threatening in nature.

    - For example, a suspect threatens to kill a store clerk if they don't cooperate in a robbery.

- causation: Refers to an act or acts that connect other elements that cause a crime.

  - For example, a suspect knowingly and intentionally shoots someone.

- legality:

  - Linking intent (*mens rea*) and knowledge (*actus reus*)

  - Consider options of self-defense.

During a suspect interrogation, one of the first steps is to put the suspect at the scene of the crime at the time of crime. Some different ways to do this are listed below:

- **forensic evidence**, scientific methods or techniques used to process an investigation, such as fingerprints or DNA

- video recordings, such as surveillance video

- eyewitness identification

- information from the suspect's initial interview

Understand that a fingerprint on a table in the room of the crime can be easily defended if the suspect had a legal reason to be in the room on an occasion prior to the crime. For example, if the suspect is an acquaintance of the victim and had been a guest of the victim in their residence prior to the crime, it's reasonable to believe their fingerprints or DNA could be on a table that they touched while visiting the victim prior to the crime. During the interrogation they will need to provide you the reasons why there is evidence possibly incriminating them. You and your legal experts can later decide if this was plausible.

However, if the same fingerprint was found in blood in the crime scene, it's reasonable to believe that fingerprint was left at the time of the crime or

FIGURE 6.1 Interrogation Room, Courtesy of Columbia, TN, Police Department

shortly thereafter because a fingerprint in blood related to the crime has a smaller timeframe due to blood drying. The window to link a bloody fingerprint is much shorter and can reasonable be linked to time of crime. Forensics experts can provide you and your department crucial information in this regard.

In the example above, we have linked the suspect not only to the crime scene but also to evidence in the crime scene (bloody fingerprint). During an interrogation, best practice is to seek information from the suspect that only a person at the scene of the crime and at the time of the crime would know. This information would be something that was not released to the public or commonly known to anyone that wasn't present. This may include victim clothing, specific environmental factors or settings within the crime scene, or any other specific details not released to the public.

You may consider having the suspect lead you to evidence, or fruits of the crime, which may assist with corroboration. If the suspect is under custodial arrest, you should be mindful of other alternative motives, such as an escape attempt. Taking a suspect directly back to the scene of a crime is not suggested but may be considered as a last resort. However, a suspect can provide specific details that may assist in recovering evidence that may not have been recovered prior to the interrogation (e.g., the body of a victim in a missing person/homicide investigation). You may have the suspect lead you to a weapon used in a crime that was tossed away while they were fleeing from the crime. This process often comes into play during plea bargains but can also come into play earlier in your investigation.

In a case like this, you could say, "I'm sure you would not want a child to find the gun and harm themselves, right? Help us recover the weapon to prevent such a tragedy." If a confessing suspect is cooperative and has any conscience, they are more likely to lead you to the evidence. Ultimately, you are seeking information that only a guilty subject would know or be privy to.

False Confessions

Your job, whether interviewing or interrogating, is to find out the truth. No investigator wants an innocent person to confess to a crime that they didn't commit. Kassin and Wrightsman (1985) describe three different false confessions: voluntary, coerced-compliant, and coerced-internalized. People who offer a self-incriminating statement to law enforcement without being pressured by the investigator give **voluntary false confessions**. Many times, their motive to falsely confess is for attention. In these cases, the confession is often recanted, typically once the pressure or stress is relieved.

Another reason for a false confession is when the suspect comes to believe they may have committed the crime. The suspect may have no independent recollection or knowledge about the crime, but they were influenced by alcohol or drugs at the time of the alleged crime. Therefore, they have what they believe is a gap in their memory. As a result, they start to believe the information the interrogators suggest and tend to conclude that they were involved in the crime. The suspect may begin to acknowledge details that the interrogator provides and doubt themselves, which causes an **internalized false confession**. In these cases, the suspect will not likely recant their confession, because they really believe that they were involved in the crime. One of the causes for this type of false confession is if the interrogator continuously describes the suspect's involvement in the crime and provides details that are believable, especially when the suspect acknowledges "blackout periods" that may be caused by alcohol and/or drugs.

There are a few reasons why people confess to crimes they did not commit. Researchers have concluded that a least one reason is the improper analysis of body language by the interviewer. We would agree that an improperly or undertrained investigator can misinterpret body language, which may lead to additional pressure being put on the subject being interviewed. Interrogations must test the confessions of suspects against known evidence or corroborating details related to the investigation. A good investigator/interrogator must be trained well and continue honing the craft of interviews and interrogations. They should also understand the reasons and causes for false confessions and then work to prevent such circumstances that cause subjects to falsely confess.

Documentation

Documenting interrogations is extremely important. There is no universal or "set way" to document interrogations or confessions. In today's digital society, one of the best ways to document interrogations is audio and video recording. However, that should not prevent investigators from taking notes during interrogations. Every confession should be either oral, written, or both. Many of the techniques that were discussed in Chapter 4 related to interviews can also be used to document interrogations. In this section, we will focus more on documenting confessions and interrogations that lack confessions.

Taking Notes

Commonly, interrogations are conducted with two interrogators/investigators. One is responsible for conducting the interrogation, and the other is responsible for documenting it or taking notes. There are times when only one investigator conducts the interrogation. It is not suggested to use three or more investigators/interrogators due to the possibility of coercion. If additional personnel are needed, it's suggested that you use a room with a two-way mirror for the additional personnel to monitor or document the interrogation.

Since interrogations are typically custodial, the Miranda warning should be used. In these cases, many law enforcement agencies require the waiver of one's rights to be documented in writing. If so, a form is commonly used to document the suspect's voluntary waiver. The form may include the Miranda warning and questions to acknowledge to rights were knowingly read, understood, and waived. The form will also have a line for the subject to sign and date, which acknowledges their waiver.

As the interrogation is being conducted, some notes that can be important are listed below:

- Suspect demeanor

- Evaluation of responses

- Observed body language indicators

  - Detail the topic being discussed and the specific indicator.

- Statements of admissions

- Statements that can be corroborated by evidence or witness statements

- Omission that can be proven or discredited

- Denials

- Whereabouts at the time of crime

  - Who can corroborate?

  - What they were doing? Why?

Your notes certainly should not be limited to the above.

During the interrogation, the suspect may agree to reduce their confession to writing. There are times when a suspect may not be able to write well. Although it's not desired, a suspect may ask an investigator to dictate their confession/statement. If this occurs, it's important to use the suspect's own words/phrases even if they aren't grammatically correct. It's their statement, not yours! In these cases, it's highly recommended that you purposely create some obvious errors that the suspect can identify and acknowledge as being incorrect. Those should be crossed out as the suspect is reading the statement. This will acknowledge the suspect's knowledge and understanding of the content. The error should include the initials of the suspect and the officer/investigator, which acknowledges the corrections. Again, this shows the suspect read, understood, and acknowledged the correction and helps show the suspect adopted the document.

There may be times when you don't take notes. If the suspect starts to watch what you are writing down or documenting, they may start to withhold information. It's important to pay attention to the suspect. If you recognize that your note-taking is starting to hinder the flow of the interrogation, you should reduce or stop taking notes. That's why it's important to use a two-way mirrored room or a video-captured (recorded) room. If it occurs within these rooms, another investigator can take notes remotely, which will not affect the suspect or the interrogation.

Audio/Video

Audio/video recording of interrogations helps reduce the accusations of a coerced confession or any other inappropriate activity. Video recording can also show the voluntariness of the suspect. For a recording to be used, the suspect does not always have to consent or have knowledge that the interrogation is being recorded. You may refer to the state in which the interrogation is being conducted to follow the proper procedures. It is extremely important to know local laws. Many states only require one party to know the conversation is being recorded. If the interrogator has knowledge the conversation is being recorded, then that is sufficient in those states. We recommend that if you record at least one interrogation, you should record them all. It's best practice to record all interrogations.

If audio or video recording are used, keep in mind that it is evidence and subject to discovery by the defense. The original recording should be treated like any other evidence in a criminal investigation. The recording admitted into evidence must be authentic, not a copy, which will be objected to as possibly being altered with omissions by the defense. It's suggested that a working copy of the recording be kept in the investigative file but not the original for security and legal purposes.

Pros	Cons
Everything is documented.	Everything is documented.
Voluntariness issues come up.	Can lead to misconceptions.
Body language can be observed.	Can lead to misinterpretations.
Eliminates complaints/allegations.	Poor quality audio/video can cause confusion.
Deters police misconduct.	Equipment can fail.
Helps protect against accusations of coercion.	Things may be incorrectly interpreted as intentional.
Helps protect against accusations of mistreatment.	
Provides the ability to review.	
Helps ensure thorough documentation.	

As with any technique, there are pros and cons, and that includes audio/video recording interrogations. In today's society, technological advances mean video recordings are extended. Below are some pros and cons to audio/video recordings.

Thorough Reports

It cannot be stated enough: Thorough and complete reporting in criminal investigations is critical. This does not exclude the interrogation process. Attention to detail is very important and can make or break a case. You should prepare a final report as soon as possible while everything is fresh on your mind. Be sure to document the mental state of the suspect at the time of the interrogation. Understand the circumstances and tactics that defense attorneys commonly employ to attack interrogations, and document what you did to circumvent those potential arguments, if possible.

Note: Review the legal aspects discussed in Chapter 5 and be sure to thoroughly document what you did or didn't do. Some aspects include the Miranda requirements, special requests (especially for long interrogations) such as bathroom breaks or food requests, lawyer/attorney requests (if applicable), witnesses, voluntariness, education level, and so on. How do you know they can read or write? How do you know they were or were not under the influence? Who was present during the interrogation (in the room, in a monitoring room, etc.)?

In your supplement report, you should include everything from the way you introduced yourself or any accusations or themes used to the way the interrogation concluded. Review the notes from the interrogation and any audio/video recordings to accurately document the interrogation. Include everything, even if is not directly beneficial to the investigation. Not leaving anything out does not mean you are hurting your case; to the contrary, it may give you more credibility in court.

When the defense attorney asks, "Investigator, why did you (do this or that)?" you might answer, "Because I wanted to ensure that (defendant)'s rights were not violated." That can be huge with juries who may have any hidden biases that you are just out to get certain people. They may think to themselves instead, "This investigator is fair and was just doing their job."

The goal of an interrogation is not a confession. Interrogations are meant to uncover the truth. Not every interrogation concludes with a confession. If your interrogation doesn't end with a confession but your suspect is the offender, it's important to document how you can corroborate their involvement. Many times, in interrogations that don't end in confessions, the suspect will provide omissions that can be proven. Maybe the suspect denies being present at the crime, but you can prove that's a lie. Then you have physical evidence that indicates the suspect's involvement, but their denial includes something that you can prove is not truthful. Documenting what the suspect's denial was and how you can corroborate why the denial is untruthful is just as important as the suspect's confession. Remember, the purpose of the interrogation is to seek and document the truth.

Remember, if you don't document it, it didn't happen. Document the details.

In *State of Tennessee vs. Dodson* (1989), presented in Case Study 6.1, the defendant didn't confess. During the interrogation, it was obvious that Dodson wasn't going to admit to any element of the crime. When that occurs, a good investigator should start focusing on what can be proven and start connecting the facts. Dodson denied being known as "Loc." Dodson was a known Crip gang member who used the nickname

---

CASE STUDY 6.1: *STATE V. DODSON* (1989)

In December 2008, a gruesome stabbing death occurred in Columbia, TN. A suspect was developed rather quickly in the investigation. The suspect was only identified by the nickname "Loc." A thorough investigation led to the identification of Dodson, who was a neighbor in the apartment complex the crime occurred in. Dodson was eventually arrested.

During the interrogation of Dodson, he adamantly denied involvement in the murder of his neighbor. During the interrogation, Dodson also denied going by the nickname of "Loc." Dodson and his girlfriend stated that the apartment that the girlfriend rented was hers, not Dodson's. Dodson was not permitted to live in the complex due to being a previously convicted felon. Dodson denied calling or talking to the victim days or hours prior to the crime. Dodson admitted to having a cell phone with a phone number near the sequence of a one-time coworker but stated he lost that cell phone.

At trial, the prosecutor showed that Dodson lived in the apartment complex with his girlfriend and argued that had the managers of the complex known, his girlfriend would have been evicted because he was a convicted felon. Dodson maintained that he lived with his mother but had clothes kept at the apartment. The "killer" who stabbed the victim was witnessed by her cousin, who was also stabbed by the killer. The cousin only knew the killer by the nickname "Loc."

The prosecutor proved that Dodson used the nickname "Loc." This was presented through the investigation and documentation of investigators, although Dodson denied using the nickname. One of the people to connect the nickname to Dodson was the coworker, whose name was also registered to a cell phone that Dodson used—the same cell phone that called the victim prior to the murder.

The cousin identified specific clothing that the killer was wearing at the time of crime. This clothing was matched to Dodson, who was wearing the same clothing on a traffic stop just a few hours prior to the murder. The traffic stop was audio/video recorded and also showed Dodson with facial hair at the time.

At the time of the crime, Dodson was at his girlfriend's apartment. There was a small window of time that Dodson had left the apartment, which we know because his girlfriend awoke and found Dodson was not in bed. Dodson maintained that he was taking the dog out and smoking a cigarette. The time that Dodson said he was outside was not consistent with his girlfriend's memory. This was also the time that the killer was in the apartment building next door and stabbing the victim.

Dodson stated that after returning from taking the dog out, he took a shower. During the shower, he decided to shave his head, his facial hair, and his eyebrows. Dodson did not provide a specific reason, but the prosecutor maintained that he did it to alter his appearance since there was a witness to the homicide.

Dodson was convicted of first-degree murder, attempted first-degree murder, and aggravated assault. He was sentence to life in prison.

"Loc," which is a common nickname for a Crip gang member. Interviews and testimony from associates, inmates, and others corroborated that Dodson used the nickname "Loc" frequently. Simply showing the jury that information showed that Dodson lied in the interrogation. But that wasn't all.

Dodson denied living at the apartment complex. He said that he lived with his mother. However, the investigation (through interviews and more) corroborated that Dodson was living at the apartment complex. It was determined one of the reasons that he and his girlfriend denied he lived there was because he, as a previously convicted felon, was not permitted to live in the government housing apartment complex. A search warrant for evidence related to the homicide was served at the girlfriend's apartment, which clearly showed that Dodson had establish residence there—another statement by Dodson proven to be a lie.

Dodson denied calling the victim prior to the crime. However, the investigation and testimony indicated that a cell phone that Dodson was using was in the name of a coworker. Evidence in the investigation was able to prove the phone was being used by Dodson, not the coworker. Yet another lie.

Dodson said that he took his dog outside, smoked a cigarette, and that was all he did when outside the apartment. Despite being outside during the time of the crime, he said that he didn't see anything suspicious while outside. Dodson stated that he was only outside for 10–15 minutes. However, his girlfriend thought it was longer than 15 minutes when she realized that he wasn't in the bedroom. At trial, she changed her story, all to benefit Dodson. At trial, she testified that he was gone for approximately 15 minutes. His girlfriend didn't know if the dog was or wasn't in the house. Although the specific time was not determined, if Dodson were the one who killed the victim, it had to have been more than 10–15 minutes. Since the eyewitness (cousin) positively identified Dodson in a photographic lineup (and in court) and knew Dodson as "Loc," Dodson's story was discredited.

Once Dodson allegedly come back from taking the dog out, he decided to take a shower. Odd timing? Sure, it was. Might he have washed evidence off? It's possible, but that could not be proven. But he shaved his head, facial hair, and eyebrows. Why? The prosecution concluded that it was to prevent witness identification. Again, very odd.

At trial, Dodson testified. However, the jury chose to convict Dodson in the case, obviously not believing Dodson's story or testimony. This is a good example of not needing a confession to complete a successful investigation. Dodson was a seasoned criminal. In the interrogation, he tried to control the conversation. He was a talker. He thought he could talk his way out of it. But it was his talking that helped discredit him. Most of his statements in the interrogation could be disproven. Obviously, there was a lot more evidence and information in this case. But it's a great example of how an interrogation without a confession works. Furthermore, thorough documentation of every omission or statement that could be proven as a lie was very beneficial.

References

Fuqua, A. (Director). (2001). *Training day* [Film]. Warner Bros.

Kassin, S. M., & Wrightsman. L. S. (1985). Confession evidence. In S. M. Kassin & L. S. Wrightsman (Eds.), *The psychology of evidence and trial procedure* (pp. 67–94). SAGE.

State v. Dodson 780 S.W2d 778 (1989). https://law.justia.com/cases/tennessee/court-of-criminal-appeals/1989/780-s-w-2d-778-0.html

Credits

Part III

Investigations

CHAPTER 7

Property Crime

Investigations encompass criminal, civil, and/or private matters. For the purposes of this text, we will only focus on criminal investigations. However, many of the same techniques can be used for any of the different types of investigations. **Criminal investigation** involves the collection of information and evidence for identifying, apprehending, and convicting suspected offenders involved in criminal activity. The initial response by patrol officers is one of the key components of any criminal investigation. The first officer(s) on scene can make or break the scene preservation and/or any subsequent prosecution. Any mistakes made early will only magnify as the case moves forward to prosecution. The initial handling by first responders can dictate the overall direction of the investigation.

FIGURE 7.1 Coauthor Korey Cooper Fingerprinting a Door During a Robbery Investigation

The Federal Bureau of Investigation (FBI) generates reliable statistics for use in law enforcement known as the **Uniform Crime Reporting Program (UCR)**. The data contained in the UCR is derived from criminal offense reports take by U.S. law enforcement agencies that is reported to the FBI through the National Incident-Based Reporting System (NIBRS).

In the next three chapters, we will discuss property crimes, personal crimes, and how to be an effective investigator. Each section will list different tactics, skills, and an investigative toolbox to help you with investigations. Be mindful that there is not one specific technique that works every time for any one specific crime. Many of the tactics, skills, and techniques discussed throughout these chapters can be universally used for any investigation.

When conducting investigations, your investigation is very likely to have been preceded by a crime and a crime scene. Unlike TV and movies, crime scenes are seldom easy to investigate and rarely lead to the arrest and incarceration of the bad guy. Rookie crime scene investigators (CSI) will often encounter far different crime scenes in the real world due to (a) inclement weather; (b) poor crime scene security leading to evidence being tampered with; (c) lack of proper equipment and staffing, especially in smaller agencies, to investigate; (d) lack of or poor packing and tracking materials for the evidence; (e) lack of good cameras and imaging-capturing devices; (f) dirty and rodent-invested crime scenes; and (g) poor maps and diagrams of crime scenes—all of which impact the role of the CSI.

Purpose

As obvious as it might seem, there are often dual or more claims over property. Obviously, if you are assigned to investigate a case, a complaint has been made by at least one party. During your investigation, another and sometimes several parties may claim ownership of property. It can get very messy sometimes, and you will likely be tasked with figuring out who has legal ownership. In these kinds of situations, court records, legal filing records, receipts, bills of sales, and so on can assist you in your efforts to investigate. A little time spent establishing the fact of ownership up front can save you a lot of wasted time later.

Property crime may be defined differently in each state. Through the UCR program, the FBI (2018b) defines **property crime** as "any offenses of burglary, larceny-theft, motor vehicle theft, and arson" (Definition section). In this chapter, we will discuss each of these as well as electronic crime or cyber-crime. Each of these crimes can be similar and overlap one another. Review the elements of each crime discussed.

Burglary

A **burglary** is an "unlawful entry of a structure" (or motor vehicle in some states) for the purpose of committing a theft or a felony (FBI, 2019, "Part I Offenses" section). Unlawful entry is better defined as entry without effective consent of the owner or occupant. "Breaking and entering" is the common-law term for burglary. A common myth about burglary is that forced entry must occur to be classified as a burglary. That is not the case. A burglary can be forcible entry or nonforcible entry if the element of the crime includes the intention to commit a theft or another felony. For reporting purposes, the FBI (2018a) defines a *structure* as a dwelling (habitat or home): "an apartment, barn, house trailer, or houseboat whenu sed as a permanent dwelling, office, railroad car (but not automobile), stable, or vessel (i.e., ship)" (Definition section). In many states, motor vehicles can also be classified as a category or type of burglary. However, the FBI does not categorize motor vehicles in their report of burglaries.

The FBI (2010) reported in a Crime Clock statistical report that a property crime occurred every 3.5 seconds in the United States and a burglary occurred every 14.6 seconds. While these statistics may seem too unbelievable, keep in mind that these are from reported incidents to law enforcement. This does not include the unreported crimes.

Different Types of Burglaries

We will discuss three of types of burglaries in the text: residential, business, and vehicle.

The most common type of burglary is a residential burglary. Each state's criminal statutes define what constitutes a residential burglary. For example, Tennessee uses the word "habitation" to define a residence that includes "structures, buildings, module units, mobile homes, trailers, and tents which are designed or adapted for overnight accommodations of a person" (Tenn. Code Ann. § 39-14-401). This includes self-propelled vehicles (boats or recreational vehicles) that are "designed or adapted for overnight accommodations of a person" (Tenn. Code Ann. § 39-14-401).

FIGURE 7.2 Photo of a Residence That Was Burglarized (Courtesy of Coauthor Korey Cooper)

A residential burglary occurs when the offender unlawfully enters a structure, as described, without the consent or permission of the owner or occupant of the structure. In cases where an occupant rents or leases a structure from the owner, only the occupant can give consent or permission. The owner has no standing to provide consent. Another element of burglary in most states and as defined by the FBI included the offender entering to commit a theft or a felony. If this element is not met, the crime is not a residential burglary. It may only constitute a criminal trespass. The three elements of burglary are:

- unlawful entry

- a structure (as described above)

- intent of theft or to commit a felony (crime)

While the majority of burglaries are perpetrated to commit a theft, there are times when a burglary is committed for other felonies. For example, a suspect who unlawfully enters a residence without consent of the owner/occupant to shoot the owner/occupant is committing a burglary because they are entering to commit a felony assault or attempted murder. If a suspect unlawfully enters a residence but does not intend to steal anything or commit a felony, then the elements of a burglary are not met.

Business burglaries are most commonly conducted afterhours. The same elements apply:

- unlawful entry without consent

- intent to commit a theft or felony

Business burglaries account for less than one third of all report burglaries (FBI, 2018a). The FBI measures residential and nonresidential burglaries. The majority of nonresidential include businesses, but it also includes some building that are not businesses as well. Those may include a building that is not a dwelling used for living space (e.g., a detached garage or outbuilding). Although businesses tend to contain more valuable content, the more preferred burglaries are residential.

Burglary can be a crime of opportunity. Very few burglaries are committed by a one-time bandit. Most burglars will continue to commit numerous burglaries until they are eventually caught. Burglars tend to seek out easy opportunities to steal. For example, a burglar may choose a specific residence because they are familiar with the resident and know they are away or out of town. Other burglars may go to a particular neighborhood and knock on doors. They may choose to burglarize the homes that no one answer the doors to. Many times, the burglar is an associate of or familiar with the victim/resident. There are burglars who work in trends and go from neighborhood to neighborhood. It's very common that the burglar is addicted to drugs and is stealing to support their drug habit.

As previously mentioned, vehicle burglaries are not reported statistically to the UCR as burglaries. However, some states still recognize the unlawful entry of a motor vehicle as burglary. Typically, these types of burglaries are a felony class lower than the residential burglary. Most vehicle burglaries are nonforcible entry because the doors are kept unlocked. There are times when the doors are locked, and forcible entry is made. In those cases, a rock or other foreign obtain is thrown through a window to make entry. Just as with any other burglary, vehicle burglaries do not require "forcible entry."

Tactics and Skills to Solve Cases

The best tactic or skill to solve burglaries is a sharp first responding officer who takes the initial incident report. The initial report is very important. The initial responding officer who uses skills discussed in the interview section of the text is more likely to provide better information that can be followed up and/or investigated. The officer should interview the victim(s) to gather information that may develop leads. If the victim of a residential burglary is interviewed properly, the officer may find out who knew the victim's schedule or when the victim was not at home. Maybe only a few people knew where the items taken were kept. Victims can provide good information to work with. It's important to ask the victim who they believe committed the burglary. Many times, they have a good idea who may have burglarized their home or business. For businesses, it's possible a disgruntled former employee is suspected.

Burglars often leave evidence behind. It could be a pry mark from forced entry, a burglary tool, or physical evidence such as fingerprints or DNA, to name a few. Additionally, some burglars may have a **modus operandi**, or a specific way they operate. This is also known as their signature practice. For example, one burglar may only enter residences by prying the rear doors with a pry bar. Others may break the front door glass to gain entry. Some burglars may seek jewelry only.

FIGURE 7.3 Depiction of a Door That Was Forcibly Entered During a Burglary (Courtesy of Coauthor Korey Cooper)

It's also important to conduct canvasses in the area. Talk to neighbors. They may have seen something suspicious but didn't report it. Use your interview skills to seek information that can develop leads to solve the crime. Today, many homes have surveillance cameras. Consider not only the victim's residence but their neighbors' as well. Crime is mobile, meaning the burglar has to get from one point to another.

Dusting for fingerprints or swabbing areas for touch DNA are two great ways to help solve burglary crimes. The sooner these methods of gathering evidence can be completed, the better. This will prevent contamination to the scene or evidence. Some government crime labs in the United States have set guidelines to submit fingerprint or DNA evidence related to property crimes. This may prevent some evidence from being processed at the lab. However, that should not prevent you from preserving and attempting to process the scene for evidence. It's possible that in time the lab procedure can change, or the evolution of new procedures may arise.

Most states require pawn shops to report their intake of property daily. This is done to report the description and serial numbers to police departments. The investigations unit can compare the reported material against reported stolen material to develop leads. With today's practices on social media and the internet, this process is counterproductive. Those listing products online are not subject to the regulation or laws that pawn shops must adhere to.

Investigative Toolbox

Online marketplaces are common in today's world. With no regulations to post or report material sold online, officers/investigators must research online themselves to develop leads or locate stolen property from burglaries. This can be a timely process. Some investigators don't have the time to monitor these websites, which makes it easier for burglars to sell their stolen material at a prime rate, rather than a reduced rate on the street.

One of the best and old-fashioned tools for solving burglaries is the use of informants or sources. The use of sources is challenging, especially if they are criminal informants. These are informants who are involved in criminal activity themselves and are providing information to reduce or abolish charges that they have incurred. Criminal informants are valuable because they are in the middle of criminal activity and know the current trends and procedures. They are "in the know." Criminal informants' information must be vetted and corroborated. Sometimes they provide information because of revenge, greed, hatred, and so on. This information may be false for these reasons, or their information is unreliable.

Noncriminal informants may be nosy neighborhoods, mail delivery persons, concerned citizens, and the like. They are people who have no specific motivation to provide information but for the betterment of the community or just doing what's right. One of the best noncriminal informants is the mailman/mailwoman. They are in neighborhoods daily and see the normal day-to-day activities. They see activity that is suspicious to them because it's outside of the norm. They know the people in the neighborhoods: where they live, what they drive, what their interests are (from the mail received), and much more. They are always around during the day, and most people really don't pay attention to the mail carriers. If you are canvassing an area after a burglary, there's always a nosy neighbor who will talk to you; you just have to find them.

Also, while canvassing, look for cameras on residences. Without endorsing any specific product, there are alarm systems and do-it-yourself surveillance systems that are readily available to residents. Some residents use doorbell cameras or floodlight cameras. All are beneficial to help identify suspect description(s), suspect vehicles, a timeline of a crime, or other leads that can assist with the investigation.

Some other considerations involving burglaries are tools used to commit the act. Many states have laws or statutes to criminally charge offenders with possession of burglary tools. Typically, a burglary tool is classified as anything that can be used, without good reason, as a tool to break into a building or vehicle. Some of the more common burglary tools include:

- pry bar or crowbar

- hammer

- screwdriver

- lock pick

- slim jim (used for vehicle doors)

- wire cutter

- gloves

Theft

Theft or larceny is defined as the "unlawful taking, carrying, leading, or riding away of property from the possession or constructive possession of another" without the effective consent of the owner, thus depriving the owner of said property (FBI, 2019, "Part I Offenses" section). This does not include the element of force or violence.

The FBI (2010) reported in a Crime Clock statistical report that a property crime occurred every 3.5 seconds in the United States. One burglary occurred every 14.6 seconds, and one motor vehicle theft occurred every 42.8 seconds.

Different Types

Thefts are classified differently in each state. A theft can range from a misdemeanor to a felony. Thefts can be categorized many different ways. Theft can include but are not limited to the following:

Pick-pocket	Purse snatching	Shoplifting
Embezzlement	Forgery	Check fraud
Theft of services	Motor vehicle theft	Identity theft
Petty theft	Grand larceny	Extortion

Most cases involving theft that are assigned to investigators involve a felony. So, a bicycle theft from a front yard may not reach an investigator's desk. In cases like this, the reporting officer may be expected to conduct any follow-up investigation. Many agencies may only take the initial report, and no follow-up would be done. Other cases, such as forgeries, embezzlement, extortion, and identity theft, could turn into in-depth investigations.

For the purposes of UCR reporting, motor vehicle theft is statistically kept separate. This includes the taking of a vehicle, not accessories to the vehicle. For example, if the wheels and tires or the stereo were stolen from a vehicle, that would not constitute a motor vehicle theft. When it comes to motor vehicles, some states include a joyriding statute, which is different from motor vehicle theft. Typically, a joyriding violation includes youthful offenders driving without consent but not necessarily to deprive the owner of the property. An example of joyriding would include a 17-year-old taking their parent's vehicle to ride around and "look cool" rather than stealing the car and keeping it from the owner.

Possession of stolen property is also categorized as theft in most states. Some states have a separate law for possessing the stolen property versus being charged with stealing the property. In those states, the charge may be reduced a level or class. Other states include possession of stolen property in with the theft law, which has equal level or classification.

Identity theft is another type of theft. Is it a property crime or personal crime? This may vary from state to state. While it may seem more personal, many states still classify identity theft as a property crime. The Identity Theft Assumption and Deterrence Act that was passed by U.S. Congress in 1998 defines *identity theft* as occurring when someone

> knowingly transfers or uses, without lawful authority, any name or number that may be used, alone or in conjunction with any other information, to identify a specific individual with the intent to commit, or to aid or abet, any unlawful activity that constitutes a violation of Federal or, or that constitutes a felony under any applicable State or local law.

Identity theft is a rather unique law because it typically involves multiple crimes as opposed to a single crime. For example, one may obtain a false identity, which is the first law violation. The purpose for obtaining the false identity may be used for financial gain with credit card fraud by purchasing merchandise with a credit card using the false identity. The most common form of identity theft involves financial crimes. Below are some of the financially related crimes associated with identity theft:

- credit card or checking account fraud
- internet scams
- forgery
- motor vehicle theft

There are other motivations for identity theft. One other primary purpose is to assume another identity. For example, one may assume another's identity to prevent being arrested. Those who are wanted by law enforcement may use someone else's identity to conceal themselves. This occurs on a local and national level. A person may use the name and identification information of someone who they are close to (e.g., associate, friend, family, etc.) on a traffic stop to elude police if their driver's license is revoked/suspended or if they have warrants for their arrest. Individuals involved in terrorism may use the identity of someone else to conceal their acts of illegal activity or to prevent them from being tracked or traced more easily. Identity theft may occur in other forms of organized crime, such as drug trafficking and human trafficking, where there is a motive to prevent true identification.

Tactics and Skills to Solve Cases

Using tools and recommendations we gave you in the Interviewing section, one of the best tools you will use to determine the facts—besides physical evidence—are interviewing witnesses to a theft crime. These are often used as supporting evidence, along with paper documentation, to determine what exactly happened.

One of the oldest and most common methods used to solve theft cases is fingerprints. However, for fingerprints to assist in these cases, the officer/investigator must process the scene of the crime for latent prints. Law enforcement have used this technique to solve crimes for years. With that being said, it is still commonly overlooked. Some officers may not take the time to dust a scene for fingerprints. It can be time consuming and a dirty job. Some agencies encourage their officers to dust for fingerprints on property crimes, and others don't. Fingerprint dust can stain or ruin uniforms or material in the area around what's being dusted. If may also get on your skin, hands, face, and inside your nose (breathing in the dust).

FIGURE 7.4 Photo of an Investigator Dusting for Latent Prints (Courtesy of Coauthor Korey Cooper)

For those reasons, some agencies have chosen to only dust for fingerprints in personal or more violent crimes or only in "major or high-profile" cases. Some crime labs have also reduced their intake of latent prints or restricted submissions to a specific criteria due to a backlog of evidence.

A **latent print** is an impression of ridged skins, also known as friction ridges, from human fingers, palms, and soles of the feet that are not visible without being processed by powder or chemical. This impression of friction ridge skin is comprised mostly of sweat/perspiration but may also contain a variety of contaminates, such as salts, oils, and dirt. Ridge patterns are unique to each individual and not duplicated; no two people have the same fingerprint. Commonly known as fingerprints, latent prints occur "when friction ridges come into contact with a suitable surface, the perspiration is transferred to that surface, leaving a print or impression of the friction ridges" (Lee & Garnsslen, 2001, p. 405).

Dusting for fingerprints is a learned skill. First, one should look at a scene and determine what may have been touched by the offender. You may notice visible prints that are plastic (ridge impression left on a soft material such as wax, putty, soap, or even household dust). Other visible prints include **patent prints**, in which the ridge impressions are visible in material such as blood, grease, ink, or paint. In these cases, there are methods that can be used to recover the impressions, but you should photograph the impression first. Add a measurement device, or scale, that can be used to show the exact size/measurement of the impression.

If a visible print is not found, you should use a fingerprint kit to dust for prints. There are different powders (graphite, charcoal, or magnetic), and each type has multiple colors. However, using a black powder on lighter colored surfaces and a white powder of dark surfaces is recommended. There may be times when you use fluorescent powders, but those are recommended more when using an alternate light source. Fingerprints can be processed with many different chemicals and solutions.

Once a latent print is developed, the print should be lifted and added to a card. We always recommend taking photographs of prints with and without a scale before lifting. It is also recommended to use a macro lens for these impressions, which will produce a 1:1 scale of the impression. These 1:1 photographs may also be used by a crime lab to help in identification of the impression. The impression is lifted with clear tape. When adding the tape over the impression, work out the air bubbles. Lift the tape from the surface. This will lift a copy of the impression from the surface. Add the

FIGURES 7.5 AND 7.6 Latent Print Card of Latent Prints Recovered During a Training Exercise (Courtesy of Coauthor Korey Cooper)

tape to a fingerprint lift card. When adding the tape to the card, again work out the air bubbles. Complete the information on the card and submit it to the evidence clerk.

When the fingerprint cards are submitted to the crime lab, the lab technician will determine if the impressions have value. If so, the impressions are searched against a database of fingerprint records maintained by the lab and/or the FBI's fingerprint database for a comparable link. These databases are known a AFIS (Automated Fingerprint Identification System). The system can read, match, and store fingerprint data for experts to use to solve crimes. If a match from the crime scene is found to a print stored in AFIS, the forensic lab expert will then be able to perform a side-by-side comparison to determine a scientific match. Prints stored in AFIS come from unidentified impressions from crime scene, **10-print cards** for arrest records, or other known sources allowed by the system.

Another technique that helps solve theft cases involves recording serial numbers. It's important for the initial responding officer to ask for serial numbers of the items stolen when a report is being taken. A known serial number can be added to the

FIGURE 7.7 Clear 10-Print Fingerprint Card

FBI's National Crime Information Center (NCIC) database. This is a national database that holds information, such as serial numbers or identifiable marks, that can help law enforcement identify stolen property in the course of their duties. For example, a stolen television from New York with the serial number added to NCIC when the crime was reported to law enforcement will stay active in the database until it's recovered and reported back to law enforcement. An officer in California may stop an individual and run a television through NCIC to check to see if it's reported stolen. If the serial number matches the one reported from New York, the database will initiate a match or "hit" to the officer. The officer would then compare the serial number, make, model, and/or any other identifiable marks to the one reported in New York. If it's a perfect match, the stolen property from New York

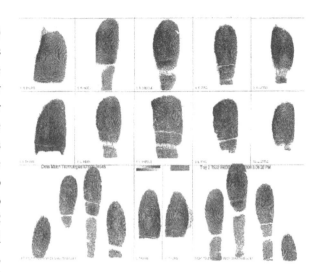

FIGURE 7.8 Sample 10-Print Fingerprint Card (Courtesy of Coauthor Korey Cooper)

would be listed as recovered and the law enforcement agency that added the television to the database would be contacted as a follow-up to the investigation.

With barcodes becoming more common today, the use of scanners makes it easier for law enforcement to record and identify stolen articles. The more information that's available to add in the description for an NCIC entry, the better the chance of positively identifying property being compared in NCIC.

For correctional workers, there may not always be criminal charges filed for stolen property that is commonly found in jail and prisons. Many times, staff do cell searches when it is discovered that property is clearly marked as belonging to another individual on their property inventory card or via other records such as from commissary. The inmate in possession of said item may have borrowed it or it was sold to them with the permission of the owner, but usually institutional rules forbid loaning out any personal property to avoid violent disagreements.

Whether property was loaned out or stolen from another inmate, you will likely have to write a rule infraction. At that point, an out-of-court disciplinary hearing may be held and a hearing officer or investigator my handle it similar to how a police investigator would.

There may be also cases where inmates have stolen institutional property and are infracted for it.

The main difference in a correctional setting is a guilty or not guilty finding and appropriate sanction will be recorded in house on their inmate jail or prison records. The theft incident may or may not be referred on to a local prosecutor. Given the low priority for property crimes in many jurisdictions today, it is very unlikely it will be picked up for legal charges.

Almost always the cell thief/culprit will be relocated away from the victim to avoid retaliation. If they have many prior incidents (just like out on the street, seldom are they a first-time offender), they may be placed in segregation for institutional safety and security or protective custody for their own protection.

Investigators should use **solvability factors** when determining which cases to work. These are determining factors related to a criminal investigation that can provide leads of information about the crime and who is involved. Many law enforcement agencies use a database or system to screen cases with the highest probability of being solved. This is typically a checklist of factors that can affect the solvability of a case (e.g., identified suspect, serial numbers listed, MO, fingerprints, etc.). Each category has a weight factor by number that is added together to determine the level of likelihood that the case can be solved from the information provided. The higher the number, the more likely the case is to be solved. That's why it's so important to get as much information when the initial report is taken.

Whether a theft case has solvability factors or not, it's always important to follow up with the victim of a theft as soon as possible. Although thefts seem to be a lesser priority than other crimes (property or personal), it's best practice to make contact with the victim, preferably face to face but at least by a phone call. They may have some additional information that can be added to the report or helpful in solving the crime. This is also good community relations. An occasionally follow-up at least 90 days after the report of the crime is recommended. If no leads or suspects are developed after 90 days, many investigative units will change the status of the case to inactive.

Arson

Arson is "any willful or malicious burning or attempt to damage, with or without intent to defraud, a dwelling house, public building, motor vehicle or aircraft, personal property of another" (FBI, 2019, "Part I Offenses" section). Arson cases are some of the most difficult criminal cases to solve. Below are the elements for arson:

- a fire or explosion
- intent: criminal act (maliciousness) and not accidental in nature
- damage (from the fire or explosion)

The nature of arson is one of the issues that causes this crime to be more difficult to solve: fire and heat. A fire can destroy evidence that may identify the offender in an arson.

Different Types
Some different types of arson include:

- Burning of a dwelling (residence or livable building)
- Burning of a building (e.g., outbuilding, nonresidential, business, etc.)
- Burning of personal property (e.g., motor vehicle, terrain/acreage, clothing, etc.)
- Malicious destruction (explosives or incendiary devices)

More focus should be put on the different motives and/or reasons related to arson. Below is a chart that lists arson motives from a 1984 journal article by O'Connor et al. (see Figure 7.9).

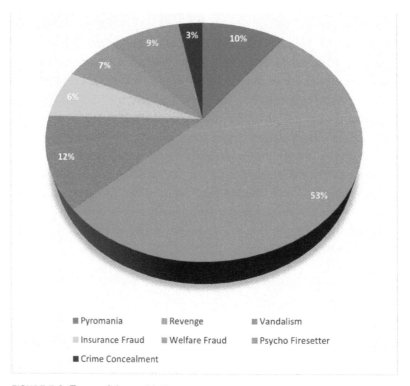

FIGURE 7.9 Types of Arson Motives

In this study by O'Connor et al. (1984), over 50% of the 138 arson cases studied in New York City had the motive of revenge. In these cases, the offender will usually threaten to set a fire prior to the actual offense. The arsonist who sets fire for revenge will use some sort of flammable accelerant to start the fire. The vandal arsonist targets something specific (e.g., residence, business, place of worship, vehicle, etc.) for the purpose of attention, ideology, and so on. For example, a White supremacist group may target a mosque to burn down because of their anti-Muslim ideology.

Some arsonists conceal other crimes by burning property. For example, an offender may shoot a victim in a residence and then burn the residence to conceal the homicide. Their motive is to prevent evidence of the homicide from being discovered. Other arsonists, known as **pyromaniacs**, set fire to objects because of uncontrollable impulses or excitement that watching the fire burn elicits.

Insurance fraud is another common motive for arson. Some motives from insurance fraud include delinquency in mortgage payments, property foreclosure, tax liens, martial issues or active divorce proceedings, unemployment, and/or gross misrepresentation of lost property, to name a few. The insurer is responsible for proving fraud/misrepresentation. Arson is not a basis for denying liability in most insurance contracts. Therefore, many insurance companies have insurance fraud investigators assigned to incidents that involve fire. This can assist criminal investigators because insurance companies have more resources to investigate these types of cases. However, there are times when an insurance investigator can cause problems in criminal investigations. If you are investigating a potential criminal arson case, it's best practice to communicate with the insurance company as soon as possible (if applicable). You and the insurance fraud investigator must work together to have a successful outcome. Otherwise, the insurance investigator can become too involved and create roadblocks with the owner and their communications with you. On the other hand, many insurance companies hire retired arson investigators with years of experience who are valuable in assisting with the criminal investigation. Communication is key! If insurance fraud is suspected, communicate early and often with the insurance investigator.

Tactics and Skills to Solve Cases

In potential arson investigations, the investigator can conduct a preliminary investigation while the fire is being extinguished or managed. While the investigator is waiting for the fire scene to cool down enough for review, there is plenty of work to be done. During that time, the investigator can interview the owner, occupants (if applicable), complainant (i.e., people who discovered the fire), eyewitnesses, and so on. The investigator should speak with fire department scene commanders as well. This is also a good time to ensure the scene security is adequate. Consider the area that's secured. Is it far enough back and all 360 degrees around secure? While doing this, it's a good idea to take a camera with you and take photographs of the security measures used. This will also document the bystanders, if any, standing around the scene and watching. If a pyromaniac is involved in the fire, they will likely be in the crowd. Remember, their motive is attention, uncontrolled impulses, and excitement to see the fire.

A skill for any criminal investigator assigned to a possible arson case is training related to arson. First, you must decide if the fire was accidental or not. Some agencies utilize their fire department investigators and state fire marshals as experts in arson cases because the law enforcement's investigators aren't properly trained in arson investigations. What does it take to determine if a fire is suspicious or accidental? Many criminal investigators aren't trained well enough in arson investigations to determine without a doubt if a fire is suspicious or not.

When investigating a fire, it's important to determine the burn patterns and the place of origin. This is not a simple as it sounds because the fire must be completely extinguished before the investigator can safely review the scene. Some complications may include the stability of the structure, how much was burned, and obstacles that may cover potential evidence. For example, the place of origin may be concealed by burned ceiling beams from the roof of the structure. Therefore, the structure may need to be strategically cleared of rubble and fire debris by firefighters before starting the investigation. In these cases, it is suggested that the investigator direct and manage the clearing to reduce contamination and preserve as much evidence as possible. During this time, the investigator should look for anything unusual or foreign to the fire scene, like a gas can. Sometimes a fire may not destroy evidence, such as a gas can, completely. So, it's important to keep an open mind and keep your eyes peeled for such evidence.

Once the potential origin of the fire can be established, next you must determine the ignition source. Many times, if a flammable liquid (e.g., gas, kerosene, barbeque lighter fluid, etc.) is used, the odor of the accelerant is obvious. If not, burning patterns may be observed. For example, if an accelerant was poured onto a floor, a burning pattern or trail may be found. A skilled arson investigator can identify other burn patterns that are consistent (or not) with the structure and air flow within the structure. At this point, the investigator will have a better hypothesis of the intent (accidental or intentional).

As mentioned at the beginning of this chapter, arson cases (including explosions) are some of the most difficult cases to investigate. Linking evidence to the fire-setter can be difficult. Moreover, proving a fire is not accidental or intentionally set can sometimes be a hurdle that cannot be overcome. That's why interviewing is important in these cases, as interviews can provide a motive for the criminal act. Many times, arson cases are circumstantial cases. Many prosecutors won't prosecute cases based off circumstantial evidence.

Investigative Toolbox

Your arson investigative toolbox is not complete without a good camera. Today, digital cameras are highly suggested. There is no reason not to take a substantial numbers of photographs with digital photography. With digital photography, you can immediately see the results of the photograph after taking each one. You can make adjustments (e.g., lighting, scale, size, ranges, etc.) as needed, as opposed to 35mm cameras that use film to be developed at a later time. If you use digital photography, DO NOT delete any photographs you take for any reason. Even if you forget to take the lens cap off and a solid black photo is developed, keep it. Don't delete it. In court proceedings, everything is discoverable. If a photograph is deleted, it gives the defense (in the criminal case) the opportunity to argue that the deleted photograph was the one photograph that could have exonerated their client. At that point, it's possible the trial judge could rule that no photograph can be admitted into evidence.

We cannot stress enough that while photographing the scene, take photographs or those standing around the security tape. Whether the suspect is a pyromaniac or not, the suspect can be documented on the scene if they are standing around the outside perimeter of the crime scene tape, especially if the suspect created the fire to cover up or conceal another crime, like the homicide we previously mentioned.

Another great tool for arson investigators is the use of accelerant or explosive detection K-9s. Dogs have a keen sense of smell. They can pinpoint traces of accelerants that they are trained to detect. Using trained K-9s on possible arson scenes reduces the time it takes investigators to search and process a fire scene. Obviously, a K-9 cannot be used on a fire scene while the scene is still hot. Therefore, allot some time to ensure that the scene is safe for the K-9 to walk through.

Fire investigation is a science. We highly recommend using a specialized investigator to investigate arson cases. The National Fire Protection Association (NFPA) has national recognized standards for fire investigators. The National Association of Fire Investigators is one recognized group that provides NFPA-certified training for fire investigators. If a law enforcement agency cannot provide such training, the agency should utilize their resources, such as state investigative agencies, federal investigative agencies (Bureau of Alcohol, Tobacco, Firearms, and Explosives) if a nexus exists, and/or fire departments that have certified fire investigators.

Electronics/Cybercrimes

Martin (2021) reported that according to 2018 U.S. Census Bureau data, 92% of American households had at least one computer. The research also indicated 85% of the households had a broadband internet subscription.

Moreover, 84% of households contained smartphones, and another 78% owned a computer (Martin, 2021, p. 4). Computer crime costs companies over a billion dollars yearly. As electronics continue to evolve, cybercrimes will become more and more common. Not all cybercrimes are property-specific crimes. For example, child pornography is not a property crime. However, it is a crime committed through electronics.

Cybercrime is often carried out anonymously. These crimes could be committed anywhere is the world, often outside of the United States. That makes it more difficult for local law enforcement agencies to investigate them. Therefore, it's important for investigators to know what resources are available to help investigate cybercrime.

Different Types

Cybercrime involves criminal activity by use of computers, networks, and/or the internet. Many electronic crimes are better classified as fraud. However, cybercrimes also involve other means, such as child pornography (as mentioned above), terrorism, and threats of violence, to name a few. One of the most common cybercrimes involves email phishing scams. *Phishing* refers to an unsolicited email, text message, or phone call "purportedly from a legitimate company requesting personal, financial, and/or login information" (Brennan & Smith, 2022, para. 6). For example, one may receive an email that appears to be legitimate and has a link to click to access data or a website. If clicked, a browser will open to a website that also has the appearance of being legitimate. However, the page isn't legitimate. The page may request the user to add a login or username and passwords to access "their account." When the user types in the requested information, it's logged and used to access the user's real account. Once the phisher has this account information, they will take control of the account. Many times, this includes banking accounts for individuals and business email compromise (BEC) schemes for businesses. The FBI's (2020) Internet Crime Complaint Center reported that BEC losses in 2019 exceeded 1.7 billion dollars. Older people are some of the most common victims of these crimes through email and phone calls. An older victim may receive a call from a phone number that appears to be local or may be **spoofed**. The caller will tell the victim they are someone who can help them with their bank account or some other account that typically relates to money. The caller will ask for personal information to assist, including full name, date of birth, social security number, account data, logins, security information, and more.

Human trafficking and internet crimes against children is a big problem in the United States and worldwide. The Internet Crimes Against Children (ICAC) Task Force Program is a national network of over 60 coordinated task forces, representing over 5,000 federal, state, and local law enforcement, dedicated to investigating, prosecuting and developing effective responses to internet crimes against children (Fuda, August, 2023).

Child pornography is a multimillion-dollar industry that involves the capturing, selling, and trading of photographs and videos of nude children under the age of 18 or children committing sexual acts. This crime is a national problem. It involves children who are trafficked from the United States as well as other countries, children who have run away from home, and children who are homeless. Most states and the federal government have strict laws that govern such activity. These laws pertain to possessing, creating, or distributing child pornographic material, whether commercially or not. While many pedophiles are arrested and convicted in the United States daily, it's still a huge problem. The advancement of electronics has increased the ability of pedophiles to conceal their criminal activity in places like the **dark web**.

The Onion Router (TOR) software is commonly used to conceal and send information through different computer relays worldwide, which helps create encrypted websites on the dark web. Often, these types of cases are long term and carried out by an agency with excellent technical capabilities, a federal law enforcement agency, or a group of law enforcement investigators working together in a task force created to reduce cybercrime.

Tactics and Skills to Solve Cybercrime Cases

Oftentimes, cybercrime is not reported. Many local law enforcement officers who are called to these complaints don't know how to respond. Others may suggest the crime be reported to a federal agency, such as the Internet Crime Complaint Center (IC3). Solving electronic crime/cybercrime will likely involve high-tech units specialized in digital forensics. With the increased growth of cybercrime in today's society, local and state law enforcement must reach out to federal law enforcement agencies for assistance. Cybercrime cannot be effectively investigated individually. Federal agencies, such as the FBI and the U.S. Secret Service (among others), have specialized units dedicated to cybercrime investigations. Many law enforcement agencies collaborate with these federal agencies to work cybercrimes in a task force. As you might imagine, the cost of these types of investigations can be high due to equipment needs and the hours of work that may go into these investigations. Local and state agencies can partner with federal agencies through a task force, which provides for manpower and financial assistance.

Digital forensics involves the processing, extraction, and analyzation of digital evidence from sources such as computers, serves, cell phones and smartphones, memory devices, networks, files, and/or any data storage device. Digital evidence can be overwhelming. There are many digital forensic solution tools that can help law enforcement extract and analyze data from electronic devices to solve crimes.

Smartphones and computers are the most commonly processed devices to recover digital evidence. These devices are not only used in cybercrimes but are also involved in just about every type of criminal activity. This includes criminal activity in correctional facilities. In most states, an inmate in a correctional facility is prohibited from possessing or using a cell phone in prison. Unfortunately, inmates using cell phones in correctional facilities is a major problem nationwide. Inmates conduct criminal activity within the prison, as well as outside the prison walls, including drug trafficking, organizing violent crimes (assaults, shootings, and murders), and identity theft scams. Processing electronic devices can be worthy in criminal investigations.

CASE STUDY 7.1: TENNESSEE DEPARTMENT OF CORRECTION

Blowing away the backlog: New mobile forensic system lets correction officials cut mobile phone processing backlog, gain fast access to critical gang intelligence.

Key achievement

The Tennessee Department of Correction had a mobile phone problem. Until April 2017, they relied on one employee to extract data from seized contraband phones from 10 correctional facilities spread across the state. Backlogs were high, processing slow, investigations impeded. But that all changed in early 2017, with the rollout of a new mobile forensic system from MSAB, using eight specialized extraction Kiosks and five PC-based XRY Office software applications. Twelve investigators have been trained to handle all extractions and analysis of phones in the field without having to use a centralized analyst. Now, there are no backlogs and the number of phones analyzed has soared 584% year over year.

The problem/challenge

Like most state prison systems, Tennessee has been fighting a battle to control the flow of contraband phones into inmates' hands and manage the large number of hardened gang members within their population. When phones were confiscated, they were sent to Nashville for processing. In some months as many as five boxes of phones would arrive, containing hundreds of phones each. In urgent, high-profile cases, phones would be driven to the Nashville office—and Tennessee is 482 miles long—consuming many hours of employee time and resources.

The phone processing backlog had the heaviest impact on the Department's investigators, who are responsible for investigations within the system, with a focus on preventing outbreaks of violence by gang members, preventing gang members from communicating with other criminals outside the prison system and identifying corrupt staff members. Phones contained critical intelligence that was needed quickly. The processing backlog was a major issue impeding their work.

The work and initial results

In early 2017, the Tennessee DOC began working with MSAB to implement a better system. The DOC staff worked with MSAB's Professional Services team to define the challenges to be solved, the goals to be achieved and other requirements. Eight easy-to-use kiosks were installed, one in each state-owned prison (with the exception of two Nashville units which are within a mile of each other), plus five XRY Office applications on standard PCs. The kiosks are computers with "wizard-like workflows" that make it easy to extract phone data by following simple steps. Every investigator received one day of training, enabling them to manage the extractions successfully in almost every case. Speed improved dramatically versus the previous technology used. The number of phones processed increased by 584% year to date in 2017 versus the same period in 2016. Reports on phones processed, gang intelligence gained, phones seized from inmates, staff and visitors are output in real time.

Now, investigators are getting updated intelligence and evidence with no delays. This is paying off in a number of ways, such as enabling the identification of high-ranking gang members, helping prison officials isolate and/or house them safely. Through the timely analysis of phone data, investigators are also able to look for evidence of potential attacks on staff members. And based on this success, the state Pardons & Paroles employees have begun using MSAB technology as well.

"Our department's mission is 'to operate safe and secure prisons and provide effective community supervision in order to enhance public safety,'" said Korey Cooper, Director, Office of Investigations and Compliance at the Department. "Our new mobile forensic system helps us to fulfil our mission daily. Contraband cellular phones can have a wealth of information stored in their memory. By extracting and analyzing more devices, the TDOC Office of Investigation & Compliance can reduce violence and contraband introduction statewide in a more timely fashion."

"Technology and Applications (Apps) improve daily. TDOC can rest assured that the new tools in our intelligence toolbox will help us stay current on today's technological progressions. Additionally, this new system allows the department to collaborate more with our partner law enforcement agencies to share intelligence gathered."

Tennessee is still a long state, but there are no longer long waiting times for mobile phone processing in the Tennessee DOC.

Investigative Toolbox

There are many different resources available to law enforcement to investigate cybercrime. These resources include training opportunities and coordinating task forces. One task force that is used for child pornography is the Internet Crimes Against Children (ICAC) program. This program provides training to law enforcement and partners with local and state agencies to investigate child exploitation.

The U.S. Secret Service also provides law enforcement training through the National Computer Forensic Institute (NCFI) to agencies in digital forensics. The agency hosts multiple different forensic classes that provide state or local law enforcement with tools to solve crimes involving digital communications, such as financial investigations. The Secret Service has nearly 40 electronic crimes task forces in the United States, as well as two in foreign countries.

Another is the FBI's Internet Crime Complaint Center (IC3), which works cybercrime and internal crime. IC3 also provides training and open-source resources to law enforcement and the public. IC3 assists and participates in research related to these crimes as well. IC3 disseminates an annual report that is provided to the public to enhance their awareness to cybercrime. IC3 also receives and investigates complaints of internet crime reported through their website (https://IC3.gov).

References

A Discussion with Jim Fuda About Worldwide Human Trafficking (2023). YouTube-Gangsters, Cops, and Politicians with Gabe Morales. https://www.youtube.com/watch?y+2rySbbo LYI

Brennan, B., & Smith, K. (2022, May 24). *FBI Tech Tuesday: Protecting against personally identifiable information (PII) theft.* Federal Bureau of Investigation. https://www.fbi.gov/contact-us/field-offices/phoenix/news/press-releases/fbi-tech-tuesday-protecting-against-pii-theft-1

Federal Bureau of Investigation. (2010). *Crime Clock.* https://ucr.fbi.gov/crime-in-the-u.s/2010/crime-in-the-u.s.-2010/offenses-known-to-law-enforcement/crime-clock

Federal Bureau of Investigation. (2018a). Burglary. https://ucr.fbi.gov/crime-in-the-u.s/2018/crime-in-the-u.s.-2018/topic-pages/burglary#:~:text=The%20UCR%20definition%20of%20"structure,vessel%20(i.e.%2C%20ship).

Federal Bureau of Investigation. (2018b). Property crime. https://ucr.fbi.gov/crime-in-the-u.s/2018/crime-in-the-u.s.-2018/topic-pages/property-crime

Federal Bureau of Investigation. (2019). Offense definitions. https://ucr.fbi.gov/crime-in-the-u.s/2019/crime-in-the-u.s.-2019/topic-pages/offense-definitions#:~:text=Burglary%20(breaking%20or%20entering)—,Attempted%20forcible%20entry%20is%20included

Federal Bureau of Investigation. (2020, February 11). 2019 Internet Crime Report *released: Data reflects an evolving threat and the importance of reporting.* https://www.fbi.gov/news/stories/2019-internet-crime-report-released-021120Identity Theft and Assumption Deterrence Act, 18 U.S.C. § 1028 (1998). https://www.ftc.gov/legal-library/browse/rules/identity-theft-assumption-deterrence-act-text

Lee, H. C., & Gaensslen, R. E. (Eds.). (2001). *Advances in fingerprint technology* (2nd ed.). CRC Press.

Martin, M. (2021). *Computer and internet use in the United States: 2018.* U.S. Census Bureau. www.census.gov/content/dam/Census/library/publications/2021/acs/acs-49.pdf

MSAB. (2018, January 11). *Case study: Tennessee Dept. of Correction.* https://www.msab.com/updates/tennessee-correction-digital/

O'Conner, D. G., Parker, W. M., Phillips; J. V., Poulsen, J. S., Reichard, D. S., & Richardson, L. L. (1984). *Fire/arson investigation research paper, February 22–March 2, 1982—Identifying revenge fires. Fire and Arson Investigator, 35*(2), 9–14.

Tennessee Code § 39-14-401 (2021). https://law.justia.com/codes/tennessee/2010/title-39/chapter-14/part-4/39-14-401/

Credits

CHAPTER 8

Personal Crime

Purpose

Personal crimes are generally categorized as crimes committed against an individual or person. In most cases, these are also violent crimes. These crimes commonly harm victims physically, mentally, and/or emotionally. U.S. 42 Code of Federal Regulation (C.F.R.) § 136.403 defines a *crime against a person* as a "crime that has as an element the use, attempted use, or threatened use of physical force or other abuse of a person and includes, but is not limited to, homicide; assault, kidnapping; false imprisonment; reckless endangerment; robbery; rape; sexual assault, molestation, exploitation, contact, or prostitution; and other sexual offenses." The Federal Bureau of Investigation's (FBI) Uniform Crime Report (UCR) categorizes crimes against person(s) as defined in the federal statute. Personal crimes may vary from state to state, just as property crimes do. However, the crimes listed in the federal statute are often recognized in most states as personal crimes.

Robbery

A **robbery** is the intentional or knowingly taking of property **(theft)** from another person or place by use or threat of violence, force, or fear. A robbery usually involves another crime when committed. For example, a person takes property from another person (theft) but uses force or a weapon to do so. The use of force or a weapon may constitute an assault as well. Crimes of assault will also be discussed in this chapter, as they are personal crimes as well. An element of robbery is the use of violence, force, or fear, which differentiates it from the property crime of theft.

From 2011–2020, the FBI (n.d.-a) reports there were over 781,000 robbery incidents reported in the United States. While that figure may seem high, the rate of robberies reported to law enforcement has dropped over the last 10 years. The chart below indicates the robbery rate per 100,000 people has decreased nearly 40% since 2010. The data collected to create the chart were from law enforcement agencies in the UCR Program (FBI, n.d.-a).

Rate of Robbery Offenses by Population

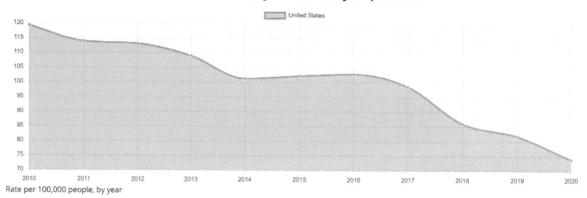

Rate per 100,000 people, by year

FIGURE 8.1 2010–2020 FBI UCR Reported Robberies

Contrary to common belief, there were more reported robberies in open areas, such as the street (27%) or parking lots (10%) than in convenience stores (8%), gas stations (4%), or banks (3%). Residences or homes made up for 19% of the robberies (FBI, n.d.-a).

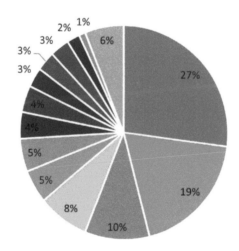

■ Street/Sidewalk   ■ Residence   ■ Parking lot   ▪ Convenience Store ■ Discount Store

■ Restaurant   ■ Gas Station   ■ Unknown   ■ Specialty Store   ■ Bank

■ Grocery Store   ■ Hotel/Motel   ■ Medical Facilty   ▪ Other

FIGURE 8.2 2011–2020 FBI Reported Robbery Data

Robberies tend to impact victims emotionally and psychologically due to the violent nature of the crime. When most people think of robbery, they envision a "hold up" similar to a bank robbery or convenience store robbery, with the offender pointing a weapon at the victim. Let us dive into the FBI (n.d.-a) UCR data of reported robberies from 2011–2020. A mere 9% of the robberies did not involve a weapon of any type. In those cases, the offender used fear or a threat of violence to commit the crime. The difference between a simple theft (property crime) and robbery (personal crime) is the offender's use of one or more of the elements of violence, fear, and/or threats. According to the FBI data, 43% of robberies involved a firearm of some type, such as handguns, firearms, shotguns, and rifles; 30% of the incidents involved personal weapons, such as fists (hitting), legs (kicking), or head (headbutt); and 11% involved a cutting instrument, knife, or blunt object as a weapon.

It should be noted that not all robberies are reported to law enforcement. Opportunistic robbers seek out vulnerable victims who may not even report the crime. Victims who are also involved in criminal activity, such as drug dealers or sex workers, are less likely to report a robbery to law enforcement, thus making them more vulnerable to robbery.

Different Types

There are several types of robberies that will change from one jurisdiction to another. Some common types of robbery are:

- aggravated robbery
- armed robbery
- bank robbery
- carjacking
- jewelry robbery
- pharmacy
- robbery

An aggravated robbery may simply be a robbery by the use of threats or physical force other than with a weapon. An armed robbery would include the element of using a weapon to commit the crime. Some jurisdictions combine aggravated robbery and armed robbery together. A carjacking is the stealing of a motor vehicle with use of violence, commonly by force involving a weapon or the display of said weapon. Some jurisdictions further categorize robberies, such as jewelry or pharmacy robberies. Others may also classify robberies by personal or business crimes. In other words, a robbery of a person would constitute a personal robbery, and a robbery of a store would constitute a business robbery. The FBI's UCR has specific criteria that it measures, most of which were listed in Figure 8.2 above.

The FBI has interests in bank robbery investigations. This has been the case since the 1930s, when it became a federal crime to rob a bank of the Federal Reserve System. This does not include financial institutions like credit unions where the institution is not in the Federal Reserve System. A local or state law enforcement agency will initiate a bank robbery investigation as soon as it occurs. The FBI will provide assistance and investigative resources to these agencies upon request as it relates to bank robberies.

Jewelry store robberies are also monitored by the FBI. The FBI has a specialized unit that investigates jewelry and gem cases. Gems and jewelry store heists are international and organized crimes. Since the jewelry and gems industry has an international nexus, the FBI delegates resources to investigate these crimes. These types of robberies are usually committed by individuals involved in sophisticated organized crime rings. However, in recent years, criminal street gangs have been known to commit mob-style jewelry store robberies or "smash and grab" burglaries to steal thousands of dollars in merchandise. The difference between the international organized crime gem and jewelry groups and these street gangs is the intention for the crime. The criminal street gangs' motive is most likely to fund their criminal enterprise or criminal activity, such as weapons and drug trafficking. The international organized crime gem and jewelry groups are violent and have resources to transport the jewelry and gems across the border quickly, thus adding to the need for international investigative resources to stop or interdict such activity. As with most any crime, the initial report is reported to a local or state agency first. Then resources from the federal government are sought to assist with the investigation.

Pharmacy robberies are less common. However, these robberies can be violent in nature, especially when the offender is addicted to drugs and is robbing to support their habit. In these cases, the robberies are spontaneous and are focused on the need of the addict/offender. Pharmacy robberies are just a snippet of the larger problem of controlled substance abuse. In Figure 8.3, a drug addict robbed a local pharmacy. Police arrived as the robber was exiting the store, and he shot toward an officer. As seen in Figure 8.4, the robber lost some of the scheduled narcotics as he fled the store.

According to the U.S. Drug Enforcement Agency Diversion Control Division (2016), the number of reported pharmacy robberies in the United States exceeded 600 or more annually since the early 2000s. While the problem is not unique to the United States, it is unique regionally within the country, with some regions being more susceptible to these types of robberies than others. For example, Georgia reported 43 pharmacy robberies in 2015 and increased to 94 in 2016. The Southeast region of the United States seems to be the most vulnerable to pharmacy robberies (see Figure 8.5).

FIGURE 8.3 Pharmacy Robbery photo (Courtesy of Coauthor Korey Cooper)

FIGURE 8.4 Pharmacy Robbery photo (Courtesy of Coauthor Korey Cooper)

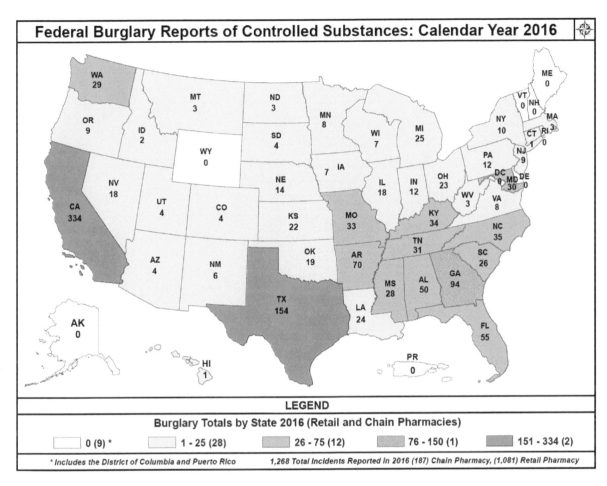

FIGURE 8.5 2016 DEA Diversion Reported Pharmacy Robberies

With the misuse of prescription medication and controlled substances (more specifically opioids) on the rise, pharmacy robberies will continue. Many experts contribute the abuse of opioids to the introduction of OxyContin in the mid-1990s, which was originally prescribed as a pain reliever. The misuse of OxyContin had developed into abusers snorting and/or injecting prescription medication with opioid derivatives. Misuse can develop into an addiction, which can lead to criminal acts, such as robberies, thefts, and burglaries, to obtain money to support the habit.

Tactics and Skills to Solve Cases

Tactics and skills to solve the different types of robberies discussed above will vary. Eyewitness information from the victim(s) of the crime may be most critical. Considerations discussed in previous chapters must be kept in mind. A robbery is a traumatic experience. Traumatic-informed interview procedures must be followed. Additionally, your ability to separate witnesses as quickly as possible is important to prevent one witness influencing another.

Although a motive is not necessary to prove or prosecute a case, motives to robbery are important. What was occurring with the offender(s) to motivate them to commit the crime? Research indicates that there are two types of robbers:

- professionals: those who plan their robberies and target a specific person or business with a purpose

- opportunistic or amateur: those who do not plan their robberies and target low-risk victims

Professional robbers are more likely to use a weapon to commit their crime. Professional robbers tend to seek out higher risk targets (banks or businesses), which provide larger dividends. Professionals may be motivated by the need for money and sometimes simply to seek the thrill. Professionals may operate by themselves or with a trusted accomplice. Their trends or modus operandi (MO) rarely changes. If it does, some elements of their MO stay the same.

Opportunistic or amateur robbers are more likely to target more vulnerable targets, such as people and businesses. They tend to be younger. Their motivation can also be for money, but more often it's to support a habit. In those cases, it's most likely a drug addiction. Robberies take less time to complete as compared to burglaries. With that said, the opportunistic robber will seek out a "quick hit" to get their loot. Knowing the type of robber you are dealing with is an important skill for solving robberies.

Robbery cases may produce less physical evidence at the scene compared to most other violent crimes. Generally, physical evidence at the scene of a robbery may include forensic evidence, such as fingerprints and DNA. These types of evidence are critical and tangible, but they are some of the most important pieces of physical evidence that can be recovered at the crime scene. It's important to preserve the crime scene of a robbery as quickly as possible to prevent contamination.

In today's world of technology, video evidence is important. Whether it's surveillance video from a business of a robbery or other video sources in the community, a technology skilled officer or investigator is extremely beneficial. Many times, video recordings have a limited expiration before being recorded over—not purposely, but in an effort to save time and money (or cost of additional memory for recording devices).

The ability to research factors, elements, motives, and other variables related to robberies is a skill needed to solve these crimes. As you will read in Part IV, research and analytical information are important to develop leads to investigate any crime, especially robberies. Most robbery offenders are not first-time offenders. Most have a history of arrest, a field interview, traffic stop, citation, and so on. Computerized incident and records management systems make it easier to develop suspects from descriptions and other information developed by the initial reporting officer.

It's important for the first responding officer/reporting officer to properly document the robbery. This includes obtaining offender descriptions, such as:

- sex

- race

- height (as close as possible)

- age range

- descriptors (tattoos, scar, marks)

- weight

- clothing (particulars)

- vehicle description (if used)

- weapon description

- any other unique descriptors (walk with limp, missing a right finger, etc.)

This information can be used by the assigned investigator to develop suspects with limited information. For example, the initial report may indicate the suspect is described as:

- White male

- approximately 20–30 years of age

- between 5'8" and 5'10", definitely less than 6'0" tall

Just this information alone can provide a great starting point if no leads have been developed. Most computer-based incident reporting systems have the ability to narrow a subject search with limited information (as listed). Keep in mind, the more specific you can be, the narrower the results will be. For example, a witness describes the offender as about 23 years old but more specifically no less than 20 years old and no older than 30 years old. Another witness is 5'9" tall and described the offender as "about the same height, but definitely not 6'0" tall." Obviously, all this information should be corroborated as much as possible. However, the information provided will generate leads to work with. As additional information or leads are developed, they can reduce the list of potential suspects developed from the incident system. If your offender has been previously added to the computer-based records management system, they will most likely be in the initial suspect list if the descriptors are correct. As the list narrows, other corroborating information and/or evidence will begin to better identify your suspect/offender. It's certainly possible that the offender isn't in the system or the descriptors don't match. In those instances, other investigative procedures should be followed.

Investigative Toolbox

Most robberies are solved by prompt actions of the victim(s), witnesses, or police response. If not concluded at the time of the report, these crimes are often time consuming to investigate and may take a considerable amount of time to successfully conclude. That's why it's so important for the first reporting officer and/or first officers on the scene to quickly obtain suspect information (e.g., direction of travel, method of travel or getaway, etc.) and get that information out with a BOLO (be on lookout) for officers in the area. Depending on the length of time (from time of crime to time of first responding officer), consider setting up a secured perimeter and working your way inward.

Canvasing the area should always be considered. Knock-and-talks door to door in the area can develop leads and information. Officers in the area should also look for items the offender dropped or discarded while fleeing the area, such as clothing, disguises, stolen material, and so on. Any item discarded is crucial because it can link the offender and the victim to the scene of the crime and establish a trail of evidence. Be careful not to contaminate the area with excessive foot traffic if a K-9 unit is available to track the offender. Heavy foot traffic can reduce the K-9's chances of a successful track.

Photographs of the crime scene are important. Photographs can be used in court to bring the crime scene to the courtroom for the jury. Document with photography any injuries the victim(s) may have received, all evidence (without evidence placards first and then with evidence placards to identify evidence), views from different angles (wide, medium, and close-ups from different angles), the crime scene boundaries, bystanders, and anything else that seems important. With digital photography, you cannot take too many photographs.

Don't forget videos. Whether it's a neighbor's doorbell camera or a business's surveillance camera, video camera footage can develop timelines and great identification images of the offender(s). These can eventually be used to create information or intelligence bulletins.

The use of social media by departments has had a significantly positive impact on solving crime. Today's society depends on social media platforms. A law enforcement agency that isn't using these platforms to assist with their investigations is missing out. Bulletins related to unsolved cases or cases with exceptional video or still photographs added to a department social media page can reach thousands of people instantly. Some agencies wait and use social media as a last resort. Others add bulletins on social media as quickly as they send the information out to other law enforcement agencies. This will depend on the agency or investigator.

Some may argue that posting investigative information on social media can expose the investigation and its potential weaknesses. That certainly could occur, so you should weigh the advantages and disadvantages.

If investigating a jewelry robbery, utilizing the Jewelers Security Alliance from New York is a resource. The FBI has access to the alliance and can assist. According to the FBI (n.d.-b), they support "an industry-operated database (maintained by the Jewelers Security Alliance), that allows law enforcement agencies to search for and identify stolen jewelry" ("FBI's Role" section).

Law enforcement agencies that are members of the Regional Information Sharing System (RISS) Program can use their services to assist in not only robbery investigations but any criminal investigation. RISS has around 10,000 members at the local, state, federal, and tribal levels. With six centers and a technology support center, RISS (n.d.) "offers secure information sharing and communication capabilities, critical analytical and investigative support services, and event deconfliction to enhance officer safety" (para. 1). They support a variety of law enforcement efforts, from organized crime to terrorism to drug activity (RISS, n.d.). RISS is congressionally funded but locally managed and operates an intelligence system that is regulated under federal law.

Another tool in the toolbox is sources or informants. As mentioned in Chapter 7, informants are valuable. Managing criminal informants or sources is challenging, but they are valuable resources if handled properly.

Homicide

One of the most violent crimes is murder (the words "murder" and "homicide" are used interchangeably). **Homicide** is the "killing of one human being by another" (Merriam-Webster, n.d.). In Early English common law, homicide was categorized as either "nonfelonious" or "felonious" (Farlex, n.d.). Nonfelonious homicide included justifiable and excusable homicide. Not every homicide is criminal in nature, and today the common law nonfelonious fall into that category. A justifiable homicide would be a homicide that occurred in self-defense. An excusable homicide would be a negligent homicide that failed to meet the elements of gross or criminal negligence.

Any unattended death should also be treated as suspicious and worked as a homicide. Figure 8.6 shows an unattended death where an elderly woman fell down some stairs in her residence. She was not able to call for assistance. Days later she was found dead by a family member. The scene was worked as a homicide due to the fact it was an unattended death. After an autopsy and a detailed investigation, it

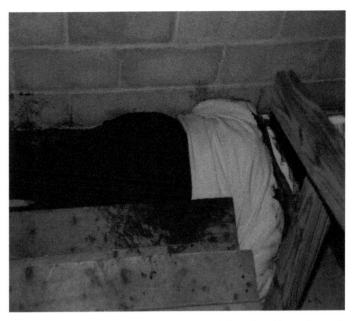

FIGURE 8.6 Unattended Death (Courtesy of Coauthor Korey Cooper)

was determined the death was a result of an accident (the fall) and a medical condition. Otherwise, you could misinterpret a staged or altered crime scene. All death investigations really should be treated as a homicide. For example, a possible self-inflicted death should always be treated and investigated like a homicide. Let the evidence direct you to a disposition of the death. Consider that some homicides are distinguished or staged to appear as a suicide/self-inflicted death. When a death is dispatched out as a suicide, it can lead investigators to develop preconceived notions. Whether it's information from the dispatcher, previous call history at the location, or simply just information provided by the complainant or potential witnesses at the scene, it's best practice to investigate any death as a homicide. Otherwise, you'll reduce the work and documentation that you provide. For example, you'll likely take less photographs and fail to collect evidence, all of which will destroy the integrity of the investigation. Once you've left the crime scene, the risk of contamination increases if you must return without the scene being kept secure.

Different Types

We have already mentioned homicides that are not always criminal, but there are several different types of criminal homicides to mention as well. Each state's laws and categorization of homicide are different. We will discuss a generalized list of homicides.

Murder is a criminal homicide. Many states categorize murder by degrees. For example, in Tennessee, first-degree murder is the most serious in a hierarchy of murders. First-degree murder is the premediated killing of another. Premeditation as it relates to murder is

> an act done after the exercise of reflection and judgment. Premeditation means that the intent
> to kill must have been formed prior to the act itself. It is not necessary that the purpose to kill

preexist in the mind of the accused for any definite period of time. The mental state of the offender at the time they decided to kill must be carefully considered in order to determine whether the offender was sufficiently free from excitement and passion as to be capable of premeditation. (Tenn. Code § 39-13-202)

As the degree of offense increases, the seriousness of the crime decreases. Second-degree murder and third-degree murder are considered less serious than first-degree murder, thus carrying a lighter sentence as well. Each of these include some culpable negligence. **Culpable negligence** is a type of negligence that occurs when a person acts in a manner that is careless and shows a reckless disregard for human life.

Another category of homicide is **manslaughter**, which is the unlawful killing of another without specific intent or culpable negligence. Voluntary manslaughter may include acting in the heat of passion, which would cause a reasonable person to act from passion rather than judgement. This would include the offender being provoked to the point of anger or rage, which creates a loss of self-control in the "heat of the moment." Involuntary manslaughter is the killing of another without intent. It is a lesser included offense than voluntary manslaughter.

Euthanasia is the practice of ending a life with the intent to end a person's suffering, which is medically know as physician-assisted suicide. As of 2022, only 10 states and the District of Columbia have legalized physician-assisted suicide (ProCon, 2022). For these states and the District of Columbia, this is considered an excusable homicide. In all but four of the remaining U.S. states, this is considered homicide. But what category of homicide? Most states classify physician-assisted suicide as manslaughter. The other four states are unclear on the legality of assisted suicide.

FIGURE 8.7 Physician-Assisted Suicide in the United States

Tactics and Skills to Solve Cases

The best tactic to solve homicide investigations is patience. A good investigator must be patient. Solving murders tends to take time. Some of the tactics that have been covered in previous sections (on interviews and interrogations) are obviously important in solving these cases. However, the scene of the crime and physical evidence are most important.

You cannot investigate a death without victimology. *Victimology* is research of a crime victim for information about what was occurring on their life at the time of crime. Information such as the victim's background, history, trends, and their associates can provide a better idea of what was going on with the victim. This includes any behavior that may have led to or contributed to their victimization. This certainly is not suggesting that all victims cause their victimization. However, there are times when a victim's habits produce the opportunity for an offender to commit a crime. For example, a drug abuser may become a victim of a robbery and shooting resulting in death. When conducting victimology research, it would be important to understand the victim was a drug abuser. That important information provides a reason the victim was at the place of the crime. Assumptions can be made, but assumptions have no place in criminal investigations. Failure to obtain a complete picture of the victim's life will make it difficult to develop motives and/or leads in the investigation.

Investigative Toolbox

Law enforcement agents who investigate homicide cases need to keep an open mind. Interview and interrogation training and experience is always suggested. Interviews include the victim, witnesses, and suspects. Initial interviews can help corroborate physical evidence. You must remember that you have to prove all elements of the crime for a successful prosecution. These include the following:

- A death occurred.
  - It occurred at the scene of the crime.
- The death was not accidental, but criminal.
  - How did the death occur?
- The death was caused by another.
  - Put the suspect at the scene of the crime at the time of crime.

The crime scene and evidence within the scene will help prove that a death occurred at the scene. But it is not as simple as it sounds. This includes evidence such as blood, fingerprints, DNA, weapons, and more that can be linked to the death at the location. Crime scene processing is critical in homicide cases. Many law enforcement agencies use specially trained officers or non-sworn civilian employees to process the crime scene for physical evidence. Other more rural agencies depend on a support agency (another local agency, state investigative agency, or even a federal agency) to help process their crime scene because of the lack of personnel or funding.

The medical examiner or coroner's office autopsy commonly indicates time of death. This can be connected to the evidence at the crime scene as well. The autopsy also provides the official cause of death. The medical examiner can provide specific details about the body and how the death occurred. They are the medical experts related to deaths and causes of deaths. This includes the method of death, accidental or criminal. The medical examiner is also critical in determining whether a death is a homicide or suicide.

In homicide investigations, the investigator must prove the homicide occurred by the suspect(s)/offender(s). This includes linking physical evidence to eyewitness or victim statements, linking the suspect(s)/offender(s) to the crime scene and physical evidence, and/or providing a motive for the crime. While a motive is not a required element of the crime, it is important to provide an overview for the judge or jury to understand why the crime occurred.

Other tools for the investigative toolbox include digital forensic evidence, such as cell phone information. Cell phones show more than just phone calls or messages to and from the device. Today's cellular phone are minicomputers. They track your every movement: GPS (Global Position System) locations, search engine searches, photographs, videos, and much more.

A good homicide investigator needs common sense, patience, an open mind, good people skills, technological skills, and to be a team player. You must work as a team with other components in the criminal justice system for a successful prosecution. It cannot be done alone.

Sex Offenses

Sex crimes can be some of the most difficult cases to investigate. Oftentimes, the primary hurdle to overcome in a sex crime investigation or prosecution is the subject of consent. *Consent* is permission or an agreement for something to happen. However, consent as it relates to sexual offenses is more than a simple definition. Consent includes the following circumstances:

- Mentally incapacitated:
  - A person under the influence of alcohol and/or drugs may be temporarily incapable of approving or agreeing to an act.
  - A person with intellectual disabilities is incapable of approving or agreeing to an act. This may also include the age of a victim.
- Physical helplessness:
  - A person who is asleep, unconscious, or for any reason not physically or verbally capable of communicating approval to an act cannot provide consent.

Sex offenses are forms of abuse. These types of investigations are more of an evidence-based investigation. While sexual offense victim interviews are important, do not forget how trauma (such as sexual offenses) can affect a person and their processes—hence the importance of physical evidence.

Keep the victim calm. Listen to what they are saying and don't jump to conclusions or preconceived notions. Assure the victim that they are doing the right thing by talking to law enforcement. Conduct an evidence-based investigation. It will be corroborated. Sex offenses related to children will be covered in more depth in another section.

Different Types

Sex crimes include but are not limited to the following:

- indecent exposure

- bestiality

- rape

- incest

- prostitution

- stalking

- sexual harassment

- sexual assault

All these crimes will vary by jurisdiction. *Indecent exposure* is the act of intentionally exposing one's genitals in a public place. This is the least invasive sex offense. However, it is generally one of the first steps of a sex offender or a key indicator for habitual offenders. In most jurisdictions, indecent exposure is a misdemeanor offense that carries little to no jail time.

Having sex with animals is known as *bestiality*. This includes other sexual contact, including touching or stroking an animal for sexual pleasure or gratification. Not all states have laws prohibiting humans to have sex with animals. According to the Animal Legal Defense Fund (ALDF, n.d.), the following states and territories have no direct laws prohibiting sex with animals: Hawaii, Kentucky, New Mexico, West Virginia, Wyoming, District of Columbia, Guam, Northern Marina Islands, and America Samoa.

Rape is the most common type of sex offense investigated by law enforcement. Rape is the "penetration ... of the vagina or anus with any body part or object, or oral penetration by a sex organ of another person, without consent of the victim" (FBI, 2018). Penetration may occur digitally (fingers) or using hands, feet, toes, sexual organ, tongue, or by foreign object. A foreign object would include anything. Throughout our careers, some objects that we have seen include broom/mop handles, sex toys, fruits, vegetables, metal rods, and more. Rape has several different forms: rape (forcible or not), aggravated rape, statutory rape, and rape of a child. We will cover the last two later in this chapter.

Rape is not always "forcible." Referring back to consent, rape victims may be mentally incapacitated or helpless. While coercion can be element of consent, coercion is considered by many to be borderline. Consider that most will agree that sexual activity is supposed to be enjoyable for both parties involved. If one feels violated, confused, guilty, or dirty after sexual activity, how effective was their consent? Is it possible that they were sexual coerced?

An aggravated rape is more heinous. It typically includes elements or factors such as violence, the use of a weapon, the age of the victim, mental incapacitation, the number of offenders, and/or if a rape is in conjunction with the commission of another crime, such as robbery or assault. Some jurisdictions have additional charges, such as especially aggravated rape, for crimes with more enhanced factors. Some

Victims by Age

- 10 to 19
- 20 to 29
- 0 to 9
- 30 to 39
- 40 to 49
- 50 to 59
- 60 to 69
- Unknown
- 70 to 79
- 80 to 89
- 90 to Older

FIGURE 8.8 Rape Victims 2011–2020, FBI

Offenders by Age

- 20 to 29
- 10 to 19
- 30 to 39
- Unknown
- 40 to 49
- 50 to 59
- 60 to 69
- 0 to 9
- 70 to 79
- 90 to Older
- 80 to 89

FIGURE 8.9 Rape Offenders 2011–2020, FBI

enhanced factors may include elements that include the crime resulting in serious bodily injury or death of the victim. Other enhancements could involve the number of offenders involved in the act.

According to FBI (n.d.-a) data for 2011–2020, there were 487,815 rape incidents reported in the United States. Of the incidents, 56% involved the offender using personal weapons to force the rape, 2% used a firearm of some type, 1% used a knife or cutting instrument, 4% used drugs or other unspecified weapons, 7% were unknown, and 30% used no force.

Although not required by law, motive is an important aspect to understand in rape investigations. Rape is not always committed for sexual gratification. Most of the time rape is committed for power, the need for power from the offender.

Let's look at age factors. In the FBI (n.d.-a) data, 14% of the victims were less than 10 years old, 42% of the victims were ages 10–19, 21% were in their 20s, and the remainder were over 30 years old or unknown. Contrarily, the majority (25%) of the offenders were in their 20s, 24% were 10–19, 18% were in their 30s, 11% were in their 40s, 7% were in their 50s, and 11% were unknown. Figure 8.9 indicates other age groups, which were lower.

Over 70% of the rapes reported in the FBI (n.d.-a) data for 2011–2020 occurred in a residence or home. Figure 8.10 (below) shows the victim relationship to the offender. Most victims know or are familiar with their offenders. Stranger rape is less common.

In Figure 8.10, you can see that the relationships between the victim and offender that involves some family member or close relative is nearly 22%. Those types of rapes are also known as incest. **Incest** involves sexual activity between family, including blood relatives and, in most states, relatives by marriage, stepfamily, adoption, or lineage.

Prostitution is another sex offense. In these cases, the prostitute is not necessarily the victim. In most states, prostitution is a crime categorized under sex crimes. For the most part, both the prostitute and the person paying for their services (commonly called the "John") are offenders. However, there are times when a prostitute is a victim. A prostitute can be raped. Consider human trafficking situations as well. Not every prostitute is willfully "conducting business." Although we will not go in-depth on human trafficking, prostitution is common within human trafficking organizations.

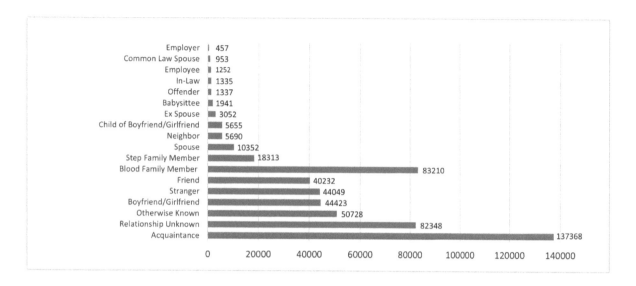

FIGURE 8.10 Victim Relationship to Offender

Stalking relates to sex offenses because most stalking behaviors are motivated by love, obsession, or lust. However, stalkers can also have motives related to politics, celebrity worship, domestic issues, or hate. Sexually offensive stalkers may stalk their victims with desire to form a relationship for sexual gratification or for obsessive love. The sexual stalker will tend to commit other sex offenses while stalking their victim. For example, a sexual stalker may watch victims at home or work and masturbate upon viewing the person they are watching. The stalker is likely indecently exposing themselves in the act. Others may further their obsessiveness to kidnap and rape their victim.

Sexual harassment is a classification under stalking in some jurisdictions. Sexual harassment would include unwelcoming or inappropriate sexual remarks or physical advances toward another. Sexual harassment is more commonly known through a workplace environment. It's not specifically criminal in all states. It is an element of harassment in some jurisdictions and may fall under sexual assault in others.

Sexual assault, also classified as sexual battery, is "contact made with someone's body that is sexual in nature and unwanted or forced" (Legal Dictionary, 2017, What Is Sexual Battery section). Some may also consider sexual assault as an attempted rape. In these cases, unwanted contact with the victim's clothes or skin in a sexual nature is the element of the crime.

Tactics and Skills to Solve Cases

Since an evidence-based investigation is so critical, the tactics and skills used when investigating sex offenses are important. Consider the following evidence at the crime scene:

- Rape kit
  - No shower, bathing, or washing of body or hands prior to is recommended.

- Hair or fibers
- Undergarments
  - These may have been taken by offender as a trophy!
- DNA
  - Check underneath fingernails.
  - Check the bed sheets or fabric where the offense occurred.
- Broken fingernails
- Bite marks
- Skin marks or abrasions
- Fingerprints

When collecting evidence from the crime scene, it's important to identify evidence that can link the victim to any offenders. You need to establish that a sexual encounter took place. If force or a weapon was used, you want to establish that force was used and link any weapon to the offender. Lastly, you need to prove the offender's presence at the scene and any additional activity prior to or after the crime.

Rape or sex assault kits vary from state to state. Most generally contain sterile material listed below:

- Oral buccal swabs: used for the purposes of locating semen
  - An oral rinse is sometimes used too. The rinse is collected from the victim and kept in a vile or tube for evidentiary purposes.
- Small combs: used to comb the victim's pubic hair for foreign trace evidence from the offender
- Anal, penile, and vaginal buccal swabs: used to detect the presence of semen in each area
- Evidence envelopes: for additional trace evidence from the victim's body and for the victim's clothing and under garments, which should be packaged separately
- Fingernail scraping kit: used to collect nail samples and scrapping from the victim for DNA (in case of struggle)
- "Catch paper": a section of sterile paper that is used for the victim to stand on while undressing or to be placed underneath during the examination. The paper will collect any falling material, fibers, or evidence that may dislodge at the time of the examination.
- Blood tubes: for toxicology
  - These are sometimes packaged separately.
- Documents: questionnaire for victim and lab submission forms

Some kits also include forceps and packaging to pull hair from the victim's pubic area and head. This step is not always used, because it's painful for an already traumatized victim. It's only used if the medical staff deems it necessary.

Most victims are transported to a medical facility where a sexual assault nurse examiner (SANE) completes a full examination of the victim. The SANE is required to stay with the kit the duration of the exam to prevent contamination. It's best practice to have the kit completed within 72 hours of the incident. It's preferred that the victim not shower or wash up prior to completing the kit for optimum effectiveness.

Best practice requires sensitivity when investigating sex-related offenses. A careless and irresponsible officer or investigator can ruin the life of a victim, or even an offender. Invasive questions are required to be asked at some point. Question about the victim's sex life and practices are important to gather, such as:

- Did the subject ejaculate?

- Was the subject wearing a condom?

- What bodily cavities were penetrated?

- Did ejaculation take place outside of the body, and if so, where was the semen deposited?

- Was the victim a child or mentally challenged or otherwise incapacitated during the incident?

- Has the victim had consensual intercourse with any other individual in the last 72 hours prior to the incident?

All are important for obvious reasons. Imagine not asking the last question about consensual sex and the DNA report coming back with more than one donor. It could be explained later, but it's certainly better to know that information prior to the kit being submitted to the crime lab.

Be aware of cultural or religious beliefs/issues that can become a possible roadblock when speaking to the victim. Some cultures find it offensive to speak to law enforcement. Other cultures accept sexual violence more than those in the United States. Male dominance in many countries is normal. In some of those countries, rape is not offensive or criminal. That's why it is necessary to understand the cultural belief of your victim. The same goes for religious beliefs, especially when the victim is a juvenile or unwed.

Documentation is the key to any successful investigation. In sex offenses, you want to be able to corroborate the victim's statement and connect it to physical evidence. Whether it's evidence at the crime scene or evidence recovered from the rape kit, you want to establish credibility of the victim.

Investigative Toolbox

You should keep an open mind when interviewing the victim. Don't ask leading questions, take good notes, and don't interrupt the victim while they're talking. It's highly recommended that you record the interview with audio and video. Provide the victim some privacy, and reduce the victim's exposure. If you are interviewing the victim at their residence, limit the number of law enforcement personnel in attendance. If possible, arrange the victim's interview in a controlled environment like the investigation's office. Again, limit exposure to the victim.

If the suspect in sex offenses is unknown, one of the first investigative steps to identify a potential offender is to review the sex offender registry in the area. Unfortunately, sex offenders are likely to recidivate. It's worthwhile to compare your known factors to previously convicted offenders. If a possible suspect is developed from the registry and they are under supervision, you may be entitled to a home visit. This can provide an opportunity to interview the subject and conduct a legal search if conditions of their supervision allow.

Create a profile of the offender from the information known, such as race, sex, height, weight, and other descriptors. Any motivational factors known can also provide valuable information to develop possible suspects, especially those who may be repeat offenders. You may be able to link the investigation to other unsolved investigations or an MO from a previously investigated case.

Be sure to review the evidence that is collecting in the case and be sure to submit the evidence to the crime lab for analysis, especially if a rape or sex assault kit was submitted. While reviewing the case, look for anything that may have been overlooked.

If the offender is known early in the investigation (within 72 hours), consider having a sexual assault kit performed on the offender. This would require consent or a search warrant but is suggested to preserve as much evidence as possible. Remember, sex offenses cases are evidence-based!

When conducting an interview with a suspect who is denying responsibility, ask some of these questions:

- Why would someone say you did this?

- Why would someone do this?

- What do you think should happen to the person who did this?

- Do you think that the person who did this should get a second chance?

Ask yourself what an innocent person would say. A person who was not involved in this type of criminal activity would not answer defensively, but someone involved may become defensive. With Question 3, an answer that downplays the incident is more likely to be from someone involved than someone who says, "Throw them under the jail." Is that what kind of sentence they want to receive? Although these questions are not specific enough to imply guilt, they can certainly express the suspect's mentality.

Assault

An **assault** is the intentionally or reckless cause of bodily injury or to cause reasonable fear of imminent bodily harm to another. A person may strike another with their fist to commit an assault. Another example of assault is when a person threatens another. For example, a person tells another by cell phone conversation that they are going to kill them. A reasonable person may fear bodily harm from the threat, and it may justify an assault. Like every other crime that we've discussed, assault is classified differently from state to state. Assault is commonly a misdemeanor in the United States.

Different Types

We have already discussed one type of assault in the sex offenses, sexual assault. The elements that make a felony or aggravated assault a felony include the use of a weapon to commit the assault and the assault resulting in serious bodily injury. Felony assaults are typically a midrange felony in the sentencing guidelines for most states. Below are different types of assault (see Table 8.1).

TABLE 8.1 Types of Assaults

Misdemeanor	Felony
Simple assault	Felony assault
Verbal assault	Aggravated assault
Sexual assault	

Tactics and Skills to Solve Cases

The tactics and skills discussed throughout this chapter can be used in assault investigations. In an aggravated assault that involves a weapon, your ability to link the weapon to the crime scene and victim is important. For example, if a handgun was used to shoot a victim, the weapon may eject a spent cartridge/casing at the crime scene. The projectile that was shot hit the victim in the leg and was recovered in surgery. You can forensically link both the cartridge and the projectile to the handgun the offender used. If, in this example, you develop a suspect and recover a possible weapon that was used, the weapon, casing, and projectile can be sent to the crime lab and analyzed against one another to determine if they are connected.

The National Integrated Ballistic Information Network (NIBIN) program automates ballistic evaluations performed and entered into the network. NIBIN provides actionable investigative leads or links to law enforcement agencies in a timely manner. NIBIN's network operates throughout the United States and is the only interstate network of its kind. Law enforcement can search against evidence from their jurisdiction and other local, state, and federal agencies across the country.

Investigative Toolbox

In most assault cases, the victim is acquainted with or knows the offender. If that is not the case, the use of social media is a popular way to identify suspects/offenders. Adding bulletins to social media outlets has become one of the best strategies used. A simple click of a button can disseminate bulletins worldwide in seconds. The more followers that the agency has, the more people the bulletin reaches. Then each of those followers can share the bulletin, and it spiderwebs out. This is much quicker than using a local newspaper outlet or even television media.

Bulletins to identify an offender who would otherwise go unknown certainly cannot hurt. Obviously, agencies should be careful to protect the rights of the accused. When the suspect is not known and has not been criminally charged, it should be noted that the subject's identity is needed for questioning and they have not been formally charged. If a surveillance photograph of the suspect and/or vehicle has been obtained, that increases the investigator's ability to identify the person.

When processing a crime scene involving an assault-type investigation, it's important to take plenty of photographs. Document the scene from every angle. Search for any evidence that can link the offender to the scene or the victim. This may include clothing and jewelry. Work the investigation and crime scene like it is a homicide because, in reality, it could result in death.

Crimes Against Children

Abuse is perpetrated by an individual or a group of individuals who are in a superior position of authority to the abused individual(s). There are many instances of abuse that occur daily, but the most persistent abuse is that inflicted on children. Crimes against children don't just encompass abuse; they also consist of exploitation and death. It's difficult to understand how or why anyone could hurt or take advantage of a child.

Conducting investigations on crimes against children can be frustrating or rewarding. These cases can take a toll on officers and investigators. They can trigger some very emotional responses from the investigator, but you will have to find ways to put those emotions aside so as not to negatively affect your work and possibly taint your case. These cases are difficult because many times the child (victim) is made out to be the guilty one or responsible for the abuse. You must understand that these investigations change lives. The safety of children is paramount.

Different Types

The different types of sexual abuse investigations against children include the following:

- rape of child

- statutory rape

- molestation

- incest

Rape of a child is typically rape as previously described but with the victim being a child under the age of 12. Some states include aggravating factors for sentencing guideline for children ages 3 and younger.

Statutory rape is sexual penetration of a juvenile under the age of consent but over the age considered to be a child (by state statute). Most states include an age differential range between the victim and the offender as well. Others use a minimal age of the offender to be prosecuted.

Some jurisdictions use molestation, which encompasses any sexual act with the minor/child, including touching of private parts (sexual assault), exposure of sexual organs (indecent exposure), child pornography, rape, or any other sexual act with children.

Incest is sexual contact between close family members who are blood kin (e.g., brothers and sisters, parents and children, aunts and uncles, nieces and nephews, grandparents and grandchildren). Incest is commonly a secondary crime to other crimes, like different categories of rape.

Child abuse/neglect has different forms as well:

- abuse: physical, emotional, neglect, or bullying

- neglect: failure to provide shelter, safety, supervision, and/or nutrition needs for a child

There are key indicators that relate to child abuse. It is crucial to understand emotional abuse indicators such as anxiety, depression, withdrawal, or aggressive behavior. These are psychological injuries in a child's emotional stability that create observable or substantial change in their behavior, emotional response, or cognitive thinking.

Exploitation of a child charges can be brought on "any person who employs, uses, persuades, induces, entices, or coerces a minor to engage in ... any sexually explicit conduct" (Child Sexual Abuse and Pornography Act, 1986). Human trafficking also plays a role in child exploitation. Unfortunately, the most common type of child exploitation is **child pornography**.

The U.S. Department of Justice (2020) defines *child pornography* as "any visual depiction of sexually explicit conduct involving a minor (person under the age of 18)" (para. 1). It's a form of child sexual exploitation. With the expansion of the internet and advanced digital technology, this crime has exploded. The dark web has promoted collaboration with pornography offenders, which has increased interest in child pornography worldwide.

Often occurring when an infant is asleep, sudden infant death syndrome (SIDS) is the sudden and unexplained death of an otherwise healthy newborn. Research suggests that a variety of genetic and environmental factors put an infant at higher risk of SIDS (Mayo Clinic, 2022). SIDS can occur with unsafe sleeping practices, accidental suffocation (sleeping with parents), or simply sleeping in a baby crib. Although the cause is unknown, a physical factor that may be associated with SIDS includes a brain defect in "the area of an infant's brain that controls breathing and waking up from from sleep" (Mayo Clinic, 2022, Overview section). A SIDS death can be criminal when suffocation occurs. These investigations are extremely difficult to prove because many remain a mystery. If criminal charges result, a manslaughter charge or its equivalent is most likely to be the charge due to negligence of the parent(s) or caretaker.

Tactics and Skills to Solve Cases

It takes a special person to work crimes against children. These cases are extremely difficult to investigative. People from all socioeconomic groups can be involved in crimes against children. Men and women, young and old, rich or poor—there is not a specific profile related to those involved in crimes against children. Child abuse can occur anywhere.

Child abuse usually takes place in secret. Oftentimes, child abuse can go undetected for years. Below are some signs of child abuse:

- problems in school

- extended absences in school

- antisocial behavior

- multiple stages of healing/bruising

- unexplained burns, cuts, bruises, welt in the shape of objects (e.g., belt, belt buckle, cord, etc.)

In crimes against children, abusers who are caretakers may delay seeking medical assistance or fail to provide treatment for the child in an effort to conceal injuries the child may have received. Children often wear oversized clothes to conceal or cover bruising.

In physical abuse case, the most common weapons used are hands, fists, and feet. If other weapons are used, it is often a belt, extension cord, mop/broom handle, or large kitchen utensil. Most often the child is struck where clothing will conceal any bruising.

Investigating these cases can take some time. You cannot rush it, although you may want to protect the child and expedite the investigation. In those instances, work with children's services to remove the child from the environment, even if just temporarily, to protect the child while the investigation continues. Below are some keys to completing a successful investigation:

- Conduct an initial interview with the child.
  - Do not collect details, just basic information.
- Assess the injuries to the child.
  - Use proper medical personnel (sexual or physical abuse).
- If a weapon was involved, identify what it would be.
  - The imprint, design, description, or configuration are important to obtain.
- Identify and document specific evidence that can be found.
- Take photographs.
- Consider a search warrant to obtain evidence as soon as possible.
- Coordinate a forensic interview with the child.
- Reconstruct what happened.
  - In sexual abuse cases, connect evidence with the statements.
- Thoroughly document all work completed in the investigation.
- Review the investigation for additional leads or actions to take.

When talking to the child, reassure them that you are glad they told you (about the incident). Be a good listener. Only ask simple open-ended questions. Allow the child to explain from their perspective and use their own terms/lingo. Use the trauma-informed approach, including scheduling a forensic interview as soon as possible.

When assessing the child for physical abuse, look for signs of extreme disciple and bruising. For sexual abuse cases, a medical assessment is highly recommended. With either case, coordinating with children's services can assist you with obtaining the proper medical attention to assess the child's welfare.

It is critical in physical abuse cases to identify the weapon used to abuse the child. Oftentimes, it's a personal weapon (e.g., hand, fist, foot, etc.). However, if another type of weapon was used, a search warrant should be sought. If you obtain a search warrant, consider any other evidence that could be found at the time of the search before completing the search warrant affidavit. Add as much information as possible to obtain any evidence related to the abuse. Understand that historically child abuse is a repetitive issue. The incident that you are investigating is likely not the first or only incident that has occurred.

When preparing for a forensic interview, consider custody issues and how a parent may influence the child prior to the interview. That's why it is important to schedule a forensic interview as quickly as possible.

In some jurisdictions the forensic interview is conducted within 24 hours of the initial report. If there may be issues of potential influence, communicate your concerns to the children's services representative.

When reconstructing the incident(s), connect the dots. Link the evidence to the facts and statements. Make sure the allegations are feasible. Be sure to use photographs that can bring the crime scene to the courtroom for a trial. Look for potential weaknesses in the investigation, and work to reduce them.

A good investigator will thoroughly document their work. It is important to document everything in your investigation. If your case goes to trial, it will likely go on for a year or longer. You may forget some things that you did. If you thoroughly document your investigative activities, it will help you become better prepared.

As long as the case is open, we always suggest that you review your case file occasionally. A good practice is to review the case file every 90 days until closed or inactive with no additional leads. Reviewing the case over time will help you think of other possible investigative actions to develop leads. Once an arrest is made, the case file can be closed. If not, it's kept open until no leads can be developed. During that time, you may be waiting on evidence processing, such as lab results.

Investigative Toolbox

There are many different resources available to use for crimes against children. One resource that is a must is to coordinate with the state or local children's services agency. These agencies are responsible for the welfare of children. They are a resource not only for law enforcement investigating cases involving children but also for families needing resources. Most states require children's services to get involved when children are abused or neglected. If the child is in immediate danger, children's services have the authority to remove the child from the home, not law enforcement.

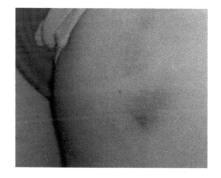

FIGURE 8.11 First Stage of Bruising

Some officers tend to treat cases involving children differently. Don't! It's not a social problem. Treat this case just like any other and preserve the crime scene. Is medical attention necessary? If so, seek treatment for the child. Is a rape kit necessary? Prepare the parents for this. Sometimes the examinations may not reveal sexual trauma (e.g., in children), but that doesn't mean that it didn't occur. This too may need to be explained to the parents or guardians.

You should be familiar with the stages of injuries and bruising:

1. The bruise will at first appear pink/red (see Figure 8.11).

2. Then it will change to blue/purple (see Figure 8.12).

3. Next, it will turn a pale green.

4. Finally, it will be yellow/brown.

The first stage of a bruise is pink at its lightest color with a fresh abrasion. The abrasion will form a reddish color as blood leaks into the tissue. There could be visible swelling, and it will become tender

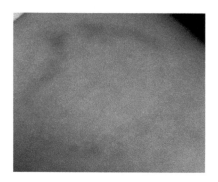

FIGURE 8.12 Second Stage of bruising

to touch, depending on depth on the injury. After about 24 hours, a bruise will start to turn to a blue or dark purple color. This is caused by the loss of oxygen within the leaking blood vessels. This stage can last up to 5 days. The bruise is sensitive to touch. In this stage, the bruise can turn as dark as black. This depends on the damage to the vessels within the tissue and the loss of more oxygen within the blood vessels. The next stage is pale green, which is an indicator that the bruise is healing. This typically occurs 5–7 days after the initial abrasion. The last stage is the yellow/brown bruise. This process starts about a week after the initial abrasion and can last up to another week. The bruising cycle lasts up to a total of 2 weeks.

If the child is mature enough, conduct a brief (not detailed) interview with the child. First responding officers should ask:

- What happened?
- Who did it?
- Where did it happen?

Neither the first responding officer nor the investigator should ask detailed questions unless they are conducting a forensic interview, which would not be at the scene. Typically, first responding officers are not certified forensic interviewers. When speaking to the child, listen for red flags (e.g., sexual knowledge, minimizing, etc.).

If the offender is known or identified, an interview should be conducted. Allow them to justify, rationalize, or excuse their behavior. Don't be judgmental. The offender may blame the child for the incident. For example, a suspect in a child sex abuse case may say "They [the child] had a desire to explore." Or they may justify their actions by saying that they were "just teaching or preparing them [the child] for life." This does not excuse or justify the crime, but it is an admission. You must acknowledge their response without being judgmental. If you are condemnatory, you risk the chances of getting the offender's statement or confession. This can be hard for any officer or investigator, but it is the best practice. Remember, you work for the victim.

ADDITIONAL RESOURCES

For more information on the relationship between teens and gang violence, watch the following 2020 interview with author Gabe Morales:

Fox 13 Seattle. (2023, January 18). *Police call recent teen violence "interpersonal conflict," gang expert says call it what it is* [Video]. YouTube. https://youtu.be/6hm6PPftcoI

References

Animal Legal Defense Fund. (n.d.). *The crime of bestiality/zoophilia: Sexual assault of an animal.* Retrieved November 20, 2020, from https://aldf.org/article/the-crime-of-bestiality-zoophilia-sexual-assault-of-an-animal/

Child Sexual Abuse and Pornography Act of 1986, 18 U.S. Code § 2251 (1986). https://www.law.cornell.edu/uscode/text/18/2251

Farlex. (n.d.). *Justifiable or excusable homicide.* The Free Dictionary. Retrieved August 8, 2023, from https://legal-dictionary. thefreedictionary.com/Justifiable+or+Excusable+Homicide

Federal Bureau of Investigation. (n.d.-a). *Crime Data Explorer.* Retrieved August 8, 2023, from https://cde.ucr.cjis.gov/LATEST/ webapp/#/pages/home

Federal Bureau of Investigation. (n.d.-b). *Jewelry and gem theft.* https://www.fbi.gov/investigate/violent-crime/jewelry-gem-theft

Federal Bureau of Investigation. (2018). *Rape.* Crime in the United States, 2018. https://ucr.fbi.gov/crime-in-the-u.s/2018/ crime-in-the-u.s.-2018/topic-pages/rape

Indian Child Protection and Family Violence Prevention Act, 42 C.F.R. § 136.403 (2017). https://law.justia.com/codes/us/2017/ title-42/chapter-136/

Legal Dictionary. (2017, February 11). *Sexual battery.* https://legaldictionary.net/sexual-battery/

Mayo Clinic. (2022, May 20). *Sudden infant death syndrome (SIDS).* https://www.mayoclinic.org/diseases-conditions/ sudden-infant-death-syndrome/symptoms-causes/syc-20352800

Merriam-Webster. (n.d.). Homicide. In *Merriam-Webster.com dictionary.* Retrieved August 8, 2023, from https://www.merriam-webster.com/dictionary/homicide

ProCon. (2022, December 19) *States with legal medical aid in dying (MAID).* https://euthanasia.procon.org/states-with-legal-physician-assisted-suicide/

Regional Information Sharing Systems. (n.d.). *About us.* https://www.riss.net/about-us/

Tenn. Code § 39-13-202 (2021). https://law.justia.com/codes/tennessee/2021/title-39/chapter-13/part-2/section-39-13-202/ #:~:text=As%20used%20in%20subdivision%20(a,any%20definite%20period%20of%20time

U.S. Department of Justice. (2020). *Child pornography.* https://www.justice.gov/criminal-ceos/child-pornography

U.S. Drug Enforcement Agency Diversion Control Division. (2016). Federal armed robbery reports of controlled substances: Calendar year 2016. U.S. Department of Justice. https://www.deadiversion.usdoj.gov/21cfr_reports/theft/maps/DTL_Armed_ Robbery_By_State_CY2016.pdf

Credits

CHAPTER 9

Being an Effective Investigator

Purpose

An effective investigator must wear many hats. Conducting investigations involves more than just sitting at a desk for a workday. It involves in-depth, thorough, and ongoing training to stay current and up to date on techniques. A good detective must possess knowledge, skills, and abilities that are not expected of the random street officer. Some of the necessary skills are trainable, but others aren't. One ability needed for an effective investigator that most people don't think about is a strong stomach. Unfortunately, investigators see the worst-case scenarios in life. One must be able to cope with dead bodies, blood, dismembered bodies, abuse to children, and much more. Not everyone is "cut out" to become a detective or investigator.

An effective investigator will manage large caseloads. Investigations involve cases from a basic theft to homicide. Few agencies have complete specialization with different types of investigations, such as property crime, family crime, violent crime, homicide, drug, or gang investigations. Therefore, most investigators have a wide variety of cases. Their ability to manage and direct resources for criminal investigation is crucial.

Lastly, an effective criminal investigator must be a good witness in court. Many times, although it's not required, investigators are considered experts in specific fields within the criminal investigations field. This is also known as a **subject matter expert (SME)**, a person who has extensive knowledge skills, and/or understanding related to a specific subject. Whether the investigator is a court-qualified expert or not, they must be able to communicate well enough to a judge and/or jury the facts of the investigation in which they are involved.

Training

For new criminal investigators to feel confident and prepared to tackle an array of complex tasks, rigorous formal training is required. For an example, see the Federal Law Enforcement Training Center's (n.d.) training program (https://www.fletc.gov/criminal-investigator-training-program). A good training program will not only cover all of the basics needed to perform job functions but also give a chance for interactions with instructors, understanding of modern technology aspects, a chance to ask questions, as well as hands-on practice. We call this "tell, show, and do" in criminal justice training so that the training becomes a useful part of your learning, on-the-job training, and professional growth opportunities.

Experience

Most criminal justice agencies will require some type of basic law enforcement or corrections training and experience prior to becoming an investigator. For example, many law enforcement agencies require at least 3 years of patrol experience prior to becoming eligible for an investigations division. Obviously, smaller agencies may differentiate from this requirement. Most correctional agencies have similar requirements. Administrators would prefer not to give investigative responsibilities to an inexperienced officer, whether in corrections or on the street.

Many times, agencies will pay for staff to attend training seminars such as the John E. Reid Interviewing, Interrogations, and Investigations seminars, and there are other such trainings that may be available in your area put on by professional nonprofit associations. There are a wide variety of these trainings, ranging from general to very specific types of investigations. We recommend that you check out each by visiting their websites and talking to peers who have taken the courses previously. Remember, when you are called in court, your expertise may be questioned as to what kind of training you've had in the area. Reading books such as ours, basic and postacademy training, public and private training, and hands-on experience can all assist in your subject matter expertise being taken seriously.

According to the Federal Law Enforcement Training Center (n.d.), investigators require "human behavior, modern technology, cultural sensitivity, law, and other interdisciplinary approaches to effective law enforcement" (Description section). An effective training program will also have good documentation by the trainer of total hours the trainee has in each subject, a grading system that can lead to improvements, and a fair evaluation.

We can't tell you how many times over our careers that probation and annual evaluations have been conducted on us by supervisors who had spent little to no time ever supervising us. Many of them admitted they were just going through the motions, as the evaluation was assigned to them outside of their power. While this may satisfy accreditation and policy requirements for an agency, it is not fair to the evaluator, nor can it be an accurate evaluation of the employee.

Education

Training will include a mixture of practical exercises, lab work, lectures, and exams (Federal Law Enforcement Training Center, n.d.). These provide opportunities for intermediate and advanced trainees to "take it to the next level." You may also want to participate in specific focused classes, such as "Working with Informants" or "Understanding Street Gangs," that may help you in your assignments with an employer.

While it may not be required to be an investigator, a college education will only assist. More specifically, a criminal justice education will help prepare you as an investigator. College courses will help you learn to research and will prepare you to write better. The higher the level of education that you receive, the more you will research and write essays or papers. Most of all, many criminal justice agencies provide pay incentives for educational degrees.

A traditional college education will also provide you social skills. You will learn how to manage your time better. Presentation and confidence in public speaking will increase. You will be tasked to problem solve and develop effective solutions and strategies to be more successful.

A college education can be of importance because it provides you with more of an open mind. As you learn from the courses and from other people's experiences, you will learn more about the real world. You will better understand and respect it. Sometimes, we, as humans, develop prejudices and/or stereotypes as we grow up. A traditional college experience can help you understand and work through those prejudices and/or stereotypes. You will develop your own opinions on social issues, which can differ from prior beliefs, when you know and understand the facts. A higher regard for the world can be one of the best benefits of a higher education.

For a list of possible class subjects, see the Federal Law Enforcement Training Center's program syllabus (https://www.fletc.gov/criminal-investigator-training-program).

https://tinyurl.com/m3s3vmcm

While these are some of the major subjects, it is not a complete list. Contact your local training academies online or in person for more information. You should also look at local colleges. We can say, there is a large variety in cost and quality of training. It is often said, "You get what you pay for." We have found free courses are often very basic unless they are supported by grants or government monies. There are also some private trainings that can be quite expensive. Some of these are good, and some are rip-offs. Another saying we'll give you is "Buyer beware." Do your homework before signing up and paying. Ask respected peers for their opinions of the training, and always keep an open mind.

Some states and/or accreditation groups requirement investigators have at least 40 hours of a basic criminal investigations course. Much of the course is a brief highlight to the long list above. The areas of basic knowledge that a criminal investigator needs to possess include:

- case management

- crime scene management and skills

- interview and interrogation skills

- informants/source of information

- evidence collection

- courtroom testimony

- property and violent crimes

- sex abuse investigations

All investigators, regardless of their affiliation or background, must hone their skills before taking on a case. Training is the first step to becoming an effective investigator, and even seasoned investigators rely on their foundational skills to communicate with witnesses, gather evidence, and ultimately solve the case (Malone, n.d.).

Disciplines

We have given a lot of focus on criminal investigations involving violence, property, and/or personal crimes. However, there are other disciplines that a law enforcement agency uses investigators for, and drug investigations are one of the other primary disciplines. Gang investigations are another.

When it comes to drug investigations, they can be long term, especially when targeting drug trafficking organizations or larger drug sales. Drug cases are not victimless crimes. Some may argue otherwise, arguing that a drug addict cannot be a victim. Of course, it's their decision to consume illegal drugs. But they are victims to the addiction, which may result in death if they overdose.

Long-term drug investigations are complex. They require planning and coordination. Drugs have no boundaries or jurisdictions. Networking with other agencies that are affected is important. A drug investigation can involve agencies from local departments, state police, and federal agencies, such as the Drug Enforcement Administration (DEA). Investigators will exchange information with agents or investigators from other jurisdictions to increase their effectiveness.

Drug investigations involve some of the same procedures as other criminal investigations. As a matter of fact, drug investigations can be more detailed because they're mostly proactive investigations. These types of cases involve quite a bit of surveillance, demanding long days and nights. They require the use of electronic surveillance techniques like global positioning system (GPS) monitoring, wiretaps (Federal Title III), trap and trace, pen registries, and so on.

Search warrants or court orders are more commonly utilized in the drug investigation discipline to obtain investigative leads and information. The techniques listed in the last paragraph all require a search warrant or court order of some type.

Most long-term drug investigations also end in **asset forfeitures**. One of the most effective tools for law enforcement in the drug investigation realm involves forfeiting the assets of the drug dealer or trafficker. An asset forfeiture is a civil proceeding that allows law enforcement to seize assets of the drug dealer or trafficker with a nexus (or connection) to the criminal activity or drug trafficking or that were purchased with funds from the sale of illegal drugs. We will not dive deep into asset forfeitures, but they are twofold.

First, this involves seizing material such as vehicles, businesses, houses, jewelry, anything of value, and most importantly money from a drug dealer or trafficker. This hits the pockets of the dealer or trafficker involved in criminal activity. The drug offender may not care as much about an arrest, even for a felony crime. But when law enforcement starts seizing their property, it's different.

Secondly, the funds from the seizures are added to the agency drug fund after (or if) the forfeiture is awarded to the agency by the court. Those funds are used by the agency to purchase equipment, salaries, and more. This is beneficial because if can reduce the cost of this expenditure to the community or taxpayers.

Additionally, the asset forfeitures take the profit of crime away, help in dismantling a drug trafficking organization, and deter crime. The process is not simple, but it is worthy of the time and effort when the agency is awarded assets of drug dealers/traffickers. Although the forfeitures are taken from the offender, there are times when the offender gets their property back. If the investigator cannot prove the property was involved in drug dealing/trafficking or is an asset of the illegal sale of drugs, then the offender (owner) is entitled to receive their property back without fine.

In Table 9.1, you can see the value in asset forfeitures from the DEA's Standardized Seizure Form (SSF).

TABLE 9.1 DEA FY2020 – FY2022 Asset Forfeiture

Fiscal year	SSF seized count	Value at seizure	Asset value
FY2022 (as of Oct. 2022)	10,635	$453,614,471.20	$443,001,136.08
FY2021	13,100	$803,017,981.73	$807,007,592.33
FY2020	11,669	$607,974,884.82	$595,886,329.36

With the recent fentanyl overdose epidemic in the United States, more focus has been given to drug investigations. As you can see in Figure 9.1, overdose deaths in the United States have dramatically increased (Elflein, 2023). Laws have changed to allow law enforcement to seek the fentanyl suppliers in overdose cases. While these types of investigations take a lot of resources, it can be a great deterrence when a fentanyl supplier is identified and criminally charged in the death of someone who overdosed. The drug dealer can be charged with murder in these cases. For example, in Tennessee, a person who supplied a drug addict fentanyl that resulted in an overdose death can be changed with second degree murder.

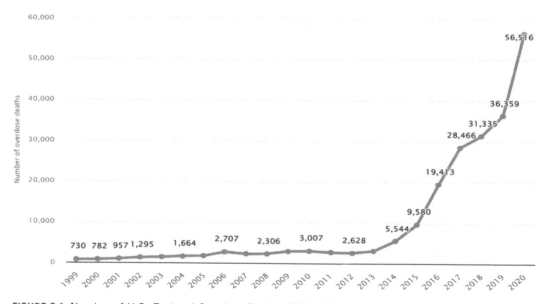

FIGURE 9.1 Number of U.S. Fentanyl Overdose Deaths 1999–2020

Another common investigative discipline is gang investigations. Both of your authors have been involved in gang investigations for over 20 years. Gang investigations are unique because they can encompass every other discipline. Gangs are a group of people who share common purpose of engaging in criminal conduct, with a recognizable structure or hierarchy, and with criminal purpose to engage in significant criminal activity, known as a criminal enterprise. They are involved in violent crimes, property crimes, personal crimes, and drug trafficking.

A gang investigator, in our humble opinion, should no doubt be a jack of all trades. In our experience, some of the best gang investigators are from the correctional side of law enforcement. Why? Because they deal with gang members on a daily basis—not only gang members but oftentimes gang leaders.

Your coauthor, Cooper, has worked gangs as a street investigator/officer in the "free world" and as a director in a state correctional agency. Some of the best gang investigators are from corrections. There is a significant difference between working gangs on the street and in a prison system. At the same time, there are some similarities.

Both are involved in drug dealing and violent crimes. Gang leaders who are incarcerated can still run their gangs from inside a correctional facility. In most states and federal prisons, cell phones are illegal for inmates to possess. Yet this is a huge issue throughout the United States. A cell phone allows a gang leader inside a prison to communicate and coordinate illegal criminal activity (violent or drug related) from inside a prison cell. These crimes are committed in the street as well as inside the prisons.

Gangs in prisons operate differently than on the street. Two different situations often occur when dealing with prison gang members or any inmates who are members of a security threat group (STG).

1. You have prior notice a STG member has been transferred to your facility via paperwork from another agency.

2. You do not have prior information or a "heads up" that you are dealing with a prison gang member.

Let's cover Situation 1 first. When an inmate is transferred to you from another professional correctional agency, they will usually include a security alert for any extraordinary handling conditions. This could be physical issues or mental health issues or things such as assaultive history toward staff and/or other inmates.

Hardcopy paperwork and/or electronic databases your agency has access to may also contain important information regarding security concerns, such as documented enemies—often referred to as "keep separate from." Documentation may also include if the inmate has been an informant previously housed in protective custody (PC).

Of course, you should never rely solely on such information, because humans recording these details can make mistakes. You should carefully read all incoming paperwork. There is usually contact information in case you have any questions regarding incoming prisoners. Be sure to call or email if you have any doubts or further concerns.

Once you feel you have a good idea of who you are dealing with, interview them and ask the inmate to clarify. Sometimes placement in another agency had to do with that environment. It may not mean they need to be in protective custody or administrative segregation at your facility. This is especially true if they have done well during a previous classification and placement at your facility. My rule of thumb was usually they go back to the security level they last left from at my facility. Then a classification review is set up to reconsider housing and program options.

For example, suppose you had an inmate 10 years ago and he was a constant behavior problem, always fighting and arguing with staff and other inmates. He would likely go back to maximum security/administrative segregation or high-security single (celled in a rack back) secure door cell. It could be he was just immature last time and may have been low security at another institution. If he adjusts well and quickly, you may decide to lower his security to an open dorm unit. The general rule in corrections is to house at the lowest level safely possible.

Your agency probably has previously documented his scars, marks, and tattoos. Be sure to check for new "ink," especially tattoos associated with known STGs. This does not necessarily mean they need their security raised. Ask him about it and call or email prior agencies that dealt with him if you have any major concerns.

In addition to visually identifying tattoos, burn mark symbols, and the like, you'll want to know the inmate's moniker(s). We would usually be upfront and ask, "So, what do your homies call you?" Nine times out of ten, they would give an answer. If they didn't, we would try looking it up in other agency's files or just ask one of my informants.

This serves several purposes. First, when there is a fight or other serious incident in your facility, many times other offenders don't know combatants' real names. During a disciplinary hearing or during an investigation, they will testify that "Capone" hit them. There may be more than one person with that moniker in that area or unit, so ask, "Do you know which Capone?" They almost always did and would respond with more specifics: Black Capone, Mexican Capone, Big Capone, Capone in the lower tier, left hand side cell, and so on. Sometimes I even carried around a "gang book" full of pictures of gang members, similar to a "six pack lineup mug shots" and had them ID'd.

Another reason for gaining insight into their moniker is to assist outside law enforcement in identifying suspects for their investigations. They may have sketchy information that their drive-by suspect last weekend was a Mexican guy named Capone from the Avenues gang. He may be the one you currently have or had in custody. You can let them know.

Nationwide, STG members have been proven to be a higher security risk. When your coauthor Morales worked at Folsom Prison in California, prison gang members were often violent. Many had committed homicides to gain entrance into the gang. Many had killed enemies while they were incarcerated, and some even tried or did kill staff.

When I worked at the King County Jail in Seattle, WA, I tracked all STG members for well over 20 years. As opposed to Folsom where a good portion of the convicts were lifers, inmates in Seattle were often housed short term unless fighting a violent felony charge. The gang population went up in the summer months, while the homeless offender population went up in the winter months. The STG/gang population only varied on average between 10% (summer) to 5% (winter), but I did several surveys showing they were responsible for almost one third of the rule violations and involved in almost half of all fights and assaults on staff.

I have conducted criminal investigations at Folsom, (CA) State Prison, King County (Seattle, WA) jail, and a federally contracted facility located in Tacoma, WA (Northwest Immigration & Customs Enforcement Processing Center). The work at the end of my career was handled by a special unit or assigned individual. I often worked closely with these individuals and was also frequently in contact with prosecutors.

They often relied on me for supplemental information during their investigations, which brings up an important tip. Whenever you are conducting interviews or interrogations, you want to know—in advance, if possible—where your best and most reliable resources are. This can save you untold hours of time and spare you some headaches. Know all intelligence databases you can access, and have names, numbers, and emails of reliable sources you can go to when you need quick and reliable information. I made up my own personal resource list for such occasions and I was very good at networking. I developed this list over the course of 30 plus years in the business.

I developed inmate informants also but was very cautious when dealing with them. I conducted required interviews and pulled guys into the office during slow or down times.

Now let's cover Situation 2.

When you run into an STG member by accident, often when it is a young offender or the first time at your facility, you will want to start off with some general questions about them and about their gang. I was always cordial even when I thought or knew they were lying, then told them we would meet again and revisit the interview or interrogation.

Once I did some fact checking with my own developed and verified information on their gang, contacted other agencies and individuals on my contact list, and sometimes after talking to my informants, I would talk to them again. I would look at and document tattoos as well as arrest reports and probable cause reports. Then I carefully documented information in official records for future use.

As Stewart (2017) puts it, "Never turn down the opportunity to talk with or interview a gang member" (para. 4). The inmate may request to speak with the correctional officer directly or via a third party (i.e., housing unit officer). In the latter case, the third party will record the request.

If time is not an issue, have the inmate put the request to speak in writing. This will assist you should the inmate or their attorney try to use this in an adverse manner against you in court at a later date.

Skills

There are several skills needed to become an effective investigator. Most of these skills are trained skills, and others come naturally to some. Even if it's not natural to you, trained skills are effective if you practice. An effective investigator never stops learning or training. We will break down some skills are they relate to the four I's.

Interview/Interrogation

The title of this book, *The Four I's: Interviewing, Interrogations, Investigations, and Intelligence in Criminal Justice*, should have given you a clue of the four main job skill areas we consider to be essential to complete tasks in this field. We've already covered some of this in previous chapters, but as a reminder and refresher, a good investigator is a good interviewer. Officers must be able to ask clear, focused questions and receive truthful, accurate responses from witnesses, victims, and suspects alike. The interviewer should be a good listener able to probe for details when needed and recognize, through body language or other tells, when the interviewee may be less than honest (Malone, n.d.).

While interrogations use many of the same skills, they may be used in a different light, such as verbally stressing a subject to get them to focus on giving a truthful and accurate answer to questioning. Ever since the beginning days of police and corrections work, effective investigators have solved the majority of their cases and made the majority of their conclusions and decisions because they were successfully able to get

Adapted from Maureen Malone, "Skills & Qualities Necessary to Be an Effective Investigator," *The Nest*. Copyright © by The Knot Worldwide.

sources to reveal critical information. Much of this is discovered by conducting thorough interviews and interrogations. While methods conducted in this area may seem harsh at times to outsiders, they should never be abusive. We are not suggesting you "waterboard" suspects or conduct yourself in a manner here that may be illegal.

Interview and interrogation skills also require good people skills to be effective. An investigator with the gift of gab (or talk) will be a successful interviewer. A shy or antisocial investigator will less likely be as effective. If you realize that this is you and that it's a weakness, prepare yourself to develop this skill. One way to develop this skill is to attend speech-related classes. These classes will prepare you to speak in front of others. Impromptu speeches are one of the best ways to develop more effective social skills.

We can't stress enough about learning different methods of interviews and interrogation. There are nationally recognized methods, like John E. Reid & Associates (https://reid.com) and Wicklander-Zulawski & Associates (https://www.w-z.com), that are available for law enforcement and the private sector to use. However, you must practice these skills to maintain your ability and broaden your skill level. It must also be stated that these are not the "end all be all" or the only way. These are each "a way."

Many other law enforcement training entities, academies, and/or businesses provide good and acceptable training, not only with interviews or interrogations but for practically any topic. We will always suggest to go to as much training as you possibly can. At the same time, we'd suggest to always vet and research the training instructor and entity. There are good ones and bad one. Always attend training with an open mind.

Investigations

An investigation starts when the first officer arrives on scene. The patrol officer needs to understand criminal investigations just as much as the seasoned investigator. Their actions or the lack thereof can make or break an investigation. The patrol officer must first take a thorough and detailed report of the offense(s) that were committed. Sometimes it's the patrol officer that must follow up on the initial report. Documentation is a key component to a successful investigation. As a matter of fact, when seeking detective applicants, we've always reviewed the reports the applicant wrote in patrol. This seems to be a good indicator of a good investigator.

We have provided you with some of the basic tools you'll need to conduct your investigations, but always rely on the standard operational procedures (SOPs) of your agency. Many of these policies were written by staff who have vast knowledge of local laws and have years of practical experience of how your department operates. SOPs are often updated as legal challenges surface and laws are changed. That brings us to a common problem some employees forget: Make sure you are looking at the most recent SOP and memos from your administration regarding written policy. It is very easy to view an old policy, and it can be very embarrassing to you later and you could even face disciplinary action and legal problems. We are not here to promote or downplay the role of unions here, but if in doubt, call your union rep or consult your own legal advice. Just because it is written policy does not mean it will protect you in court. We covered personal crimes in Chapter 8; don't become your own statistic.

While conducting investigations, you must control your emotions. In case you didn't already know, this can be a very stressful line of work. We can't tell you how many times our coworkers have told us they fear some of their own coworkers more than suspects. The work can be a mental drain in itself without having to deal with the fact that sometimes you may have coworkers or other agencies interfere with your investigations, whether intentionally or unintentionally. While these situations can be frustrating, don't let your anger get the best of you. Doing so can destroy relations with coworkers and outside agencies, jeopardize the case, and cause witnesses to withhold information. As Malone (n.d.) notes, "The investigator must show empathy to victims and clients and create a safe environment for them to share important details" (Control Emotions section).

A successful investigator must be an active listener. We've mentioned it in the interview and interrogation sections of this book. You have to listen to what people are telling you and match it to their body language and other nonverbal communication, as well as the physical evidence. If you are not paying attention to what a suspect or victim is saying, you are likely missing crucial information or indicators.

There are many other specialized skills that are considered "advanced" by most investigators. One such skill is bloodstain analysis. Blood can tell an investigator a lot about a crime and what occurred. Obviously, blood will most likely be found at violent crime scenes, like homicides. Blood may also be found at burglary scenes, where the offender may have cut themselves while entering. This is common is cases involving broken glass. The value of blood evidence is high because DNA from the blood can identify the contributor. In some cases, that may be the offender. Depending on the investigation, the blood contributor could be the victim.

Every criminal investigator should attend a bloodstain school. There are chemicals that can be used for presumptive blood tests. Some of those are:

- luminol

- tetramethyl benzidine

- reduced phenolphthalein

- leuco-malachite

- hemin crystals

Bloody crime scene can be reconstructed—again, signifying the importance of bloodstain. Keep in mind that blood reconstruction involves advanced mathematic skills. Additionally, you must continue to practice the skill after training. Otherwise, you will lose the skill.

We cannot stress enough about thorough documentation. Investigations are typically long and drawn out, especially through the court process. We are human, and we forget things. That's why it's so important to document everything, even things that may seem minimal. Do not cut corners. Remember, you work for the victims.

Investigators have to be able to adjust well and occasionally very quickly. On television, it may appear the detective works a 9–5 dayshift job and is at their desk most of the time. That's certainly not the case, especially for an effective investigator. Investigations include long and odd hours, working holidays and nights. Overtime is highly likely. This can be a hardship on family life. All of this must be taken into consideration when seeking a job in investigations.

Good communication skills are also important. Investigators communicate with victims, offenders, families of both, witnesses, the media, and the court. A good detective must be able to talk to different types of people and keep an open mind. Investigations is a profession. Although it's a position in the criminal justice field, it's really a profession of its own. It requires skills of a car salesman, a psychologist, a counselor, and a builder, amongst many others.

We've said it before but will say it again, and you should remind yourself daily because it is very easy to forget and become callous and careless. If a case goes to court and uncovers that an investigator lied or employed unethical methods, this could prevent a conviction and cost the investigator their career. As such, it is essential that investigators remain credible and ethical (Malone, n.d.). We are sure there are some current or past prisoners who worked in law enforcement or corrections that look back and regret some of the decisions they made. Be smart, prevent it from ever happening to you, and remind yourself of your duty. Should you ever doubt that, it might be a good time to consider other employment. This work is not meant for everybody. It takes a certain kind of individual who can keep their mind, body, and spirt in order.

Intelligence

Some of the better intelligence-related training can be found in the military. Since 2001, law enforcement intelligence has been developing. Today, the law enforcement intelligence function is very capable. Although some of the best intelligence-based training stills come from the military, for obvious reasons, law enforcement fusion centers throughout the United States provide valuable training as well.

WHAT CHARACTERISTICS ARE DESIRED IN A GOOD ANALYST?

General factors
- Impeccable standards of honesty and integrity a thorough understanding of the concepts of:
  - Intelligence
  - Civil liberties
  - Criminal law enforcement
- The capacity to think in a logical and rational manner
- The capacity to approach situations from broad and divergent perspectives
- The ability to comprehend complex masses of data and communicate its contents to others
- Background factors
  - Broad range of interests
  - Developed research ability (library, qualitative, quantitative)
  - Helpful previous experience (law enforcement, military, security)
- Mental traits
  - Intellectual curiosity
  - Rapid assimilation of information
  - Keen recall of information
  - Tenacity
  - Willingness and capacity to make judgments
- Communication skills
  - Developed writing ability
  - Skill in oral briefing
  - Interviewing and interrogating skills
  - Eliciting information from officers

- Liberal arts skills
  - Good writing ability
  - Fluency in a second language desirable
  - Good knowledge of geography
- Work style
  - Initiative and self-direction
  - Effective personal interaction
  - Disciplined intellectual courage

Not all intelligence analysts are sworn law enforcement personnel. There is disagreement amongst the law enforcement intelligence community about whether analysts should be sworn or not. Some argue that an analyst should not be sworn personnel because it opens the position up to less restrictions and requirements expected on sworn personnel. An analyst possesses some different characteristics that may not be the best fit for a sworn officer, investigator, or agent. To the contrary, the argument is that many will use an analyst position as a steppingstone or for promotional purposes to transfer to a position as an investigator, officer, or agent. In this case, the position would be a revolving door.

Both arguments have merit. Whether the intelligence analyst is sworn or not, it's the dedication of the person that is critical for the position. It's the qualifications that are most important to review when determining who is the best fit for the position.

Case Management

The Investigation Case Management (ICM) system generates a report of an incident or incidents that assists with a case to be resolved over a relatively quick but careful period of time to achieve a satisfactory result for all involved. As a case evolves and progresses, it often involves a series of spelled out processes under which an investigator is expected to operate. These can range from simple to complex, from single to multiple persons inside and outside the organization, and specify the manner in which documents, messages, digital data, and other third-party material can be processed, analyzed, and cataloged for later reference. This can take the form of hard files, digital files, or both.

Some part of case management involves solvability factors. Investigators are assigned cases based on agency guidelines and/or focus. Investigative units may assign cases based on solvability factors that are developed from the initial report and/or additional investigative resources available to develop leads to solve the case. Some agencies have developed matrixes that rate the solvability of cases, which may determine if the case is assigned to an investigator or not. If not, the case may be listed as inactive and the only follow-up is a courtesy call to the victim(s).

Case management embraces the principles of an investigation. It is a legal and systematic gathering of evidence and details of a case for later possible legal discovery, checkable facts, and accurate information that can show you respected a subject's rights and gave due process while conducting your investigation, that you used your SOP and all legal laws of your area in all fairness. If you conducted your investigation thoroughly, a good defense attorney will realize it and recommend your subject take a plea bargain rather than take it to trial. This is often referred to as an "open and shut case." If a subject decides to take it to trial, you will be operating on information that you will feel confident about when up on the trial stand. If you did not conduct your investigation in the best manner or even if you did, you can bet a good defense attorney will cast doubt in court and make you feel at times it is you who is on trial.

Investigators have to multitask well. You will have multiple cases open at one time. You'll have to balance out priorities in cases and follow-up investigations. Whether provided by the law enforcement agency or created by the investigator themselves, an assessment tool to manage or prioritize case investigation is critical. Otherwise, you will bounce from one case to another without solving anything. As new cases are assigned, they become more of a priority. However, the cases that were assigned a week prior may have better solvability.

Cases such as homicides are often complex to investigate. These cases take a lot of time to work. Some larger agencies have specialized investigators (homicide units) that only investigate homicides or death cases. However, most midsized and smaller agencies operate with a general detective's division. These investigators are assigned cases that range from theft to homicide. As an investigator in a general investigations unit, it is sometime difficult managing cases. The workload may be overwhelming. This is because a "smaller case" may have a large priority due to community needs, politics, or simply just because of criminal trends.

An effective investigator will create a uniform or organized case file. Developing a case file checklist is a great way to ensure that everything is in your case file, and it can be a way to make sure that you don't forget an investigative task. If you create your own checklist, you can add to it as needed. For example, if you determine that a specific task such as checking pawn tickets in theft or burglary cases is always done, then add the task to your checklist. That way, you'll never forgot to complete the task.

If you have managed your case in an orderly and well-documented manner, prosecutors will love you. If you did not, they may not think very highly of you and you may find yourself reassigned to another unit in the future. This business can be very competitive; there are very likely other employees who already feel they can do it better than you. Don't let this distract you. Just do the best job you can do and follow our recommendations on case management and other subjects described in this book, and you likely won't go wrong.

Crime Scene Management

As an investigator, crime scene management is a duty that you'll be responsible for. Depending on the agency size, you may have to manage the personnel securing the crime scene and process the scene as well. That includes communicating with agency leaders, legal counsel or prosecutors, family contacts, and so on. Crime scene management call be overwhelming, especially with limited personnel.

First and foremost, you must ensure that the scene is secured to preserve evidence. That includes creating a barrier, commonly done with plastic crime scene label tape. This barrier shall always be larger than you expect the crime occurred in. Personnel should be scattered out around the perimeter of the tape to make sure no one crosses the barrier.

Evidence collection is one of the most important tasks of crime scene management. Before evidence can be recovered, you need to ensure that you follow all legal requirements. The Fourth Amendment of the U.S. Constitution does not have a crime scene exception. Therefore, consent to search or a search warrant must be obtained. There may be times when exigent circumstances may apply. Be careful! Always err on the side caution, and seek a search warrant when at all possible.

It's a good idea to keep a notepad with you to keep up with a to-do list. A crime scene checklist can also be valuable. It will assist you with tasks that otherwise may forget. Refer to the crime scene checklist in Appendix 1 for a reference.

Once the crime scene has been processed, you are accountable for releasing the scene to someone. Typically, that is a family member or the victim. When releasing any crime scene, we'd suggest that you document the person it's being released to. You can ask for identification (or a driver's license) and photograph it. That time and date stamps the release. The photograph should be stored in your case file and evidence.

Photographs are critical for any crime scene. As the crime scene manager, make sure the photographer doesn't delete any digital photographs, even if the exposure was black or the lens cap wasn't taken off. Any photographs are discoverable in court proceedings. If a photograph is deleted, it may cause evidentiary issues when providing discovery for prosecution. A defense attorney may argue that the deleted photo is exculpatory evidence.

Courtroom Testimony

We already described some of the "dos and don'ts" in the previous sections, but let us cover a little more of the end processes that can make or break a case and make you look good or bad in the courtroom. Almost always, a prosecutor will question you before trial to make sure you are a good witness or, if you are the officer providing a good chuck of the evidence, so that they get a good feel for how you will present yourself in court. They cannot tell you what to say, and you will be taking an oath to "tell the truth and nothing but the truth." They just don't want to be blindsided. There is also often a pretrial for both sides, the prosecution and the defense, to know the charges and evidence against a defendant.

PERSONAL EXPERIENCES

Morales

I was testifying in the case of a Mara Salvatrucha (MS) member who was on trial for a drive-by shooting that was charged as an attempted assault since, I believe due to very liberal local politics, a drive-by shooting charge may have been considered prejudicial. In fact, while we had gang laws on the books, they were very rarely used, as using the "g" word was often rebuffed or objected to.

The assistant prosecutor asked me how I knew the subject, and I replied that I had dealt with him previously in jail. She then asked me his name, and I answered and that I also knew him as "Solo" (his gang name). She asked me if I knew if he had any gang affiliation, and I was actually surprised she was allowed to do so by the judge because, as I previously stated, this was a very liberal court. I told her that I did know his affiliation as being a member of MS. She asked me how I knew, and I stated because he self-admitted to me he was a member and it was documented in his inmate record and file. She asked me how did I know that he wasn't lying, and I stated that he has tattoos of a large "M" on one shoulder and an "S" on the other. She then asked me how did I not know that they were not the initials of somebody or something else. I answered that it was because he was let out to the inmate yard one day, and when I checked the yard for damage and contraband before the inmates went back in, there was multiple gang graffiti written on the walls that said, "Solo MS13." I stated "Solo" was his moniker, MS his gang, and the 13 stood for the umbrella group Surenos 13 that MS fell under.

I then stated something that almost resulted in a retrial. I stated that I found this out right before we reclassified him to a higher security level after he got into a gang fight.

"Objection, Your Honor!" the defense attorney said.

The judge instructed to jury to disregard that last statement, but I'm not sure they could.

The lesson of this story is not to say anything until asked. Had that case been set for retrial, I'm sure the prosecutors would not have been happy with me.

In spite of me making a blunder in court and scaring the prosecutors, the accused received 40 years in prison. I did not conduct that case. I was only a witness, but the detectives did their homework with a "little assistance" from me.

The investigator has to bring the crime scene or the investigation of the crime to the courtroom for the judge and/or jury. This is another reason why being detail-oriented is so important. You will have to swear to investigative facts to obtain warrants, such as search warrants or arrest warrants. In previous chapters, we mentioned elements of the crime. This is when those element are important. You must have probable cause to believe a crime was committed to obtain a warrant. To show probable cause, the elements of the crime have to be shown to the court. That's why knowing the elements is so important: first to show probable cause and in the end to prove guilt beyond a reasonable doubt for a conviction.

A good investigator must be confident in their work, including all parts of the investigation. If you, as the investigator, are doubtful or lack confidence, can that produce reasonable doubt to the judge or jury? Absolutely!

A criminal investigation may include court testimony in preliminary hearing, the grand jury, and during trials. Oftentimes, there are pretrial hearings that require the investigator's testimony as well. For example, the offender/defendant may file a motion to suppress evidence from the investigation. A judge must determine if the evidence was lawfully obtained and/or if it should be admitted in whole or in part during a trial.

If an investigation is presented to the grand jury, the investigator is most likely the primary witness in the presentation of evidence. There are times in long-term or complex cases that multiple witnesses testify before a grand jury. However, in most cases the primary investigator presents the facts of the case or investigation to the grand jury for consideration.

An investigator's testimony should support the facts of the investigation. An investigator must explain in layman's terms about technical or scientific material in a way that can be understood. Consider yourself being on a jury that will determine the fate of someone else's life. Wouldn't you want to understand the facts? Of course, if it were more technical or scientific than you could comprehend, you might reserve judgement. Keep that in mind when you are preparing investigations and testifying in court. You may understand exactly what you see, did, or know because of your training and experience as an investigator. But can you explain it to a layman in terms that anyone can understand without being confused? If not, consider your approach to the testimony as you are planning for a criminal investigative trial.

There are times when the prosecutors use investigators as expert witnesses to better explain the skills used in investigation cases. Expert witness are used to provide the court (judge and jury) with special knowledge or proficiencies in a specific field that is relevant to the case. An investigator with advanced training and experience in bloodstain pattern analysis could be called as an expert witness to better explain to the court particularities of blood spatter in a criminal case. An investigator cannot just claim to be an expert witness. There is a process to qualify as an expert witness. Those qualification include knowledge, skill, education, experience, or training in the specialized field.

Courtroom testimony is a critical part of the investigative process. Before a judge or jury can decide guilt, there has to be some sort of testimony of facts. Even in a plea agreement, the judge must be provided facts of a crime, and the law enforcement officer or investigator typically provides that testimony. Integrity is the most important concept in the code of conduct. Never testify to anything other than the truth, even if it means that you open yourself up to mistakes that you made or something that you failed to do that may make you look "bad." It's not worth it. Your integrity says a lot about who you are. Integrity indicates your dependability and the confidence that the public has in you. Lying or falsifying information on the witness stand will destroy your career in the criminal justice system. It should not be tolerated and should be punished.

References

Carter, D. L. (2009). *Law enforcement intelligence: A guide for state, local, and tribal law enforcement agencies* (p. 399). U.S. Deptartment of Justice, Office of Community Oriented Policing Services. https://cops.usdoj.gov/ric/Publications/cops-p064-pub.pdf

Drug Enforcement Agency. (n.d.). *DEA asset forfeiture.* Retrieved October 2, 2022, from https://www.dea.gov/operations/asset-forfeiture

Elflein, J. (2023, January 19). *Fentanyl overdose deaths U.S. 1999–2020.* Statista. https://www.statista.com/statistics/895945/fentanyl-overdose-deaths-us/

Federal Law Enforcement Training Centers. (n.d.). *Criminal Investigator Training Program.* https://www.fletc.gov/criminal-investigator-training-program

Frost, C. C., & Morris, J. (1983). *Police intelligence reports.* Palmer Enterprises.

Malone, M. (n.d.). *Skills & qualities necessary to be an effective investigator.* The Nest. https://woman.thenest.com/skills-qualities-necessary-effective-investigator-4903.html

Stewart, S. (2017, October 10). *How to interview gang members.* Corrections1. https://www.corrections1.com/corrections-training/articles/how-to-interview-gang-members-5JMY65NEC1DLiw97/

Credits

Part IV

Intelligence

CHAPTER 10

Intelligence-Led Policing and Corrections

Law enforcement intelligence includes police and correctional data. Intelligence is critical for law enforcement agency decision making, planning, crime prevention, strategic targeting, and operational planning. Sources of information collected in the intelligence-led policing process should involve the corrections component. However, many practitioners fail to seek or use correctional information. Why? Some simply forget about the correctional resources. Others choose not to utilize the correctional resources for a variety of reasons, including but not limited to lack of trust, lack of correctional understanding, and/or lack of networking availability. Law enforcement intelligence includes protocols and procedures to develop or disseminate a final product. These guidelines ensure that the information gathered is reliable, valuable, accurate, and trustworthy. The intelligence cycle (see Figure 10.1) provides a means to plan, collect, evaluate, collate, disseminate, and evaluate intelligence and the product. The cycle provides analysts with the ability to evaluate and/or reevaluate the intelligence product at any stage as additional information is developed. An **intelligence product** is a report or document that contain assessments, forecast, association, links, and other outputs from the analytic process.

Let's briefly highlight the intelligence cycle (Figure 10.1):

- *plan*: Define the purpose, need, requirements, and/or problem for analysis.

- *collect*: Gather data from sources (open source or investigative/covert).

- *process*: Assess the data for reliability, and process the collected data to determine if the **raw data** (information that's not yet intelligence) can exploit the problem.

- *collation and analysis*: Data is filtered, studied, and corroborated to provide a logical forecast related to criminal activity.

- *reporting and dissemination*: Develop a timely and accurate product that fits the purpose or need for the intelligence plan.

- *reevaluation*: The is a continuous process to identify changes or additional needs.

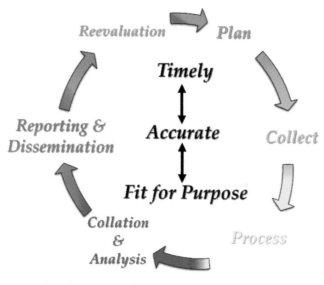

FIGURE 10.1 Intelligence Cycle

There is a difference between an investigation and intelligence, just as there is a difference between information and intelligence. Information is not intelligence. Information plus analysis equals intelligence. Investigations and intelligence each have different objectives and goals. Their focus is different, and the information gathered has different purposes (see Table 10.1).

TABLE 10.1 Investigation Versus Intelligence

Investigation	Intelligence
Crime-driven	Threat-driven
Primary goal is arrest and prosecution.	Primary goal is prevention.
Offender-specific information collection	Broad, threat-specific information collection
Information deals with facts and evidence to support burden of proof.	Information deals with facts and probabilities.

Coauthor Gabe Morales has written or assisted in writing several assessment documents for criminal justice agencies, worked at the U.S. Marine Corps Tactical Air Commend Center under a security clearance by the federal government, as well as recently working as a lieutenant with a security clearance from the Department of Homeland Security at a contracted federal immigration detention center, and understands intelligence issues. He formally exchanged intelligence on criminals with agencies all across the United States in his job as a jail classification officer and informally exchanged intelligence while working as a correctional officer at Folsom Prison in California.

East Coast Gang Investigators Association Founding President Wes Daily who was a detective in the state of New York for decades was often fond of stating, "Intelligence not shared is information wasted."

Coauthor Korey Cooper started working in a law enforcement intelligence function in 2002. This was just after the terrorist attack on the United States in 2001. He became the terrorism liaison officer (TLO) for a local police department to collaborate with state and federal homeland security agencies. In 2009, he created a gang and intelligence unit within the Columbia Police Department in Tennessee. This unit worked daily with state and federal law enforcement agencies involving information and intelligence on gangs as well as domestic terrorism. Additionally, the unit processed weekly intelligence using the intelligence-led policing philosophy. The department created a weekly accountability-driven leadership (ADL) meeting, which brought leadership within the department together weekly for a roundtable discussion on issues and strategies to overcome these issues that effected the community.

He continued the intelligence process after being appointed to the Tennessee Department of Correction's Office of Investigation and Compliance. He was tasked with creating a unit to oversee intelligence and security threat group (gang) activities with a nexus to corrections. That included being the TLO for the state correctional agency, which collaborated with the FBI's Joint Terrorism Task Force (JTTF) frequently. That's when he realized how important the corrections function was to the law enforcement intelligence process. He will share his experiences in the text to help the readers better understand the intelligence function as it relates to the four I's.

Another trailblazer in the world of interviewing, interrogation, and investigations was Robert "Moco" Morrill, who was a detective and investigator for almost 50 years. When he went through the police academy was back in the 1950s, he was taught, "Police and intelligence, never the two shall they mix." But Morrill did not believe that, so he sought out previously gathered intelligence and generated his own credible information and shared it with the California Gang Task Force (the first task force of its kind), which went on to bust several key criminal organizations.

To this very day, some people feel such information should remain secret, and agencies and individuals assigned to such duties often are hypervigilant not to share intelligence with many in the fear that it may end up in the wrong hands because, to be frank, knowledge is power. Some individuals assigned to key intelligence functions like to hold on to information because they may feel it makes them invaluable as job security.

For purposes of safer communities, law enforcement needs to maintain information on some people and/or organizations for two reasons. They either have the potential to commit crimes or they pose a threat to safety or security. If no criminality exists but the risk of a danger or threat is reasonably justified and a link of criminality to a person or group can be presented, intelligence can be kept and/or disseminated. In Chapter 11, we will discuss some legal aspects of intelligence gathering, storage, and dissemination.

Intelligence-Led Policing

Intelligence is the "product of systematic gathering, evaluation, and synthesis of raw data on individuals or activities suspected of being or known to be criminal in nature" (National Advisory Committee on Criminal Justice Standards and Goals, 1976, p. 122). **Information** is "data compiled, analyzed, and/or disseminated in an effort to anticipate, prevent, or monitor criminal activity" (International Association of Chiefs of Police, National Law Enforcement Policy Center, 1998, p. 11). **Intelligence-led policing (ILP)** is a law enforcement model that emphasizes the use of data analytics, community outreach, and cooperation between various law enforcement agencies and organizations. First developed in the 1990s, ILP grew in popularity following the 9/11 terrorist attacks, as law enforcement professionals sought a proactive, rather than reactive, approach to preventing crime (Kent State University, 2020).

Intelligence-led policing requires a team of highly trained analysts to comb through larger amounts of data. The New Jersey State Police define intelligence-led policing as "a collaborative philosophy that starts with information, gathered at all levels of the organization that is analyzed to create actionable intelligence and an improved understanding of their operational environment" (Fuentes, 2006, p. 3). With this information, police are equipped with the tools they need to prevent crime and interact with a variety of communities, particularly those with diverse backgrounds (Kent State University, 2020).

While the 9/11 terrorist attack provided a critical lesson learned because of need to collaborate with law enforcement agencies at all levels, it also provided an opportunity to develop different systems to ensure information and intelligence are communicated better. The **fusion center** concept for law enforcement was developed post-9/11 to exchange information and intelligence amongst federal, state, local, and tribal law enforcement agencies. This process facilitates and manages the flow of information and intelligence across each level of law enforcement and some private-sector organizations with the "need to know." As such, the Bureau of Justice Assistance (2013) explains that fusion centers provide a central hub of information, allowing public safety officials to cut down on digging for information so that they can better serve and project the communities in their jurisdiction.

Established to facilitate the National Criminal Intelligence Sharing Plan (NCISP), the fusion center focus group consisted of practitioners from the local, state, and federal levels of law enforcement. The group even boasted representatives from Homeland Security, the FBI, and the DOJ. You can see how these groups distribute information in Figure 10.2. The fusion center focus group stressed that fusion centers should be scalable at the city and state levels, providing a variety of intelligence services and functions to support investigations.

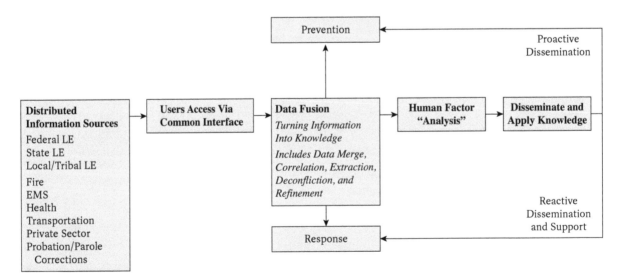

FIGURE 10.2 Fusion Centers

As a result of the focus group's work, guidelines were developed in 18 areas (Bureau of Justice Assistance, 2013):

1. The NCISP and the intelligence and fusion processes

2. Mission statement and goals

3. Governance

4. Collaboration

5. Memorandum of understanding (MOU) and nondisclosure agreement (NDA)

6. Database resources

7. Interconnectivity

8. Privacy and civil liberties

9. Security

10. Facility, location, and physical infrastructure

11. Human resources

12. Training of center personnel

13. Multidisciplinary awareness and education

14. Intelligence services and products

15. Policies and procedures

16. Center performance measurement and evaluation

17. Funding

18. Communications plan

Intelligence-led policing and the fusion center concept embrace one another. The NCISP provides guidance to law enforcement agencies with a model of standards and policies to communicate and share criminal intelligence. The NCISP provides 28 recommendations for agencies to gather, process, and disseminate credible intelligence to protect "the security of our homeland and preserve the rights and freedoms of all Americans" (Bureau of Justice Assistance, 2003, p. 2).

Some components of intelligence-led policing include (Heinen et al., 2020; Kent State University, 2020):

- Community-oriented policing (COPS)

Intelligence-led policing emphasizes developing a positive relationship between law enforcement and the community they serve. Also known as **community policing**, officers and other law enforcement personnel are encouraged to become actively engaged in the community via regular patrols, informal conversations with citizens, and transparent policing practices. Likewise, law enforcement

U.S. Department of Justice, Selection from "Fusion Centers and Intelligence Sharing," https://bja.ojp.gov/program/it/national-initiatives/fusion-centers, Bureau of Justice Assistance.

should prioritize addressing issues identified by and unique to the community, such as vandalism, petty theft, and noise violations. Fostering a strong rapport with the citizenry allows officers to solicit information, tips, and support for larger initiatives such as budget increases.

- **Problem-oriented policing (POP)**

  Once a criminal, community-based issue has been identified, law enforcement agencies must evaluate and analyze the problem to develop an effective response. This involves addressing the root causes of the issue, considering relevant, community-based factors at play, and predicting how the community might be impacted or react to a particular strategy. After potential practices have been drafted, law enforcement agencies can further refine them with community input to maximize efficacy.

- Scanning, analysis, response, and assessment (SARA)

  The four SARA techniques—scanning, analysis, response, and assessment—allow officers to gather and deploy intelligence effectively. Definitions are as follows:

  - *Scanning* involves utilizing a wide variety of police and community resources to identify a criminal problem. Once a problem has been scanned, it can be addressed.

  - ***Analysis*** occurs when data collected from law enforcement resources, the community, and research into the problem is used to develop solutions.

  - *Response* refers to the deployment of law enforcement actions to address the problem. The goal is to create community-based, long-term solutions to reduce or remove the issue and create a safer community.

  - ***Assessment*** involves evaluating the effects of the response on the problem and community. Law enforcement should follow-up with the community members to assure its efforts were effective, and crime trends may be used to determine the impact on immediate conditions.

- Policing of hot spots

  Hot spots are areas where crime is commonplace and frequent. Using data and intelligence, U.S. law enforcement agencies can identify hot spots and employ a number of strategies to combat crime in these areas. This can include routine patrol assignments and duties, increased use of zero-tolerance policies, and greater visibility of officers.

- Collaborative approach

  Because crime doesn't adhere to jurisdictions, it's important for federal, state, and local law enforcement agencies to cooperate. The sharing of information and data between these agencies is a crucial aspect of intelligence-led policing, as it allows officers and other personnel to track criminals across borders and boundaries. Investigative units focusing on international or national crimes, such as counterterrorism units, may utilize multiple law enforcement resources, like the Regional Information Sharing Systems (RISS) program.

Since intelligence-led policing heavily relies on data and identifying general trends, it's important to avoid engaging in racial profiling or other behaviors that rely solely on an individual's race, ethnicity, and/or national origins. Actions should also be based concrete criminal behaviors of the individual or intelligence gathered during the course of an investigation that indicate criminal behavior. Violations of an individual's civil rights hurt the agency and can damage its relationship with the community.

As you might expect, technology and hardware play a significant role in intelligence-led policing and the sharing of information. In "Technology Isn't the (Biggest) Problem for Information Sharing in Law Enforcement," Doug Wyllie (2009) addresses how technology can be leveraged to create positive outcomes in communities and how law enforcement officials might start integrating this technology:

> For example, the networking and hardware purchases you make can have an enormous (and positive) effect on the ability for your agency to adopt new software and new devices as they become available in the marketplace. Sure, making a big "back end" infrastructure purchase can be a tough sell to the city council or the mayor, but when you can demonstrate that such an investment enables your department to have interoperability with evolving technology, that argument becomes much easier to make.
>
> Some of the usability issues can be resolved by having members of your department actively participate when technology vendors invite feedback on "Beta" tests of their solutions. Sure, those studies are time-consuming and sometimes fraught with frustrations, but if you don't have a seat at the table when the products are being developed, you effectively forfeit your ability to complain about the end result.
>
> Some of the cultural, operational, structural, and legal issues that prevent data from being shared will never go away, but there are some fairly simple things you can do to chip away at the problem. ("Taking Steps" section)

So, in summary, it is very important when using Intelligence Led Policing to have collaboration, a clear written understanding between all parties, use of databases while respecting privacy laws, civil liberties, following Code of Federal Regulations (CFR) rules, policies and procedures. You want to ensure your information is secure and classified correctly as far as who can have access to it. You will want to make sure you have the best technological tools as well as the best human resources available and that staff are well trained in intelligence and associated fields. Intelligence led policing requires that you have follow up reports, evaluations, and audits to make sure you are addressing problems correctly or are able to make adjustments where needed. You will also want to make sure you have sufficient funding and support. This will require good communications and outreach on your part.

Intelligence-Led Corrections

There is a wealth of information within the corrections community as it relates to criminal activity. This includes information about gangs or security threat groups (STGs), terrorism, and/or radicalization efforts. Correctional facilities are small, controlled access communities. The incoming and (under some circumstances) outgoing mail is searched. Phone calls are monitored. Contraband phones are evidence and can be processed without a search warrant to develop information and/or intelligence. There is a significant need to enhance collection and information-sharing between law enforcement, corrections, and probation/parole.

In most states, probation/parole officers are associated with state correctional agencies. Some misdemeanor probation officers are not related to state agencies. They are part of private businesses that are managed by local courts. For those probation/parole officers who are related to state correctional agencies, they too have a significant involvement in the intelligence process.

Probation/parole officers monitor offenders who are allowed to live in their community instead of serving their sentence in a jail or prison. With that comes restrictions (e.g., periodic and/or unannounced home visits, warrantless property searches, etc.). These restrictions provide law enforcement with a plethora of resources to use for information- or intelligence-gathering purposes.

Intelligence-led corrections can also provide the correctional agency with valuable information/intelligence to keep their correctional facilities and community safe. Strategical intelligence examples include data-driven information that can be used to prevent issues such as gang violence. An example of tactical intelligence, which we will detail later in this chapter, may be for targeted searches.

In the collection process of intelligence-led corrections (ILC), information may be derived from outside agencies and the correctional institution staff (e.g., correction officer, investigators, tactical teams, etc.). Additionally, information can be collected from mail review, monitoring phone calls, processing contraband cell phones, searching cells, and/or other investigative techniques. The expectation of privacy in a correctional facility is limited to none. Therefore, information is more easily accessible. Once the information is gathered and collected, it must be processed. Typically, the agency investigative staff will utilize investigators or analysts to sift through the information.

Analysis or an intelligence product can be created to measure activity within the system. An intelligence bulletin may also be created to provide information to reduce or prevent ongoing criminal activity or activity related to contraband or violence in the facility. If there is a need for the information or intelligence to be utilized, a product will be developed for those with the "need to know." The need to know may not include everyone within the correctional facility. The need to know is determined by the agency prior to being disseminated. An example of this could be a limiting intelligence on contraband-introduction techniques to line staff corrections officers. This may be due to officers being involved in such activity, which may compromise investigation techniques.

Feedback and reevaluation are consistently completed throughout the cycle. As information changes, there may be a need to reevaluate the product, add or subtract details, and so on.

Both of your authors have extensive knowledge of correctional intelligence. Coauthor Korey Cooper developed the ILC process in the Tennessee Department of Correction. At the time, the unit he was assigned to measured a variety of incidents related to prisons within the state. The system that was created was based on the COMSTAT process but was called accountability-driven leadership (ADL). Since gangs or STGs were involved in a majority of the measured incidents, the gangs, their involvement, and their membership numbers were also evaluated.

Technology was used to deploy systems within each of the state prisons that could process and extract data from recovered contraband cell phones—most of which were recovered from inmates. The extracted data was used to link inmates to other inmates (statewide), visitors, and staff (staff that may be involved in criminal activity, such as contraband introductions). Additionally, the technology allowed investigators the ability to intercept gang communications in the cell phones. This helped prevent and reduce gang-related violence and provided information about another incident that had already occurred.

While intelligence procedures were very important for law enforcement on the street after the 9/11 attacks on the United States, it was just as important in corrections, if not more important! Terrorist/radical group have targeted prison populations. This was directly mentioned in the Al-Qaeda training manuals and debriefs seized in prisons. Prisons are full of the "worse of the worst" in society. Prisons are a target-rich environment for radical recruitment.

Prisoners may be antigovernment simply because the government was involved in their incarceration. Inmates have lost liberty and contact with the "outside world." Some correctional facilities are not equipped to adequately vet prison staff and/or volunteers who may be involved with terrorist organizations. Gang and STG influences are also conducive to prison radicalization. Not all correctional agencies collaborate with other state, federal, local, or tribal law enforcement agencies related to prison radicalization. All of these circumstances make correctional facility populations vulnerable to radicalization.

That's why intelligence-led corrections is so important. This concept encourages effective communication with law enforcement, correctional facilities, fusion centers, and some private organizations with a need to know. Correctional policy should encourage social research within prisons to provide a better understanding of the vulnerability of prisoners to radicalization. Correctional agencies should provide adequate staff training and develop intelligence-sharing networks with criminal justice partners.

Corrections is a unique environment, but it plays a critical role in the criminal justice intelligence process. Law enforcement agencies that fail to communicate with corrections are lacking a full component of information gathering. Unfortunately, it happens daily. At the same time, correctional agencies must reach out and create collaborative networks. Corrections and "the police" are all just members of law enforcement and the criminal justice system. Working with one another creates a strong intelligence process.

Strategic Analysis

Strategic intelligence includes statistic crime trends and patterns that have been analyzed and evaluated for law enforcement administrative use in decision making, resource deployment, and policy planning. The primary purposes for strategic intelligence analysis in law enforcement is crime prevention and controlling crime behavior. The result of strategic analysis is providing a final product that includes recommendations for future actions. This may include identifying and describing trends and patterns in criminal activity from credible sources. Strategic intelligence products are also used for operational planning in law enforcement. The information may be obtained from incident report data, informants, and/or investigative techniques. The information is then processed and analyzed to provide interactive intelligence that can be disseminated to agency personnel on a need-to-know basis. The intelligence can be used to in decision making to prevent or control crime.

Product Types

One strategic product that many don't think about relating to role of intelligence is budget planning. With agency personnel shortages or reductions budgets related to personnel, an agency's intelligence analyst may be tasked with providing data that provides better resource allocations. Agencies are having to do more with less. Therefore, intelligence analysts are tasked with providing information and intelligence that allow investigators to work more efficiently. Intelligence can be used to prioritize and focus strategies. This can be translated to a more efficient use of resources.

For example, an agency with a neighborhood car burglary problem will examine criminal predicates, target analysis, target locations, crime characteristics, and intervention techniques that will identify possible offenders or responses that will prevent and/or deter the car burglaries. By reviewing the intelligence provided, an agency can allocate resources more efficiently. Additionally, the agency can provide awareness, such as "lock it or lose it" initiatives to notify their citizens to remember to lock their car doors.

Most strategic intelligence provides long-term planning solutions for data collected over time. Information collected from incident reports over a period of time can be analyzed for indicators and/or crime trends. Those can be compared to crimes of similarity in other jurisdictions or areas to identify offenders or common characteristics (MO), which may provide leads or preventative measures to mitigate the impact of the crimes committed. Once an intelligence product is created and disseminated, that is not the end of the intelligence process. The intelligence cycle may start all over again, and the intelligence is reevaluated.

Operational intelligence is another type of strategic intelligence. This is actionable intelligence that is used to develop and implement preventative responses or actions. Operational intelligence, as it relates to law enforcement, is information gathered and analyzed to assist and plan with investigative efforts or target identification. Identifying specific targets or threats involved in criminal activity is important for public safety. For example, it is important to provide indicators of threats that officers should be aware of for their safety or the safety of the communities the officers serve.

Specialized law enforcement units, such as narcotics investigative units, may utilize operational intelligence as a resource to identify suppression or intervention strategies. In a long-term drug trafficking investigation, operational intelligence can be used plan surveillance, search, and/or arrest operations of a drug trafficking organization.

Crime analysis is scientific data analysis. In a small- to midsized police department, crime analysis and strategic intelligence could be performed by the same unit. In larger police departments, criminal analysis is a specific unit. Law enforcement administrators use data from reported criminal incidents to compare. The data is mined for crime patterns and comparison activity to link and/or track criminal activity. The New York Police Department created a program in the 1990s called COMPSTAT, short for computer statistics. The purpose of this program is to gather timely and accurate information about crime in the different precincts that are considered a problem. The program will map out crime, which shows when and where crime occurred.

Department heads meet weekly to discuss strategies to rapidly deploy officers and resources to reduce the criminal activity in a timely manner. COMPSTAT is designed to hold police supervisors and leaders accountable for their areas of responsibility. The program focuses on providing effective police responses and tactics to reduce the criminal activity that had increased. The program is designed to follow up to see if their responses did, in fact, reduce the targeted criminal activity. If so, data would continue to be measured to ensure the problem didn't reoccur. If it did reoccur, they would readdress and refocus, which would include different responses.

COMPSTAT forces precinct commanders to monitor the criminal activity in their areas and holds them accountable for their areas of responsibility. Oftentimes, the COMPSTAT process will create competition between precincts to identify crime and push crime from their precinct on to others, which will indicate a decrease in their numbers and an increase in the neighboring precincts' statistics.

Critics of the COMSTAT program argue that the statistics could be adjusted by the reporting officer or commanders. Officers may be discouraged from taking a report in order to create a false appearance of a reduction in criminal activity in the assigned area. Others say that the program focuses too much on statistics and doesn't address the problem of crime or provide an open exchange with the community it affects. Some critics call for an evidence-based approach rather than statistical approach.

No matter which strategical intelligence approach that is uses, it must be based on either **quantitative** analysis methods (measurements) or **qualitative** analysis methods (conclusion based on a cumulative interpretation). Many products may use both methods. Quantitative references information in a numerical form. One example of strategic intelligence related to quantitative measurements is the number of home burglaries in a specific area during a period of time. Quantitative measurements may also include information related to patterns and trends, which can be used to prevent criminal activity.

Trends

Crime patterns are similar crimes that are in a defined geographic area. A **crime trend** is a specific crime pattern that develops a significant change in a defined measurement within a geographic area and period of time. Trends are represented as an increase or decrease over the measured time. In the chart in Figure 10.3 from Memphis, TN, you can see major violent crime has increased since 1985. Since 2019, violent crime has increased from 1,941.3 to 2,465.2 per 100,000 in population.

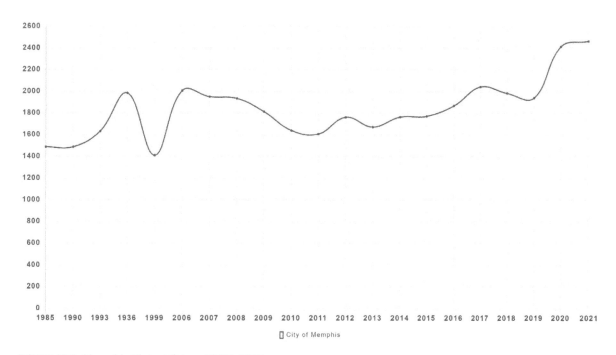

FIGURE 10.3 Memphis Violent Crime 1985–2021

Since the early 1900s, the Uniform Crime Reports (UCR) has been the primary source of information about crime data recorded in the United States. The FBI's National Incident-Based Reporting System (NIBRS) began in the 1980s. The NIBRS allows crime data to be compared by reporting agencies throughout the United States. NIBRS more accurately reflects crime in communities than the UCR. It also includes victim and offender demographics, their relationships, property data, and arrest information. Agencies also have the ability to the develop evidence-based strategic plans and intervention processes from the statistics derived from NIBRS.

According to Gardner et al. (2022), more than half (28) of state UCR programs accepted NIBRS-compliant data from at least 90% of their local agencies by the end of 2021, with 15 of those programs achieving 100% reporting (see Figure 10.4). They report that agencies of all types and sizes have transitioned to NIBRS in recent years, with notable gains seen across large law enforcement agencies (those employing 750 or more full-time sworn officers) and tribal agencies. Among the United States' 115 large law enforcement agencies, NIBRS reporting increased from 27 agencies in 2017 to 62 agencies in 2021. Using the FBI's web-based NIBRS Collection Application, transitions to incident-based reporting also increased significantly in tribal jurisdictions, where 87% of the 207 tribal agencies reported NIBRS data in 2021 compared to 10% in 2017 (Gardner et al., 2022).

Geographic information system (GIS) technology has increased law enforcement intelligence analysts' ability to track and describe crime trends in recent years. GIS has significantly increased an analyst's

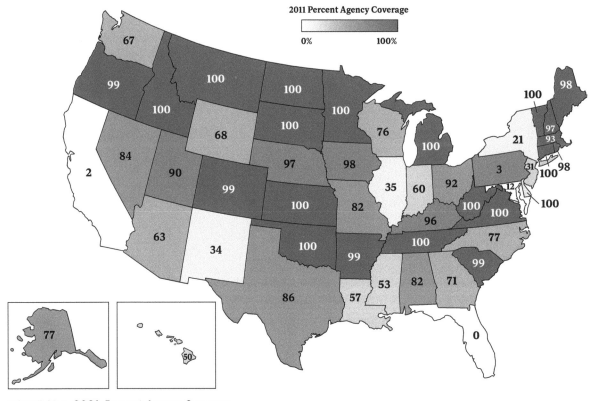

FIGURE 10.4 2021 Percent Agency Coverage

ability to identify **hot spots** through new computer-based analytical tools. By identifying these areas of increased needs, or hot spots, law enforcement may direct resources and asset accordingly. Not only may a commander increase patrols in a hot spot but they may also develop additional strategies to provide crime prevention techniques in their problem-solving efforts.

Law enforcement agencies also use commercial software programs developed to filter data and create link analysis to identify trends and patterns in criminal activity. The process is performed during the collation and analysis phase of the intelligence cycle. The goal is to filter or remove useless or incorrect data.

Activity

INFORMATION-SHARING OBSTACLES BETWEEN LAW ENFORCEMENT DATABASES

Modern law enforcement practices require police to effectively share information between databases. While law enforcement is limited by jurisdictional boundaries, criminals are not restricted by these confines. With streamlined information-sharing capabilities, law enforcement agencies can compare cases with one another, avoiding duplicated efforts and time wasted chasing dead ends.

While there are many benefits of information sharing in the law enforcement industry, police continue to face challenges that make their jobs more difficult. Some agencies do not have adequate business models that support advanced information sharing, while others may encounter barriers due to outdated or inferior technologies.

It is important to understand what information-sharing obstacles exist between law enforcement databases and how to resolve these issues for a more comprehensive sharing of data.

Importance of Information Sharing in Law Enforcement

In today's high-tech environment, law enforcement requires more than just a willingness to work together to remain successful. Police officers must have the ability to share data, information, and intelligence effectively across jurisdictional boundaries.

Advances in technology have granted law enforcement amazing opportunities to collect, organize, cross-reference and share information in a way that helps agencies across the United States perform their jobs more effectively.

Efficient data sharing can provide law enforcement agencies with a wide range of benefits, such as increased apprehension rates and reduced victimization.

When police can proactively share data, public safety agencies gain greater insight into crime patterns and trends to better understand and potentially anticipate future crimes within a community. Information databases provide law enforcement agencies with the data they need to increase police presence when needed and better allocate their resources.

Challenges in Information Sharing Between Law Enforcement Databases

Law enforcement agencies across the country face a number of obstacles when sharing information between databases. Some of the most common challenges encountered include:

1. Unreasonable technology costs

   Cost is one of the most common concerns for law enforcement agencies seeking new technologies for information sharing. This is especially common among smaller agencies with tight budgets. The cost of computer-aided dispatch (CAD) systems, record management systems (RMS), and other data systems can be exorbitant, making it financially difficult for agencies to upgrade their current systems.

2. Siloed information systems

    Law enforcement officials often have difficulty leveraging information across databases when systems remain siloed. Police data can be found from a wide variety of sources, such as warrant records, CAD records, license plate reader results, and other information.

    Officials rely on RMS to document reports of encounters and incidents, and many other record-keeping tools are used to store and share data. Unfortunately, these different tools do not always sync, resulting in extensive time spent organizing and consolidating relevant data.

3. Limited data available from N-DEx

    The National Data Exchange (N-DEx) is considered one of the most widely used law enforcement databases provided by the U.S. federal government. This database enables law enforcement agencies to share certain documents, such as arrest reports, booking reports, incident reports, pretrial investigations, parole records and probation records.

    While useful, the N-DEx does not always provide sufficient data to help investigators move forward with their cases. In addition, the N-DEx does not consolidate entries into unified records that can be investigated from a sole point of reference.

4. Complex information-sharing architecture

    Another common obstacle that occurs within information-sharing between law enforcement databases is complexity within database systems. Law enforcement information-sharing architecture can often be complicated with just a small fraction of the interfaces being covered by standards. In addition, these standards often overlap or even conflict with one another.

5. Inconsistencies in narratives

    Law enforcement agencies often use record management systems that store a combination of structured, semi-structured and unstructured information, making data sharing more difficult. Structured data often includes fields for data, make, model, type of call, and other similar elements.

    The unstructured narrative section usually explains the story from the officer's point of view. These reports may have inconsistencies that can interfere with investigations. Information can also become trapped in siloes, preventing law enforcement from accessing the data they need.

Police officers are often tasked with sorting through large amounts of data to access the information they need to do their jobs effectively. Having the right law enforcement software can help eliminate information-sharing obstacles between law enforcement databases and optimize an agency's ability to store and share information.

CPI OpenFox offers comprehensive law enforcement software solutions to police departments and other public safety agencies across the United States. These enterprise-grade programs work seamlessly to streamline important law enforcement processes and workflows. OpenFox's high-level software solutions are scalable and fully encrypted to protect sensitive information.

Finding solutions to common challenges that affect the law enforcement industry is not always easy. Fortunately, OpenFox law enforcement software solutions can help. CPI OpenFox offers comprehensive law enforcement software solutions to police departments and other public safety agencies across the United States. These enterprise-grade programs work seamlessly to streamline important law enforcement processes and workflows. OpenFox's high-level software solutions are scalable and fully encrypted to protect sensitive information.

Handling Intelligence

The issue over how to best gather, store, and disseminate intelligence, often via an official agency criminal analyst or analysts, is not new. This subject has been around ever since police and corrections agencies started.

The Federal Bureau of Investigation (FBI, n.d.) official website states, "The FBI uses intelligence to drive its decision-making. The information we get through intelligence gathering and sharing guides us in our mission to protect the American people and uphold the Constitution. Gathering intelligence has always been critical to fulfilling the FBI's mission" (para. 1). Within the Intelligence Branch (IB) of the FBI, surveillance specialists, agents, and analysts gather and disseminate intelligence on a need-to-know basis. Their goal is to uphold and defend national and homeland security. There are a number of stakeholders involved in the intelligence field, and the IB works closely with the U.S. intelligence community, law enforcement, and key members of the private sector (FBI, n.d.).

The ability of criminal justice staff to be trusted and respected was brought into question when it was later discovered during hearings of the 9/11 Commission that some intelligence community members may have known some details about the 9/11 hijackers that was not pushed up the FBI and other federal agencies chains of command due to the sentiment by some staff that it would or did fall on deaf ears.

Due to some of the post-9/11 assessments of this problem, several federal agencies were revamped or newly created to assist in avoiding such disasters in the future. For instance, the FBI's Intelligence Branch was created as a result of the 9/11 terrorist attacks in the United States. Analyzing intelligence has become a critical focus for national security, as well as state and local law enforcement efforts. The FBI Counterterrorism Division (CTD) integrated to include an Office of Intelligence within the CTD in 2002. The 9/11 Commission recommended strengthening efforts to recognize the role intelligence played within the FBI's structure. In 2004, the Intelligence Reform and Terrorism Prevention Act was passed. The United States Attorney General directed that intelligence unit be created that would operate independently from the CTD; therefore, in 2005 the Intelligence Branch was formed. In 2006, the Intelligence Branch, along with the FBI's Counterintelligence Division and the FBI Weapons of Mass Destruction Directorate, became part of a newly established FBI National Security Branch.

Some of the same issues that have faced the FBI have been present in smaller agencies. The main issue seems to be arguments over what is "need to know" information and what is "nice to know." Intelligence files not handled properly can possibly aid criminals and/or impede investigations. One can view the internet today and see plenty of documents clearly marked classified that are posted online for anybody to see. The FBI often posts documents, typically after a significant amount of time has passed, but even then, there are often large portions of the document blacked out (redacted) on the basis of national security and for legal reasons.

Individuals employed with criminal justice agencies usually have to get a security clearance in order to view and handle intelligence documents. There are usually very clear policies controlling what can be viewed and warnings that the individual can be disciplined, even legally prosecuted, for mishandling said documents. This usually is considered a very serious matter. The 2022 discovery of classified documents in the hands of former U.S. president Donald Trump underscores the seriousness of such policies and will likely be part of the national debate for years to come.

Situational Awareness

Situational awareness in law enforcement is of great importance. Intelligence and information bulletins are created to make law enforcement personnel aware of situations and individuals that may pose a threat to the community, themselves, and/or law enforcement. Many of these types of notifications are disseminated through fusion centers. A situational awareness intelligence bulletin can be strategic or tactical analysis.

Strategic analysis may be related to crime trends or specific information related to type of crime. For example, a bulletin may be disseminated related to a group of individuals involved in a transient theft ring that has been identified. The bulletin would include any photographs or still video shots of individuals believed to be involved, their vehicles, and so on. If the group targets specific merchandise or items, that information could be listed as well. Any other known trends may be included in the bulletin to notify law enforcement personnel to be looking out for the individuals, their vehicles, and/or their crime trends—all of which are elements of situational awareness.

Situation awareness can also be used for tactical analysis. This would include intelligence disseminated with a more timely focus than based on a specific crime or trend. Another tactical analysis approach would include intelligence related to a specific person or event that involved an imminent threat.

Tactical Analysis

Tactical analysis contributes to the success of specific investigations. **Tactical intelligence** is intelligence provided to law enforcement agencies so that they can develop strategies that stop and prevent oncoming threats (Carter, 2022). The intent for tactical intelligence is for an immediate response.

Tactical intelligence contributes directly to the success of a specific investigation. As Carter (2004) writes:

> Tactical intelligence is used in the development of a criminal case that usually is a continuing criminal enterprise, a major multijurisdictional crime, or other form of complex criminal investigation, such as terrorism. Tactical intelligence seeks to gather and manage diverse information to facilitate a successful prosecution of the intelligence target. Tactical intelligence is also used for specific decision making or problem solving to deal with an immediate situation or crisis. For example, if there is a terrorist threat to a target, tactical intelligence should provide insight into the nature of both the threat and the target. As a result, decisions can be made on how to best secure the target and capture the offenders in a way that increases the probability of some form of action, such as prosecution or expulsion from the country if the person(s) involved is (are) not United States citizen(s). (p. 83)

While tactical intelligence has many benefits, critics of departments who rely solely on this process feel this is too narrow of an approach. They argue that tactical intelligence will not provide long-term solutions for crime reduction and safety without implementing a range of intelligence methods. Many smaller to midsized agency may fall into this category for their intelligence units or function. Some may not even have an intelligence unit. It's not difficult to see why agencies may prefer tactical intelligence over other methods, in part because it's easier to explain to front-line officers and provides clear objectives. However, in these cases, tactical intelligence creates a vicious cycle: Officers focus too much on arrests, which require more tactical intelligences, which creates an even narrower focus on arrest activity, and so on (Ratcliffe, 2007, p. 10).

Product Types

Some may separate operational intelligence into a different category of intelligence, especially in the military arena. However, operational intelligence and tactical intelligence share some similarities. Therefore, we will discuss operational intelligence as a tactical product. Operational intelligence supports law enforcement officers who are planning activities, such as crime reduction, and utilizing resources to complete an operational objective.

One type of operational product, for example, may be related to a narcotics investigation. If during the course of an investigation probable cause for a search warrant is developed, then a operational plan may be created that details the execution of the search warrant. Information included in the operation plan would include targets or suspect(s), known hazards or problems that may be encountered, the personnel involved in the execution of the warrant, and the duties for each of the personnel. Additionally, the operation plan should include exigent planning, such as the closest medical facility or any other special need for the operation.

Target Analysis

An example of target analysis related to tactical intelligence would be investigating a community gang and their criminal activity. The gang may be the target. or the individual members or leaders within the gang may be the target. The target should be identified early in the intelligence phase, during the planning cycle. Target analysis involves gathering as much information about the target as possible. Target analysis involves:

1. Obtaining a target profile.

2. Selecting a target.

3. Conducting statistical analysis related to the target.

A *threat assessment* is a "document which looks at a group's propensity for violence or criminality or the possible occurrence of a criminal activity in a certain time or place" (Bureau of Justice Assistance, 2013, p. 48). It is an assessment of a criminal or terrorist presence within a jurisdiction integrated with an assessment of potential targets of that presence and a statement of probability that the criminal or terrorist will commit an unlawful act. The assessment focuses on the criminal's or terrorist's opportunity, capability, and willingness to fulfill the threat (Federal Emergency Management Agency, 2010).

Target analysis includes examining priorities, including the importance of the information/intelligence, a timeline (if involving operational planning), available or needed resources, and/or analysis of any potential threats related to the target(s). While target analysis may be used more commonly for military intelligence, law enforcement uses it more for specific operational needs.

Statistical Analysis

The United Nations Office on Drugs and Crime (2010) *Criminal Intelligence Manual for Front-line Law Enforcement* defines **statistical analysis** as "the review of numerical data to summarize it and to draw conclusions about its meaning. It incorporates several different techniques including frequency distribution" (p. 47). There are seven different types of statistical analysis:

- *descriptive:* collective analysis that is summarized or presented in the form of charts, graphs, and/or tables (see Figures 10.5 and 10.6).

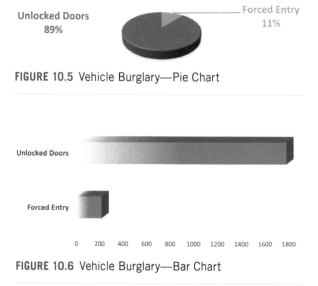

FIGURE 10.5 Vehicle Burglary—Pie Chart

FIGURE 10.6 Vehicle Burglary—Bar Chart

- *inferential:* analysis that draws a meaningful and predictable conclusion based on different variables (see Figure 10.7).

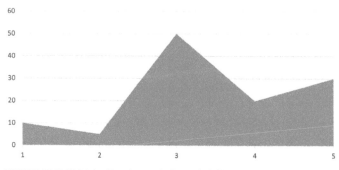

FIGURE 10.7 Vehicle Burglary—Inferential Chart

- *predictive:* analysis that analyzes data based on past trends and will predict future issues or problem events (outcomes) from the derived data.

What happened?	**Why did it happen?**	**What's happening?**	**What will happen?**
• Incident Reports • Statistics	• Analysis by spreadsheet or software	• Monitoring • Dashboards	• Prediction based on statistics, data mining, etc.

FIGURE 10.8 Predictive Analysis Chart

- *prescriptive:* analysis that helps make informed decisions; analysis of data that prescribes the best course of action (what "should be done") based on the results of the analysis. This may be in a dashboard (see Figure 10.9).

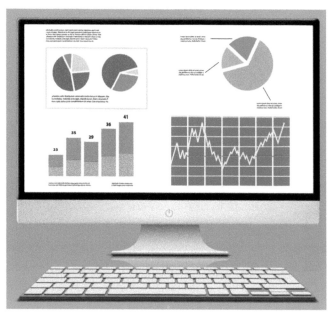

FIGURE 10.9 Prescriptive Analysis Details

- *exploratory data:* similar to inferential analysis, but it explores the unknown data associations for key patterns and recognizes potential relationships within the data (see Figure 10.10).

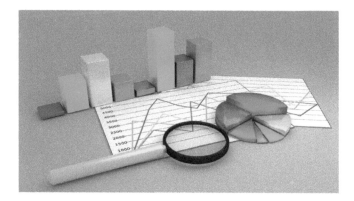

FIGURE 10.10 Exploratory Data

- *causal:* analysis that focuses on the cause-and-effect relationships (the who, what, when, why, and how's) between different variables within raw data (see Figure 10.11).

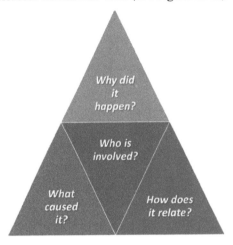

FIGURE 10.11 Causal Analysis

- *mechanistic:* analysis used to understand the specific changes in variables that can make changes to other variables or a link analysis (see Figure 10.12).

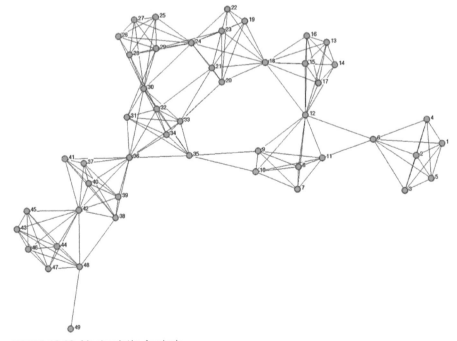

FIGURE 10.12 Mechanistic Analysis

When properly used, statistically data can help law enforcement agencies become more proactive by identifying trends in crime and criminal activity. Statistical analysis is also important for law enforcement executives when requesting additional funding. Visual statistical analysis may consist of pie charts, circle graphs, diagrams, bar graphs, dot plots, scatterplots, or series graphs, as listed above. Those interested in a career in crime analysis will need to be proficient in a variety of tasks:

> Given the aim of exploring both crime events and broader trends in crime patterns, good crime analysts have to understand a wide range of technical and theoretical areas. For example, an experienced crime analyst might have an understanding of quantitative research skills using a variety of software packages, probably uses a geographical information system to analyze spatiotemporal crime activity, creates analysis products and conducts officer briefings, and has a knowledge of the basics of environmental criminology. However, the perception sometimes is that crime analysts just provide management with charts and breakdowns of overtime and sick leave or simple counts of the numbers of different crime types that have happened in the last week. These tasks are not crime analysis but are simply the provision of management statistics. Such requests for help in areas unrelated to crime can often be a considerable drain on the enthusiasm of some analysts, and police executives should be wary of allowing their analysts to engage in work that is far removed from the central aims of crime reduction and prevention. (Ratcliffe, 2007, p. 15)

If you find that you are getting bogged down in management statistics tasks, it is important to address this right away with management. While critical to the management of police agency, management statistics should not detract from your goal of reducing crime.

References

Bureau of Justice Assistance. (2003). *The National Criminal Intelligence Sharing Plan: Solutions and approaches for a cohesive plan to improve our nation's ability to develop and share criminal intelligence.* U.S. Department of Justice. https://bja.ojp.gov/sites/g/files/xyckuh186/files/media/document/national_criminal_intelligence_sharing_plan.pdf

Bureau of Justice Assistance. (2013). *National Criminal Intelligence Sharing Plan: Building a national capability for effective criminal intelligence development and the nationwide sharing of intelligence and information.* https://bja.ojp.gov/sites/g/files/xyckuh186/files/media/document/National%20Criminal%20Intelligence%20Sharing%20Plan%20version%202_0.pdf

Carter, D. (2004). *Law enforcement intelligence: A guide for state, local, and tribal law enforcement agencies* (1st ed.). Bureau of Justice Assistance. https://irp.fas.org/agency/doj/lei/guide.pdf

Carter, D. (2022). *Law enforcement intelligence: A guide for state, local, and tribal law enforcement agencies* (3rd ed.). Bureau of Justice Assistance. https://bja.ojp.gov/sites/g/files/xyckuh186/files/media/document/Law_Enforcement_Intelligence_Guide_508.pdf

Federal Bureau of Investigation. (n.d.). *Intelligence.* https://www.fbi.gov/investigate/how-we-investigate/intelligence

Federal Emergency Management Agency. (2010). *Considerations for fusion center and emergency operations center coordination.* U.S. Department of Justice. https://www.fema.gov/pdf/about/divisions/npd/cpg_502_eoc-fusion_final_7_20_2010.pdf

Fuentes, J. (2006). *Practical guide to intelligence-led policing.* New Jersey State Police. https://nj.gov/njsp/divorg/invest/pdf/njsp_ilpguide_010907.pdf

Gardner, A., Pope, M., & Smith, E. (2022, August). Better data for evolving crime trends (2012–2022 NIBRS transition). *Police Chief Magazine.* https://www.theiacp.org/resources/better-data-for-evolving-crime-trends-2012-2022-nibrs-transition

Heinen, B., Mulvaney, R., Fien-Helfman, D., Mihalco, K., Silverman, J., & Thompson, C. (2020). *Community Policing Self-Assessment Tool (CP-SAT): Final Report.* Office of Community Oriented Policing Services.

International Association of Chiefs of Police National Law Enforcement Policy Center. (1998). *Criminal intelligence.*

Jacobson, N. (2022, September 26). *Information-sharing obstacles between law enforcement databases.* CPI OpenFox. https://web.archive.org/web/20221226212018/https://www.openfox.com/information-sharing-obstacles-between-law-enforcement-databases/

Kent State University. (2020, October 2). *What is intelligence-led policing?.* Kent State Online. https://onlinedegrees.kent.edu/sociology/criminal-justice/community/intelligence-led-policing

National Advisory Committee on Criminal Justice Standards and Goals. (1976). *Organized crime: Report of the Task Force on Organized Crime*. U.S. Department of Justice.

Ratcliffe, J. (2007). *Integrated intelligence and crime analysis: Enhanced information management for law enforcement leaders* (2nd ed.). Community Oriented Policing Services. https://cops.usdoj.gov/RIC/Publications/cops-w0690-pub.pdf

Tsvetovat, M., & Kouznetsov, A. (n.d.). *Social network analysis for startups*. O'Reilly Online Learning. https://www.oreilly.com/library/view/social-network-analysis/9781449311377/ch01.html

United Nations Office on Drugs and Crime. (2010). *Criminal intelligence manual for front-line law enforcement*. https://www.unodc.org/documents/organized-crime/Law-Enforcement/Criminal_Intelligence_for_Front_Line_Law_Enforcement.pdf

Wyllie, D. (2009, April 30). *Technology isn't the (biggest) problem for information sharing in law enforcement*. Police1. https://www.police1.com/police-products/communications/articles/technology-isnt-the-biggest-problem-for-information-sharing-in-law-enforcement-x5XzuiFPyCwl8gUC/

Credits

CHAPTER 11

Intelligence Planning

Legal Aspects

We will be covering 28 C.F.R. Part 23, a federal regulation that provides law enforcement guidance "on the implementation standards for operating multijurisdictional intelligence systems" funded by the federal government under the Omnibus Crime Control and Safe Streets Act of 1968 (Bureau of Justice Assistance, 2015, p. 1). The purpose of 28 C.F.R. Part 23 is to protect constitutional rights (civil rights and civil liberties) and the expectation of privacy of individuals. Some of the guidelines governed by 28 C.F.R. Part 23 include:

- submission/entry (collection) of criminal intelligence data

- inquiries

- dissemination of intelligence

- review and purge processes and standards

- validations

- audits and inspections

- data security

The regulation was first implemented in 1980 and it was revised in 1993. It lays out a framework and identifies principles that need to be adopted by law enforcement agencies in their policy and procedures. The regulation provides a "foundation for collecting, maintaining, and sharing criminal intelligence while ensuring privacy and protecting the rights afforded to all Americans" (Bureau of Justice Assistance, 2015, p. 1).

Law enforcement agencies maintain several different types of reports, files, and data that contain investigative and management information, some of which is considered public record. Information in an agency database must be relevant to criminal activity. Multiple databases are used to store this data, whether it's information from reports or databases with investigative files or data stored in commercial platforms. All of this is subject to the 28 C.F.R. Part 23 regulations. Information not relevant to criminal activity must be purged from the agency database. For example, information gathered may initially have value or relevance to criminal activity. But after being processed, any information not related to criminal activity must be removed or purged from the system/database.

An individual's right to **privacy** ensures that criminal justice agencies will use and disclose "personally identifiable information" only as needed for an investigation or other legal process (Carter, 2022, p. 444). This includes the person's information (e.g., phone number, home address, etc.) and their behaviors (e.g., who they communicate with, where they shop, etc.).

Information can be collected if there is reasonable suspicion of criminal conduct or activity. Information cannot be collected concerning a subject's "political, religious, or social views, associations, or activities" unless a direct and "relevant" relation to criminal activity can be established (Bureau of Justice Assistance, 2015, p. 2). No information that has been obtained in violation of any laws, regulations, or ordinances can be maintained in a criminal intelligence system/database.

Information that is maintained in a criminal intelligence database must be properly labeled as to its:

- sensitivity (public, for official use only, unclassified, secret, etc.)

- reliability

- validity

While 28 C.F.R. Part 23 is a federal statute, it is the standard for the intelligence community. State and local law enforcement agencies are not required to follow 28 C.F.R. Part 23 specifically unless the agency receives federal funds (supported by the Crime Control Act) to operate any part of their intelligence function. However, being the intelligence community standard, 28 C.F.R. Part 23 is a best practice. It should be noted that correctional information has more latitude. We will discuss this further in this chapter.

When it comes to legal concerns and issues to consider related to intelligence, ensuring that privacy and constitutional rights are protected is a high priority. Adopting the standards and guideline of 28 C.F.R. Part 23 will ensure you are operating properly. Other sources of intelligence guidelines can be found in the Law Enforcement Intelligence Unit (LEIU) Criminal Intelligence File Guidelines or Justice Information Privacy Guidelines. The websites below can be used to guide you:

- 28 C.F.R. Part 23: https://bja.ojp.gov/sites/g/files/xyckuh186/files/media/document/28cfr_part_23.pdf

- LEIU: https://bja.ojp.gov/sites/g/files/xyckuh186/files/media/document/leiu_crim_intell_file_guidelines.pdf

- Department of Justice Guidelines: https://www.justice.gov/opcl/docs/doj-ise-privacy-policy.pdf

Intelligence Planning

It might seem elementary, but you will want to have a game plan before you embark on using intelligence for your work or you may waste a lot of precious time. You will want to correctly identify the problem but not be too quick to jump to conclusions regarding a solution. You will want to determine realistic goals and objectives early on. For instance, currently, many laws are very weak concerning juveniles, so while you may know that a group of juvenile males are involved in car thefts, does it make a lot of sense to spend too much time gathering intelligence on them when you know they will most likely be released from custody quickly after arrest? Or, does it make more sense to take note of them, while obeying current laws regarding juveniles whether you like it or not, but focus more attention on the adults who are very likely ringleaders, chop shop owners, and drug suppliers to them?

You will want to lawfully collect intelligence on suspects or convicted criminals and use all tools and technology you can. You will also want to meet and discuss with your peers on how to best proceed. Determine among your work group or task force, is it best to go for a state prosecution or try to make a federal case?

Problem: What Is the Need?

Information may be gathered for police administrators or leaders to use for decision making in crime prevention and/or law enforcement operational guidance. Crime analysis for COMPSTAT or department accountability can strengthen an agency's service to their community. Many times, law enforcement administrators plan ineffectively because they don't understand the crime problem in their community. In those situations, "strategic planning bears no resemblance to strategic analysis or strategic intelligence. Instead, it relates only to funding issues and operational constraints" (Peterson, 2005, p. 4).

You must have an identified criminal subject (individual or organization) when planning or gathering information/intelligence related to an investigation. Analysts should understand the need and define the problem. Your analysis/evaluation of the available information must result in a determination that there is reasonable suspicion that the subject is engaging in an identifiable criminal activity or enterprise. Specific steps to complete the task shall include potential sources of information and projected timelines. The analyst should develop collection and/or investigative plans to meet the goals and/or objectives of the assignment.

Goals/Objectives

In the intelligence community and at a national level, there are two primary goals to develop intelligence. Those are to maintain national and homeland security. Generally, intelligence in law enforcement at a state or local level has three primary goals:

- Allocate and deploy agency resources.
- Develop evidence in criminal investigations.
- Identify specific criminal activity and/or criminal organizations.

With these in mind, objectives can be developed for the basic purposes below:

- Identify criminal activity and crime trends.

- Identify criminals.

- Develop and integrate information.

- Create or open criminal investigations.

- Support criminal investigators in more complex investigations.

The overall goal for any intelligence product is to develop a report that fits the purpose or need of the customer, law enforcement, and correctional personnel. A final product should connect information in a meaningful manner that provides logical, reliable, and valid details that explain the needs or purpose of the product. When a specific threat has been identified, the goal is to create an intervention, whether strategical or tactical, to stop or prevent the threat.

The Office of the Director of National Intelligence's (2006) *Information Sharing Environment Implementation Plan* (2006) articulated six objectives that can serve as guideposts for the collection plan:

- Sharing information to manage risks to business enterprises and in a manner that protects the information privacy and other legal rights of Americans

- Creating a national framework and culture for sharing information that rationalizes requests for terrorism information to the private sector and that adequately protects the risks and proprietary interests of corporations

- Creating an integrated, trusted environment in which information can be shared, maintained, and protected

- Ensuring access to the integration and analysis of data from multiple sources to provide industry with indicators of impending threats or current attacks

- Receiving actionable alerts and warnings concerning specific industries that improve their situational awareness of terrorist threats and enable them to prioritize risks and security investments, and shape the development of plans to ensure the security, continuity, and resiliency of infrastructure operations

- Implementing policies and mechanisms that provide liability and antitrust protections to the private sector in connection with sharing information in good faith (p. 20)

Notice that one of the primary purposes related to intelligence is terrorism. That's because terrorism is the reason intelligence needs for law enforcement were created. Terrorism certainly has a place for collecting and sharing intelligence, but state and local agencies can utilize the process for so much more. At the same time, we cannot underestimate or take for granted the terrorism link and need for intelligence sharing as it relates to terrorism.

Thomas E. McNamara, Information Sharing Environment Implementation Plan, p. 20, Information Sharing Environment, 2009.

Plan

The intelligence cycle starts at planning. **Planning** is the preparation for future law enforcement operational situations, estimating agency requirements or needs and resources needed to address the know problem(s), and creating strategies to solve the problems. If you conduct an in-depth study of intelligence processes, there are many different intelligence plans or cycles. We have provided one intelligence cycle that incorporates a broad group of cycles. The Bureau of Justice Assistance's (2003) National Criminal Intelligence Sharing Plan (NCISP) provides its intelligence process or cycles (see Figure 11.1). The FBI adds a phase at the beginning of their cycle and lists it as a requirement. Requirements are what they must know to safeguard the nation. While "requirements" are important, many other agencies add the requirements to the planning phase in their intelligence cycle.

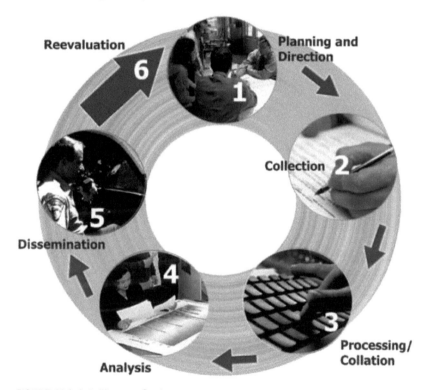

FIGURE 11.1 Intelligence Cycle

Resources

First, determine the outcomes you want to achieve from data collection. Planning how data and information will be gathered is important to the intelligence process. By identifying your outcomes, you can start planning how to direct resources such as investigators and/or analysts. You can utilize existing data and collect any additional potentially related information to fill in intelligence gaps from existing information.

Providing information-sharing solutions, the Regional Information Sharing Systems (RISS, n.d.) program allows those in the criminal justice sector to share information, provide safety measures, and collaborate on criminal investigations. Each RISS center has a criminal investigation unit and provides analytical services such as flowcharts, link charts, telephone toll analysis, financial analysis, computer forensics, phone forensic analysis, and so on. Below is a breakdown of each of the RISS centers in the United States (RISS, n.d.).

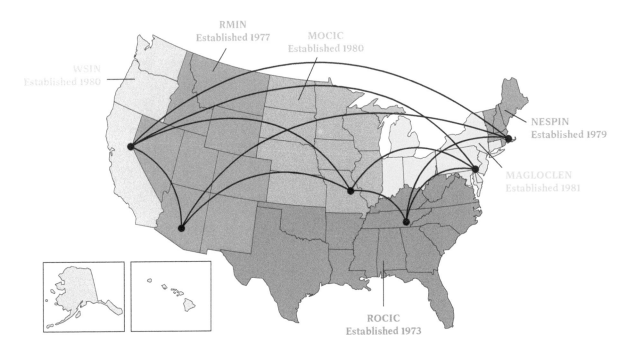

FIGURE 11.2 Regional Information Sharing Systems

Partnerships in law enforcement are valuable. It is vital that law enforcement agencies (including corrections) develop and enhance partnerships—not only with other law enforcement agencies but also with the private sector. Partnerships with agencies at every level, including local, state, federal, and tribal law enforcement agencies, will broaden your ability to network and collaborate. Some may draw concern with partnering with the private sector for intelligence purposes. But the private sector has information that law enforcement may not have access to.

An example would be a car rental company. This company is certainly not a government-run company, but the information kept by a car rental company could be extremely valuable to law enforcement needs. Rental car companies use contracts to rent cars out to the general public. Those contracts include names, addresses, phone numbers, identification information, payment methods, signatures, and the list goes on. Might some of that information be valuable to a criminal investigation? Absolutely. By developing a partnership with the private sector, such as a rental car company, law enforcement can reduce valuable time inquiring for information.

That is just one example. We've already mention the RISS centers, which are also private entities. Other considerations include privacy advocates, other public safety disciples, community groups, and so forth. Keep in mind that a partnership does not mean that the law enforcement agency must share all of their information or intelligence with the private sector. Later on in this chapter, we will discuss disseminating information/intelligence to those with the right or need to know.

Decision

Planning is where the decision is made on how the intelligence function can assist with the needs and/or goals the agency. For example, an investigation may have already been started. Over time, law enforcement agencies have determined that getting an intelligence analyst involved at the beginning of an investigation is more beneficial. Once a problem or target subject has been identified, the intelligence function should be involved to start collecting information. They can identify intelligence gaps or what needs to be known to assist with the investigation. An **intelligence gap** is simply an unanswered question relating to criminal activity or a threat of criminal activity or national security.

Involving the intelligence function, whether it's a designated analyst or another officer/investigator assigned to the task, can also develop investigative leads as the intelligence process develops. Sometimes investigators are overwhelmed with the investigation, information, and management of the case. Obvious information or links can be missed. If that occurs, the assigned intelligence analyst can add what they found to the investigative plan. It may likely develop more information that can also be utilized in the intelligence plan as well.

With a combined effort with the investigator(s) and the intelligence analyst, a plan of action can be determined to identify goals and objectives. The direction process begins at this point. Departmental management can direct resources to fulfill the needs of the investigation if that's the case or collect more information for intelligence purposes.

The intelligence management function continues as well. It doesn't stop. A manager of the intelligence function continues to task their resources or analysts with obtaining new sources of information that can be reevaluated and compared against the known or prior information. The intelligence manager also ensures that every phase of the intelligence cycle is completed properly and effectively.

Direction also involves guiding the law enforcement agencies or unit toward fulfilling the goals/objectives set in the intelligence plan. Direction ensures compliance with mandate and policy, such as 28 C.F.R. Part 23, and monitors the intelligence processes safeguarding privacy and constitutional protections of the subject or target group. Direction keeps the intelligence function within policy, procedure, and the law.

Collection

Collection is the process of gathering information or raw data needed to produce an intelligence product. Information collection must be not only planned but focused. Planning and collection are joint efforts and require collaboration between intelligence analysts, investigators, and managers. The collection process may include two different methods: overt collection and covert collection. Overt includes open-source material, and covert includes investigative techniques.

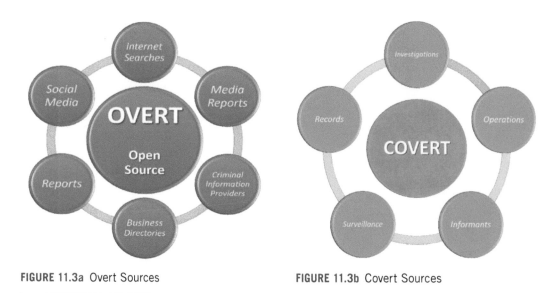

FIGURE 11.3a Overt Sources   FIGURE 11.3b Covert Sources

Overt Collection

This is the collection of raw information or data to be processed and analyzed. Some overt methods include searching or monitoring social media posts and/or internet searches. The internet is open to the public. Social media or phone applications (e.g., Facebook, Instagram, etc.) are open to the public as well, but account security features may restrict some visibility from the public. Information databases that use open-source information could also be used. These third-party solutions provide a variety of options to search, including:

- phone numbers

- addresses

- court records

- vehicle registrations

- family links

- email addresses

- property ownership

- financial data

Some businesses provide their directories and data to the third-party systems too. For example, a private utility business may provide data from their recorded material such as applications and/or account details that are provided by their customers.

Law enforcement incident reports are considered open source, with exceptions in some limited cases. Juvenile records are protected. Some personal identifiers can be redacted in police reports, but the majority of a police report is open record.

Covert Collection

Some covert methods include informants, surveillance, travel records, CCTV, banking transactions, trap and trace, pen register, wiretaps, trash pulls, forensic evidence, document evidence, phone extractions, undercover operations, and more (Carter, 2009). As we mentioned in the Interview section, informants or human sources are important throughout the processes of the four I's. Surveillance techniques may include physical surveillance involving operations of watching subjects or targets. Electronic surveillance has become an essential law enforcement tool in today's technological world. Electronic devices are becoming easier to track, whether in real time or as it's stored in the device. Most electronic surveillance requires a search warrant or court order. Electronic surveillance includes observing and documenting another individual's actions using cameras, long-range microphones, and/or listening devices, as well as by monitoring cell phone, office, and home phone services. "Trap and trace" and pen registers are also part of electronic surveillance.

As cell phones become more sophisticated, they also have larger data storage capabilities. This allows law enforcement the ability to obtain a plethora of information that can be collected and processed for intelligence. Extracting data from a cell phone requires consent or a search warrant for law enforcement to collect the data, but extracted cell phone data can be utilized in different ways for intelligence purposes. The data can provide location information, link communications (e.g., calls, text messages, etc.), application information and communications, contact information, photographs, search and view browser histories, and so much more.

Cell phones are illegal in most correctional institutions. When a correctional agency seizes a cell phone from an inmate, it's considered contraband, so a search warrant or consent is not required to process or extract data from the phone. There is a large amount of data and information that links to criminal activity, not only inside a correctional facility but on the street (in the real world). That's one reason why the correctional component is so important to utilize with investigations and intelligence law enforcement units.

The investigative techniques discussed in Section III are considered covert methods. This could include telephone tolls or cell phone tower dumps. These are investigative techniques that request a court order or search warrant for historical data, rather than real-time monitoring (**pen registry** or trap and trace). A *pen registry* is "a device or process which records or decodes dialing, routing, addressing, or signaling information transmitted by an instrument or facility from which a wire or electronic communication is transmitted" (Cornell Law, n.d.).

Trap and trace is a device or process that finds the source of a wire or electronic communication via "incoming electronic or other impulses" that can pinpoint information like a phone number, address, routing number, and more (18 U.S. Code § 3127). Both pen registry and trap and trace do not include the content of a communication. The primary difference between a pen registry and trap and trace is that the trap and trace records incoming data only.

Trash pulls are another covert method. A *trash pull* is an investigative technique that permits law enforcement to remove and/or sift through a subject's trash. The U.S. Supreme Court has held that trash left for collection (curbside) is not subject to a reasonable expectation of privacy. Therefore, law enforcement may search or pull the trash to be searched at a different location without a warrant (*California v. Greenwood*, 1988).

Trash pulls are most used in drug investigations to find drugs, drug paraphernalia, drug residue, or any other possible evidence to indicate drug activity. If such evidence is located within the trash, it can provide corroborating information to support probable cause for a search warrant for the residence. If you plan to use trash pulls as part of an investigation, we suggest that you pull trash on multiple occasions to establish trends and stronger corroborating evidence.

Other sources of information that could be collected that may not fall into overt or covert methods include techniques previously discussed in this book: interviews and interrogations. Additionally, it could include information gathered from traffic stops, cell phone extractions, jail or prison calls, tips, and/or leads.

Processing

Some intelligence cycles combine processing, collation, and analysis. That is certainly plausible. Others, like the NCISP, combine processing and collation but separate analysis. We have separated processing in our intelligence cycle because we feel that the collected data needs to be sifted through first as a separate process or phase. You will need to determine which way will best fit your needs.

Action

You should have collected a large amount of data, but you must determine what is more valuable. The first step is to assess the raw data and process the collected data to determine if the raw data can exploit the problem. Then separate the data that can be sorted or categorized better in the next phase. If you are involved in an investigation that needs information processed for intelligence, you may have interviews, forensic data from a crime scene, investigative information from similar cases, and previous incident reports from recent armed robberies. Some of the information may not be valuable for analysis. The processing step can eliminate the data that would not be useful. The data will not be discarded, just set aside.

The processing phase can be one of the most time-consuming processes. That's because all the raw data must be reviewed for valuable content. There are databases or applications available for agencies to utilize and streamline this process. We will detail those later in the collation phase. However, there are times when this process must be manually performed. Sometimes it's because you cannot afford to miss anything, and other times it's because the agency doesn't have the ability (electronically or financially).

As mentioned above, there are resources available to assist law enforcement agencies. In the processing phase, one resource that's available to member agencies is RISSNET. Each regional center has analytic assistance available to assist. As we mentioned before, the process can be time consuming, and the RISS-NET center will likely need additional time to assist as well. They are working for numerous agencies with limited personnel. However, they typically have the software or applications to perform the needed analysis. It will just take more time because there may likely be a waitlist.

Evaluation

The NCISP model uses the processing phase to evaluate source reliability and information validity. We agree. **Processing** is sifting through collected raw data to determine what is most valuable to the mission. Others may evaluate the data in the collation or analysis phases. Information kept in the intelligence process or in a database must be evaluated. It must also be designated for reliability and rated for content validity. **Reliability** is asking yourself, is the source of the information consistent and dependable? This is a critical stage because most of the information and data collected may be unverified. The evaluation process determines the collected information's value or worth and its usefulness. Furthermore, the validity of the information must be rated. **Validity** should ask the question, does the information actually represent what we believe it represents? If the information can be corroborated by a reliable source, it is rated as "confirmed." An example of reliable sources include evidence from an investigation, an investigator, eyewitness statements, and/or other independent sources. Below are some examples of the evaluation process (Law Enforcement Intelligence Unit, 2002):

- Reliable source evaluation:
  - reliable: The reliability of the source has been tested and determined to be reliable or the source has been reliable and/or tested in the past, which was also corroborated with other independent information and sources.
  - usually reliable: The reliability of the source has been proven reliable in the past. The source has provided information in the past that has been determined as factual and reliable.
  - unreliable: The reliability of the source has been irregular in the past, both reliable and/or unknown.
  - unknown: The reliability of the source cannot be tested or judged. The trustworthiness of the source may not have been determined due to time, experience, or an ongoing investigation.
- Content validity:
  - confirmed: The information has been corroborated by the investigation and other independent resources.
  - probable: The information is consistent with past accounts (crimes, trends, patterns, etc.).
  - doubtful: The information is inconsistent with past accounts (crimes, trends, patterns, etc.).
  - cannot be determined: The information cannot be judged due to time, experience, or an ongoing investigation. (p. 7)

The source reliability and content validity should be added in the criminal intelligence database. It should also be added to the final product, when disseminated, as well. The reliability and validity could change as additional information is gathered. As it changes, each version of a saved product or the worksheet should be saved as well. If the changes occur after the product was originally disseminated, updates shall be sent to every customer the product was originally disseminated to. **Customers** in intelligence are any agency, investigator, analyst, or a group that may receive an intelligence product.

Collation and Analysis

Processing and collation involve analyzing the information's reliability and validity. Reliability and validity should always be tested throughout the intelligence process. We start it in the process phase. As you

Law Enforcement Intelligence Units, Selection from Criminal Intelligence File Guidelines, p. 7, Law Enforcement Intelligence Units, 2002.

analyze data, you will determine if it corroborates with the facts and evidence. Conclusions can be drawn to develop reporting components. At this point, your information or data may become an intelligence product. When it does, the storage of intelligence has restrictions.

Collation

Collation involves sorting, categorizing, combining, and arranging the data collected to determine relationships and connection, also known as connecting the dots. Analysis of the raw data will transform it into a product that is timely and useful.

The collation and analysis phase separates "information" from "intelligence." Without this phase, you will only have fragments of information with individual meanings. The analyst should compile the information, being careful to sort and organize the data so that they may recognize any patterns, trends, or missing pieces in the data collection (International Association of Law Enforcement Intelligence Analysts, 2012, p. 16).

Collation is when data is added to different software tools, if not previously used in the processing phase. In today's modern and computerized age, different applications and software assets can streamline and enhance the intelligence analyst's ability to process and analyze data. A wide variety of software tools are available to support the processing and analysis function. The International Association of Law Enforcement Intelligence Analysts (2012) outlines five categories for this kind of software:

- databases: used to store, organize, or manage information from disparate sources so it can be retrieved and analyzed.

- spreadsheets: used to organize, tabulate, display, and to graphically depict mathematical or financial data.

- visualization: used to assist the analyst in extracting information from all sources, databases, and spreadsheets to produce and change charts as new information is developed.

- mapping: a subset of visualization used to geographically depict criminal activity from the street, local, county, state, regional, or national level.

- text/data mining: using search engines to review and cull multiple sources (databases, spreadsheets, text files, etc.) for further analysis. (p. 17)

Analysis determines what information is present or missing from the facts and evidence analyzed. The results of analysis are **hypotheses**, conclusions, and recommendation for action. Multiple hypotheses can be drawn and recommended for action. For the most part in law enforcement, data is analyzed to develop leads in investigations, present hypotheses to assess threats, predict crime patterns or trends, determine how a crime was committed, or determine who committed the crime. In *Psychology of Intelligence Analysis*, Richard "Dick" Heuer, Jr. (1999), a 45-year veteran of the Central Intelligence Agency (CIA), described how to evaluate known hypotheses and all evidence to eliminate all but the most likely hypothesis. Which of several possible outcomes is the most likely one? Heuer (1999) explains:

> The way most analysts go about their business is to pick out what they suspect intuitively is the most likely answer, then look at the available information from their point of view of whether or

The International Association of Law Enforcement Intelligence Analysts, Selection from Law Enforcement Analytic Standards, pp. 16–17, 2012.

not it supports this answer. If the evidence seems to support the favorite hypothesis, analysts pat themselves on the back and look no further. If it does not, they either reject the evidence as misleading or develop another hypothesis and go through the same process again. (pp. 95–96)

Below are eight steps Heuer (1999) outlined to analyze competing hypotheses (see Exhibit 11.1).

EXHIBIT 11.1 STEP-BY-STEP OUTLINE OF ANALYSIS OF COMPETING HYPOTHESES

1. Identify the possible hypotheses to be considered. Use a group of analysts with different perspectives to brainstorm the possibilities.
2. Make a list of significant evidence and arguments for and against each hypothesis.
3. Prepare a matrix with hypotheses across the top and evidence down the side. Analyze the "diagnosticity" of the evidence and arguments; that is, identify which items are most helpful in judging the relative likelihood of the hypotheses.
4. Refine the matrix. Reconsider the hypotheses and delete evidence and arguments that have no diagnostic value.
5. Draw tentative conclusions about the relative likelihood of each hypothesis. Proceed by trying to disprove the hypotheses rather than prove them.
6. Analyze how sensitive your conclusion is to a few critical items of evidence. Consider the consequences for your analysis if that evidence were wrong, misleading, or subject to a different interpretation.
7. Report conclusions. Discuss the relative likelihood of all the hypotheses, not just the most likely one.
8. Identify milestones for future observation that may indicate events are taking a different course than expected.

Source: Heuer, R. J. (1999). Psychology of intelligence analysis. *Center for the Study of Intelligence, Central Intelligence Agency, p. 97.*

Storage

Law enforcement must take care when labeling intelligence for storage. The majority of local/state law enforcement information is considered unclassified but controlled. **Unclassified** information does not require safeguarding or dissemination controls. This is also known in the intelligence community as controlled unclassified information (CUI). Some information or intelligence may be classified as **secret**. In these cases, secret information may be related to material that affects national security. Secret information is highly protected and sparingly used in law enforcement or corrections. This type of information/intelligence is mostly stored by federal agencies. There is a higher tier of information/intelligence that can be stored, and that is **top secret**. This information/intelligence refers to national security or any information that may cause exceptionally grave damage to national security.

Secret and top-secret material is stored in a sensitive compartmented information facility, commonly known as a SCIF. This can be a single secured room or a secured data center. These accredited areas are heavily guarded against electronic surveillance. Cellular phones, thumb drives, or any electronic device capable of storing data are strictly prohibited. A SCIF is designed to store and protect highly sensitive and protected information/intelligence. However, that information, also known as **sensitive compartmented information (SCI)** is not to be taken outside of the SCIF. This information is also labeled as **classified**.

For law enforcement intelligence purposes, those handling intelligence such as an intelligence analyst or investigators should obtain a "secret" security level clearance from the U.S. Department of Homeland Security. While not required for the majority of local- and state-level law enforcement intelligence, we would recommend it as a best practice. Those operating in fusion centers may be required to obtain at least a secret clearance because one of their primary goals is it disseminate information and intelligence to public safety agencies and/or the private sector. One job of the fusion center is to declassify information and intelligence to share outside of the classification barrier. It may be small fragments of information or intelligence from a more secure document to disseminate the fragments (and only the fragments) to those that need it outside of a secret clearance.

This is not as easy as it may sound. Declassifying information is a process in itself. Additionally, collaborating with the original disseminator of the product is critical. You can't just take a piece or two from a secret product and place it in another. If the classification of the original document is secret and an analysts want to disseminate parts from that document to non-secret-classified personnel, a process must first be completed to declassify the information. Otherwise, it should not be disseminated or forwarded. We will discuss permissions in dissemination later in that section.

Information labelled as public information may have a criminal nexus, but the information can be disseminated to the public. Some examples of public information are:

- *wanted bulletins*: bulletins of subjects wanted for criminal offenses.

- *missing person bulletins*: bulletins that are provided to the public to assist in finding a subject reported as missing.

One of the most common law enforcement intelligence products is labelled as For Official Use Only (FOUO). Most of this information is also considered Law Enforcement Sensitive (LES). This means that the information should not be transmitted outside of the "customer network." The customers are law enforcement personnel with the "need to know" only. This should be law enforcement personnel with legitimate purpose or need for the information. Some common LES intelligence products include:

- information related to specific criminals or criminal activity

- information related to specific groups (gangs, extremist, drug trafficking organizations, terrorists, etc.)

- crime trends (which likely involve at least one of the above)

Evaluation and information classification are part of dissemination controls. Classification provides criteria on who may receive the information/intelligence. Classification also provides an internal approval process in most intelligence units. With that being said, classifying stored information should follow a system (see Table 11.1).

TABLE 11.1 Intelligence Security Levels

Security Level	Dissemination Criteria	Approval Process
Unclassified	Not restricted	Intelligence unit designee
Restricted	Restricted to law enforcement personnel having a specific need to know and right to know	Intelligence unit supervisor
Confidential	Restricted to law enforcement personnel having a specific need to know and right to know	Intelligence unit manager
Sensitive	Restricted to law enforcement personnel having a specific need to know and right to know	Intelligence unit command staff

Data source: Law Enforcement Intelligence Units, Criminal Intelligence File Guidelines, 2002.

The maximum retention period for intelligence files is 5 years. A record must either be purged at the end of the established retention period or undergo a review and validation process before the end of the retention period. A **purge** is a process to permanently remove, erase, or eliminate data from storage. Information or intelligence that has not been updated must be purged after 5 years. When a product or file has no further informational value, it should be purged after the 5-year retention period. The disseminating agency should maintain a record of purged files. This should be kept by the intelligence manager or supervisor.

Agency policies and procedures should be in place that specify auditing and purging intelligence files. Some agencies purges file annually. If, for example, an intelligence file has no value after a 2-year period, the file can be purged at that point. The agency does not have to wait for the 5-year period. That is a maximum timeline range to retain files after no value of continued criminal activity.

If the file or subject of the product is still involved in criminal activity and that activity has been documented within the file, then the file can continue to be kept. Don't be confused by this process. See Table 11.2 for a better explanation.

TABLE 11.2 Information Log

Date	Information
March 30, 2000	Intel product disseminated on John Smith for drug trafficking.
January 31, 2002	John Smith arrested for possession of methamphetamine.
February 16, 2006	Validated human source provided information detailing how John Smith is arranging drug sales from prison.
December 27, 2010	John Smith released from prison.
February 1, 2011	John Smith stopped on a traffic stop and found in possession of a small amount of drugs and drug scales.

The initial intelligence product was created on subject John Smith on February 1, 2000, relating to his drug trafficking. At that point, the information can be kept no longer than the 5-year period using the standard set forth in 29 C.F.R. Part 23. However, on January 31, 2002 (nearly 2 years later), John Smith was arrested for a criminal activity, and it was specifically related to the original intelligence disseminated in 2000. Therefore, the 5-year period is now calculated from the 2002 date.

After nearly 5 years had passed, information was received that Smith was still involved in drug sales, but this time from prison. On February 16, 2006, a validated source provided information that corroborates the previous information and thus indicates continuous criminal activity. It should also be noted that the 2006 information mentioned that Smith was operating from prison. It's reasonable to believe that Smith was convicted and serving a prison sentence after his 2002 drug arrest.

An analyst or investigator could easily verify the prison sentence with open-source records from the prison or by checking Smith's criminal history as part of an ongoing investigation. Although the release from prison on December 27, 2010, has no value of criminal activity, it is worthy of noting that information in the file. It can show the reason for limited information in the timeframe that Smith was in prison.

The last note was within days of a 5-year period of the last information related to criminal activity. On February 1, 2011, Smith was found in possession of drugs and drug scales. All of this is criminal activity, and it supports the original intelligence product. Therefore, the 5-year retention period continues up to February 1, 2016. Since Smith was incarcerated for a period of time, information obtained during that time may not always apply to the 5-year purge requirement.

A criminal intelligence submission requires that the criminal subject be currently involved in criminal activity or enterprise. The purge requirement does not apply to correctional/parolee subjects or information. However, most state correctional facilities have policies in place to match the 28 C.F.R. Part 23 requirements. For example, in Tennessee, the policy related to gangs or security threat groups (STGs) allows an inmate's/member's active status to be changed from "active" to "inactive" if the inmate has not been involved in defined gang/STG activities over a period of 5 years. Each institutional STG investigator is required to update an inmate's STG file at minimum annually. If the inmate is involved in STG activity (e.g., contraband, disciplinaries, fights, etc.), their file is updated immediately. If not, their file is reviewed annually. Any gang/STG activity, such as correspondence to another gang member or being involved in fights amongst gang/STG members, is considered activity. Fights (or assaults) are criminal activity, as is contraband introductions or possession in a correctional institution.

After 5 years of good behavior and no additional gang information being obtained, the inmate can be changed to "inactive" status. However, the file is saved and kept. It is still part of the inmate's institutional file, not an intelligence file. This process assists when sharing information with agencies related to gang/STG members. While 28 C.F.R. Part 23 provides some leeway for correctional data, some agencies prefer to follow the guidelines without using a correctional exception. If correctional agencies develop guidelines that correspond to the 28 C.F.R. Part 23 standard, it makes intelligence sharing easier amongst law enforcement.

Another exception is a gang/STG member being released from prison. By being a member of a criminal organization while in prison, even over the 5-year purge requirement, it doesn't prohibit the correctional agency from notifying law enforcement agencies of a gang/STG inmate's release. The release notification is not solely based on the inmate being released but the inmate being connected to a criminal organization being released.

Reporting and Dissemination

Know your audience. As the International Association of Law Enforcement Intelligence Analysts (2012) indicate, it's important the analysis product "aligns" with the customer's needs. They continue:

> If the report has been assigned as part of a specific investigation, the audience would be the investigators, officers, and possibly attorneys involved. If it was assigned to inform a wider number of agencies involved in a cooperative effort, they would form the audience. A written dissemination plan for the product is essential, even if it is only a paragraph stating the specific audience, to avoid intelligence sharing misunderstandings. The report may require multiple versions, depending on its sensitivity and intended purpose and/or recipient: one with specific recommendations for a target audience and another for a more general audience. (International Association of Law Enforcement Intelligence Analysts, 2012, p. 18)

Dissemination should not be openly published. An intelligence product should only be disseminated to someone or an organized that has a purpose or need for the information. Intelligence sharing is important, but intelligence products should only be disseminated sparingly. We will discuss a two-prong test that you may used to determine who needs the information.

Reporting

Next is preparing a report of your finding. Reports should be written clearly and facts documented thoroughly. Reports are not always an intelligence product, matrix, or worksheet. There may be times when the data don't produce an information or intelligence product. Whether in the product or a separate report, it's important to organize the analysis into a strong, analytical conclusion that outlines the thought process and indicates where more intelligence is necessary. Intelligence gaps may be processed and answered as additional data is obtained or developed. As the product and/or information is reassessed, intelligence gaps that are answered can be added or changed. Prioritize concise writing that features "objective and dispassionate language" (International Association of Law Enforcement Intelligence Analysts, 2012, p. 20).

Dissemination

What good is collecting information without sharing it? **Dissemination** is the distribution of analyzed intelligence that uses specific processes and formats to provide those with the need to know of information to accomplish their intelligence needs or goals. Analysts will determine who should receive certain intelligence based on the concepts of "right to know" and "need to know" (Bureau of Justice Assistance, 2003, p. 7). The **right to know** and **need to know** determine who should receive intelligence products with the ability to act on the intelligence. The integrity of criminal intelligence can be best maintained by proper dissemination guidelines. Products should not just be sent out to anyone or everyone. Intelligence should be a protected product. An accepted standard to determine who should receive the intelligence is a two-pronged test (Carter, 2022, p. 77):

1. Does the person have the authority required to receive the information? That is, do they have the right to know?

2. Is this information necessary for the recipient to perform their job, either to assist with an investigation or stop a potential threat?

The International Association of Law Enforcement Intelligence Analysts, Selection from Law Enforcement Analytic Standards, p. 18, 2012.

As we previously discussed, the purpose for a law enforcement intelligence product is either tactical or strategic. A final intelligence product will be disseminated to law enforcement agencies, the intelligence community, fusion centers, other public safety agencies, or in some cases the private sector. This is known as **intelligence sharing**.

Intelligence has no value if it is not shared. Intelligence products are developed to support short- or long-term investigations or goals, as well as to support specific agency needs. Products can also support multijurisdictional efforts.

An information-sharing guideline that you may want to consider is called the "third-party rule." This rule prohibits a recipient who receives intelligence from an intelligence source/agency from further sharing, forwarding, or disseminating the intelligence without permission from the original source. This intelligence sharing is expected to be shared "confidentially." For example, an officer receives intelligence from their state fusion center. That officer should not forward the intelligence directly to a fellow officer without first receiving permission to pass on or forward the intelligence from the fusion center that originally sent it.

From time to time, intelligence sources/agencies will list in the product or in the message in which the product was sent if the product needs permission to forward or waives permission for specific recipients with the need and right to know. As Carter (2022) writes:

> It should be reinforced that in law enforcement intelligence, both the right-to-know and need-to-know provisions as well as the **Third Agency Rule** serve two purposes: to protect individuals' civil rights and to maintain operations security of intelligence inquiries. That being said, such dissemination practices do not carry the force of law and typically have minimal or no sanctions if a person does not comply with the guidelines. In a few cases, there are regulatory obligations for following the guidelines—such as an agreement to abide by the rules as a user of a criminal intelligence information system—but in most cases, it is a professional agreement. (p. 78)

There is some confusion about labelling law enforcement intelligence. As we have already mentioned, most law enforcement intelligence is Law Enforcement Sensitive (LES) or For Official Use Only (FOUO). Some agencies use Sensitive but Unclassified (SBU) labels for their intelligence products. With this said, there is a lack of definitive guidance in labelling law enforcement intelligence. The federal government is in the process of recreating Unclassified labels with a new label called Controlled Unclassified Information (CUI).

Law enforcement intelligence is an everchanging process. Prior to September 11, 2001, law enforcement officers hardly received intelligence products. After the terrorist attack, that has changed. There is an increased emphasis on information and intelligence sharing amongst law enforcement agencies, including local, state, federal, and tribal agencies.

There were times just after 2001 when law enforcement agencies or their personnel were overwhelmed with information being shared throughout the United States. So much information was passed around the roll call table at shift briefing. Or officers emails were filled with information and/or intelligence bulletins—all of which had little or no direct value or nexus to their jurisdictions.

There should be a balance. Otherwise, an officer or investigator will discard information or intelligence forwarded to them that in valuable to their needs. For example, a threat to New York City during an event likely won't effective officers in Tennessee. Therefore, there would be not need to disseminate information or intelligence about the New York event to Tennessee law enforcement agencies.

Reevaluation

Intelligence gathering is an ongoing system. Intelligence does not exist in a vacuum, but rather is evaluated and incorporated into the existing data. Throughout this process, analysts continually reevaluate the intelligence they have as they learn new information. In doing so, analysts can determine if threats are being accurately identified and intelligence provides clear next steps. This also ensures that information is as up to date and precise as possible. If you choose a career in analysis, you can ask yourself, "Is this information providing value? Where do we need to make adjustments? Is our system for evaluating intelligence working efficiently?" (Carter, 2022, pp. 80–81). **Reevaluation** is an assessment or review of intelligence within the intelligence process to assess the value of information or intelligence output.

Situational Awareness

Gang intelligence databases are a good example of the pros and cons of collecting, storing, and disseminating intelligence. These gang databases often contain the names, dates of birth, physical characteristics, criminal justice tracking numbers, gang affiliation, notes who they associated with, and other personal information.

This information can come in very handy for officers after a crime has been committed in the free world or even after a serious incident involving the incarcerated. But it doesn't come without challenges or criticism.

Lawsuits occurred with the CalGang database of 80,000+ California residents suspected of having gang affiliations. It's claimed LAPD violated public trust by routinely filing false information classifying people as gang members, then entering it in CalGang. One lawsuit claims LAPD criminalizes innocent residents under auspices of state law to arrest individuals suspected of committing a crime at the direction of a gang (Macias, 2020).

Intelligence can also be used to prevent crime through crime trends and crime data analysis. These methods can provide law enforcement with situational awareness, such as information related to violent criminal activity. For example, a community could see an increase in homicides involving guns. Gun crime data can be collected, analyzed, and evaluated to develop crime reduction analysis and provide situational awareness for officers.

For example, analysis can determine a specific area of the community where these types of crimes may occur more often. A particular subject or group of subjects, possibly a criminal street gang, can be identified and can provide officers with more awareness. A crime trend may be identified that indicates that a subject(s) is breaking and entering unlocked vehicles in a particular neighborhood. Additionally, crime data could determine a day and/or time frame in which these crimes are occurring. All of this is significant situational awareness for law enforcement.

Situational awareness can lead to the development of proactive investigative and/or intelligence planning.

Assessment

The final process of the intelligence cycle (before it starts over again) involves assessment and management planning. This phase reevaluates to entire processes, cycles, and information. New information may be developed that identifies potential weaknesses and/or additional threats. This process also strives to corroborate previous information or strengthen less reliable sources. This phase can remove information that's validity has been proven more doubtful than probable. Information that's validity may not have been determined could be later corroborated and updated.

The assessment includes feedback that can help determine the effectiveness of the disseminated product. Feedback comes from the users who the intelligence product was disseminated to. Feedback includes assessing the intelligence process and the value of the product to the user(s).

Conclusion

As you should have noticed, the four I's are all interchangeable in different ways. No specific one must be completed before the other, with the exception of a preferred interview prior to the interrogation. However, you may not be afforded the opportunity to interview a subject before an arrest or interrogation. Other than that, each of the four I's are interchangeable.

Many times, a criminal investigation starts the process because it's reactionary. In other cases, you may be able to proactively work a criminal investigation (mostly in drug cases) where the intelligence component starts or drives the investigation. Interviews can be associated with information collection for intelligence purposes or for the investigative process. Or it may be that a field interview started an investigation from the information gathered in the interview process. Interviews and interrogations can help reassess everything or connect to other previously unknowns (circumstances or activities) within the investigation.

At that point, you should have options: Conduct additional interviews, collect information for the intelligence process, conduct an investigation into criminal activity, or even go into an interrogation after developing probable cause from evidence and/or the interview. Remember, the intelligence process is a continuous cycle, even after an investigative arrest or interrogation.

The most universal "I" of the Four I's is intelligence. That's because the intelligence process can assist with each of the other three I's (interview, interrogation, or investigation). Intelligence can stand alone as well. But any of the other three I's can be performed without intelligence as well. Intelligence is a great benefit, but it's not the be-all and end-all.

Throughout this book, you should have been able to see when intelligence could be a vital asset. You should have also been able to see where the other three I's could assist with the intelligence process. All the four I's are a critical component in law enforcement and corrections.

We have provided you with a good foundation to utilize each of the four I's. Develop a way that fits you and your needs to apply what you have learned from each of the four I's, and you'll be successful. Good luck!

References

Bureau of Justice Assistance. (2003). *The National Criminal Intelligence Sharing Plan: Solutions and approaches for a cohesive plan to improve our nation's ability to develop and share criminal intelligence*. U.S. Department of Justice. https://bja.ojp.gov/sites/g/files/xyckuh186/files/media/document/national_criminal_intelligence_sharing_plan.pdf

Bureau of Justice Assistance. (2015). 28 C.F.R. Part 23: A guide to criminal intelligence policies. https://bja.ojp.gov/sites/g/files/xyckuh186/files/media/document/28C.F.R._part_23.pdf

California v. Greenwood, 486 U.S. 35 (1988). https://supreme.justia.com/cases/federal/us/486/35/

Carter, D. (2009). *Law enforcement intelligence: A guide for state, local, and tribal law enforcement agencies* (2nd ed.). Bureau of Justice Assistance.

Carter, D. (2022). *Law enforcement intelligence: A guide for state, local, and tribal law enforcement agencies* (3rd ed.). Bureau of Justice Assistance. https://bja.ojp.gov/sites/g/files/xyckuh186/files/media/document/Law_Enforcement_Intelligence_Guide_508.pdf

Heuer, R. J. (1999). *Psychology of intelligence analysis.* Center for the Study of Intelligence, Central Intelligence Agency.

International Association of Law Enforcement Intelligence Analysts. (2012). *Law enforcement analytic standards* (2nd ed.). U.S. Department of Justice. https://www.publicsafety.gc.ca/lbrr/archives/cnmcs-plcng/cn89655285-eng.pdf

Law Enforcement Intelligence Unit. (2002). *Criminal intelligence file guidelines.* U.S. Department of Justice. https://bja.ojp.gov/sites/g/files/xyckuh186/files/media/document/leiu_crim_intell_file_guidelines.pdf

Macias, M. (2020). *LAPD faces lawsuit over false gang reports in state database.* Courthouse News Service. https://www.courthousenews.com/lapd-faces-lawsuit-over-false-gang-reports-in-state-database/

Office of the Director of National Intelligence. (2006). *Information Sharing Environment Implementation Plan.* https://irp.fas.org/agency/ise/plan1106.pdf

Peterson, M. (2005). *Intelligence-led policing: The new intelligence architecture.* Bureau of Justice Assistance. https://www.policinginstitute.org/publication/intelligence-led-policing-the-new-intelligence-architecture/

Regional Information Sharing Systems. (n.d.). *About us.* https://www.riss.net/about-us/

U.S. Department of Justice. (2010). *Department of Justice's privacy, civil rights, and civil liberties protection policy for the information sharing environment.* (https://www.justice.gov/opcl/docs/doj-ise-privacy-policy.pdf

Credits

Closing

Some final thoughts for you: Police-Community Relations is a big topic today in our society, probably more now than ever. We cannot overemphasize the need to also have good Police to Police, Corrections to Corrections, and Police to Corrections good relations. You may have heard the saying, "It is not what you know, but who you know."

Networking in this business is very important and, like it or not, other people may have access to and control very important information that will assist you greatly in your work. Now, you could seek legal action to force them to cooperate but we have discovered it is a lot easier and less of a headache if you simply use common courtesy and good communications skills with all people you encounter on and off the job. Most of the time you will be happy you did.

We hope you've found this book to be useful as a criminal justice student. We also hope that you retain it as a reference manual to help remind yourself of some key considerations when interviewing, interrogating, investigating, or sharing intelligence.

It has been a learning experience for us also. It is not easy to write a book. As with most things, there is a lot more to it than what first meets the eye. But we are proud of our project and happy to assist others in learning some things we had to learn the hard way. We hope that you have found this book unique in that the book is written based upon experience in the field. Many times, you will only get an academic conclusion.

We both continue to be involved in the criminal justice field and hope to never stop learning, as things in our line of work are always changing in great part due to changing laws and technology.

Stay safe out there!

Sincerely,

Korey Cooper
Gabe Morales

Appendix 1: Crime Scene Checklist

Case number	
Date:	
Initial Notification of Detective	
Date and time of initial report	
Notified by whom (supervisor, dispatch, etc.)?	
Who notified police?	
Name	
Address	
Phone number	
Date and time of notification to police	
Was notification by phone?	
Phone number used	
Location	
***Obtain Copy of Dispatch Recordings and 911 Tape/Printout	
Information Upon Arrival at Scene	
Time of arrival by primary detective(s)	
Address of crime scene	
Type of structure	
Outside weather/temperature conditions	
Outside lighting conditions	
Interview with first officer on scene to establish sequence of events from their arrival	
Name and badge number of first officer to arrive	

Adapted from Vernon J. Geberth, *Sex-Related Homicide and Death Investigation: Practical and Clinical Perspectives*, pp. 163–164, 189, 219–220, 223, 226, 227, 229–233. Copyright © 2010 by Taylor & Francis Group.

Time of call	
Time of arrival	
Crime discovered by	
Name	
Address	
Hold and obtain formal written adopted statement (FWAS)! Also determine if this is the person who notified police. If not, locate notifier and obtain their FWAS.	
Patrol officer's preliminary investigative findings	

Preliminary Inspection of the Body at the Crime Scene	
Is the victim alive?	
If possible, obtain FWAS.	
Is death possible?	
If yes, OBTAIN DYING DECLARATION! Reduce it to writing, and have a witness present.	
Taken by	
Witnessed by	
If victim is dead, HOLD BODY AT SCENE!	
Has the victim been removed from the scene?	
If yes, where to?	
Who transported the victim?	
If by ambulance, SEIZE LINENS AND VICTIM'S CLOTHING! Interview transporter and passenger to determine if any statements or dying declaration was made by victim. If so, OBTAIN FWAS.	
Victim pedigree	
Name	
Address	
Date of birth	
Race	
Sex/gender	

Location of victim	
Description of the scene	
Have the initial patrol officer escort you through the crime scene to the body using the <u>same path</u> that was used by them upon responding to the call.	
Condition of the body	
Are there any additional victims? (If yes, provide for additional documentation, separate from the first victim.)	
If identity of victim is known, background check/criminal history?	
Implementation of Crime Scene Control Procedures	
Has the crime scene been protected?	
If not, what has been disturbed, and why?	
Persons present at the crime scene:	
Patrol	
Supervisors	
Detectives	
Medical	
Fire	
Relatives and friends of victim	

Witnesses, including detainees: _____

*Keep witnesses <u>separated</u> and provide for security and protection.

1. Who is in charge of the crime scene (before detective's)?

2. Are any suspects in custody? _____ If yes, do the following:

    a. Ensure that the suspect is removed from the scene!

    b. Safeguard all evidence found on the suspect.

    c. Do not allow suspect to wash their hands or do anything that may alter or destroy evidence.

    d. <u>DO NOT</u> permit any conversation between the suspect and any other person.

    e. Advise any officers transporting the suspect not to engage in any conversation or questioning and <u>not to</u> advise suspect of their Miranda warnings. <u>However,</u> if the suspect makes any spontaneous statements, these should be recorded (in-car video). Alibi and any self-serving statements should be documented.

3. Who is the suspect? _____

4. Run a complete background/criminal history check. _____

5. Is there a crime scene log? _____ If not, assign a patrol officer to record the names of all persons at the crime scene.

6. Who is assigned to the crime scene log? _____

    a. Identify and establish crime scene perimeters. (Use rope, tape, barriers, etc.) <u>Only authorized personnel enter the crime scene.</u> Determine the outer and inner perimeters, and determine who is authorized to enter these areas.

7. Establish a single path of entry and exit to these areas.

8. Is the Crime Scene Unit processing the scene? _____

9. If so, list the crime scene technicians: _____

Crime Scene Integrity

	Yes	No
Do I need a search warrant or consent to search prior to entering the scene?		
Has a search warrant been obtained?		
Has consent to search been obtained?		

1. <u>DO NOT</u> touch, move, or alter anything at the scene until full documentation has been completed. This includes photographs, descriptions, and sketches.

2. Record any crime scene alternations made in the course of investigation or emergency police intervention.

3. Were any lights turned on or off?_____ If yes, where? _____

4. Were any doors or windows opened, closed, locked, or unlocked? _____ If yes, describe: _____

5. Was the body moved or cut down? _____ If yes, by whom and why? _____

6. Was any furniture moved? _____ If yes, describe:_____

7. Is there a vehicle involved? ___ If yes, is engine cold, cool, warm, or hot?

8. DO NOT use any telephones located inside the crime scene!

9. Conditions of light, lamps, and electric appliances? _____

---

1. If emergency medical service (EMS) personnel were present before detective's arrival, determine if the crew or anyone else moved the body or any other items within the crime scene. If yes, record the following:

   a. When were alterations made? _____

   b. Purpose of movement: _____

   c. Person(s) who made alterations: _____

   d. Time of death as pronounced by EMS:_____

2. If a weapon is discovered, do the following:

   a. Firearms: Do not immediately attempt to unload (unless this is a danger or threat).

   b. Photograph the cylinder of a revolver to show the shell location.

   c. Where is the weapon located? _____

   d. Determine if the weapon is from the premises.

   e. Is there blood or other trace evidence on the weapon? If so, what? _____

   f. Safeguard the weapon for forensic examination!

   g. Photograph the weapon before further examination!

   h. If the weapon is a firearm, consider an examination of the suspect's hands for gunshot residue analysis. _____

Firearm Information

Firearm # 1
Make: _____ Model: _____ Serial number: _____
Caliber: _____ Revolver: _____ Semi-Auto Pistol: _____ Rifle: _____ Shotgun: _____

Loaded:	
Unloaded:	
Number of bullets in magazine:	
Number of bullets in cylinder:	
Number of spent casings in cylinder:	

	Yes	No
Is there blood evidence on the firearm?		
Is there blowback on the firearm?		
Was the firearm superglue fumed?		

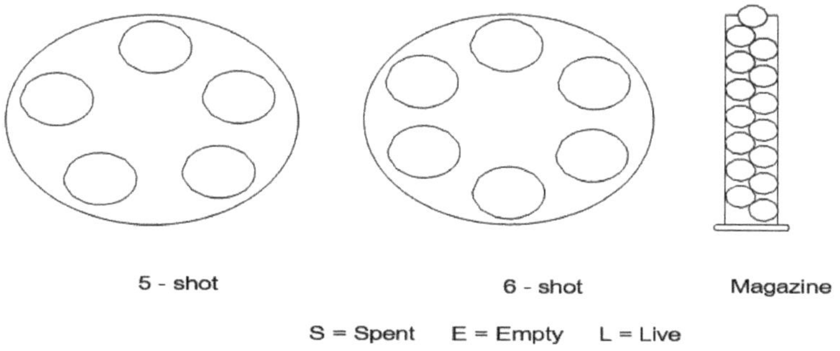

5 - shot   6 - shot   Magazine

S = Spent   E = Empty   L = Live

IMAGE A1.1

Firearm # 2
Make: _____ Model: _____ Serial number: _____
Caliber: _____ Revolver: _____ Semi-Auto Pistol: _____ Rifle: _____ Shotgun: _____

Loaded	
Unloaded	
Number of bullets in magazine	
Number of bullets in cylinder	
Number of spent casings in cylinder	

	Yes	No
Is there blood evidence on the firearm?		
Is there blowback on the firearm?		
Was the firearm superglue fumed?		

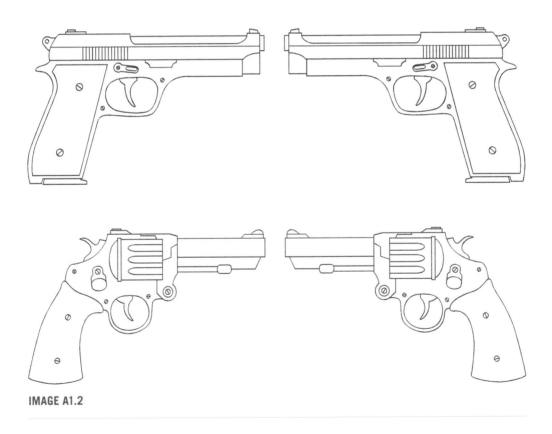

IMAGE A1.2

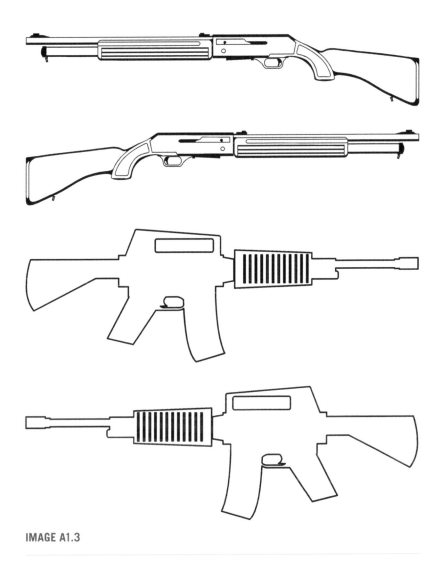

IMAGE A1.3

Are the wounds consistent with the suspected weapon?	

Alternate Light Source (ALS)

	Yes	No
Was the ALS used at the scene?		
Was the victim's body processed at the scene with the ALS?		
If not, where?		
Victim's body processed by:		
Was the scene processed for inherent luminescent prints?		
Was the body processed for bloody fingerprints?		
Was the body processed for bite mark evidence?		
Were bruises or bruising photographed on the body?		
Was UV light used to search for bruising not yet visible?		
Were scales used when photographing items on the body?		
Was the body processed for hairs?		
Was the body processed for fibers?		
Was the body superglue fumed?		
Did you find amido black on the body?		
Did you find fluorescent powders on the body?		

What evidence was collected or documented?
Hairs ___
Fibers _____
Blood evidence _____ Fingerprints ____
Shoe impressions _____
Tire impressions _____
Bite marks _____
Ligature markings _____
Stab wounds _____
Gunshot wounds _____
Blunt force trauma _____ Burn marks _____ Lividity _____ Marbling _____ Tattoos _____
Other ___

Electronic Evidence

	Yes	No	Recovered to process?	Notes (Why?)	
Cell phone(s)					
Computer/tablets					
Smart watches					
Other devices:					

Crime Scene Search

	Yes	No
Strip method		
Spiral method		
Wheel method		
Grid method		
Zone method		
Was a metal detector used?		
Were there any shell casings on the scene?		
Did you find bullet holes in walls, doors, furniture, etc.?		
Can you document a bullet trajectory?		

Did you search under the body?		
Weapon?		
Evidence		
Projectile under carpeting (beneath body)?		
What is the point of entry (POE)?		
Front door _____ Rear door _____ Garage door ___ Side door _____ Patio door _____		
Window AC unit ___ Knocked hole in wall ___ Roof vent ___ Unknown ___		
Other ___		

Were shoe impressions observed?	Yes	No
If yes, where?		
Were tire impressions observed?	Yes	No
If yes, where?		
Were bloody prints observed?	Yes	No
If yes, where?		
Were tool mark impressions found?	Yes	No
If yes, where?		

	Yes	No
Was the electrostatic dust print lifter used?		
Were shoe or tire impressions cast with dental stone after photography?		
Were tool mark impressions cast with a casting material after photography?		
Was a GSR test performed on the victim?		
Was a GSR test performed on the suspect?		

Suspect in Custody

Is the suspect(s) known? _____ If yes, who are they? ____
Did the suspect make any statements? ____ If yes, who took it? _____
Has it been reduced to writing? ___ If not, do so NOW! FWAS if possible!
Was the suspect advised of their Miranda Warning? ___ If yes, by whom? If no, why not? _____
Was the suspect questioned? _____ If yes, by whom? _____
Does the suspect have an interest in the crime scene? _____
If the suspect is <u>NOT</u> in custody, how was the escape (from crime scene) effected? ____
Is there probable cause for arrest? If so, broadcast BOLO!
Are there any witnesses to the suspect's escape? ___ If yes, OBTAIN FWAS! Determine their relationship to suspect or victim.

Crime Scene Photographs

Photograph log sheet used? _____If no, why? _____
Documentation of crime scene photographs:
Date and time photographs are taken:
Exact location of photographs:
Description of the item photographed:
Compass direction (if possible):
Focus distance:
Type of film and camera used:
Lights and weather conditions:
Identification of photographers:
Recommended photographs:
The entire location where the crime took place
The crowd or any bystanders (surreptitiously with the crime scene)
The suspect and/or any witnesses, if applicable. Any injuries to the suspect should also be photographed and the suspect's clothing, shoes, etc.
The front entrance of the building
Entrance to the room or apartment where the victim is located
Body shots from four different sides
General view of the body and the crime scene
Close-up shot of body
Any visible wounds
If the body has been removed, photos should be taken of the original location.
The possible entrance or escape routes of the suspect
Area and close-up views of any physical evidence
Fingerprints should be photographed before lifting.

*** Do not add any markers (chalk or otherwise) until the original crime scene photos have been taken. Markers can be added later for close-up shots.

	Yes	No
Photos of the scene: Overall & long-range		
Photos of the scene: Medium range		
Photos of the scene: Close-up		
Evidence photographed first without a scale		
Evidence photographed with a scale in place		
Photographed the following:	Mark with "X"	
Point of entry		
Point of exit		
Doors		
Windows		
Damage to doors or windows		
Objects as they relate to the scene		
Evidence as it relates to the scene		
Evidence as it relates to other evidence		
"North" arrow		
Front of building, structure, vehicle		
Sides of building, structure, vehicle		
Rear of building, structure, vehicle		
Entrances to rooms		
Views of each room from corners		
Photographs of body (from four sides and minimum of two overall)		
Photographs of the body as it relates to the scene		
Photographs of the scene as it relates to the body		
Photographs of all tire and shoe impressions		
Photographs of visible wounds		
Photographs of location where body found (if move/removed prior to arrival)		
Close-ups of evidence with evidence markers		
Photographed latent, patent, or plastic fingerprints		
Photographs of all involved vehicles		

Photographs of all vehicle tags	
Photographs taken of adjacent buildings and structures	
Photographs taken discretely of the crowd or bystanders	
Photographs taken of the suspect, clothing, shoes, or injuries	
Record and photograph injuries observed on suspect:	
Hands	
Feet	
Head	
Chest	
Back	
Legs	
Arms	
Neck	

	Yes	No
Photographed suspect's clothing?		
Photographs taken from locations of witnesses?		
Timed exposures taken?		
Painting with light?		
Was black-and-white film used for fingerprint photography?		
Was black-and-white film used for tire or shoe impression photography?		
Was the scene videotaped?		
Were bullet trajectories photographed?		
Dowels		
String		
Laser light		
Was blood spatter photographed?		
Are aerial photographs needed?		
Were monopod photographs taken?		

Fire Scene Photography

(Taken in addition to the above photographs)

Photographed the following:	Mark with "X"
Exterior of structure	
Point of entry	
Windows	
Doors	
Pour or burn patterns	
Flammable containers	
Stove and oven and positions of knobs	
Position of light switches	
Settings on heater/air conditioner	
Electric meter box	
Circuit breaker box	
Smoke demarcation lines	
Fire damage	
Burglar bars on doors and windows	
Space heaters	
Fireplaces	
Extension cords	

Crime Scene Sketch

1. Make a simple line drawing of the crime scene.

2. Include the following information:

   a. Measurements and distances

   b. A title block consisting of:

      i. Name and title of sketcher

      ii. Date and time of sketch

      iii. Classification of the crime

      iv. Identification of the victim(s)

      v. Agency case number

      vi. Names of any persons assisting in taking measurements

      vii. Address of the location sketched

      viii. Compass direction "North"

3. Include a legend to identify any object or articles of evidence in the crime scene.

4. Include a scale to depict measurements used or a "Not to Scale" statement.

***Note: If a rough draft is made at the scene, it must be included in the case file along with the smooth sketch.

Crime Scene Search and Processing

I. Search

The crime scene search should not be started until the perimeters of the crime scene have been documented with photographs and the crime scene sketch. Recreate aspects of the crime while conducting the search. Determine the legality of the search before seizing evidence. Locate physical evidence and determine how and if it should be collected prior to further alteration of the crime scene. Determine the method of search depending on your investigative theory, the size of the search area, and any other relevant factors.

II. Processing

1. <u>Dust for fingerprints.</u> Note first that any evidence that can be bagged and taken to the lab for processing should not be processed at the scene.

2. The following areas should be processed for latent prints:

    a. Areas of entry and exit

    b. Door handles

    c. Telephone instruments

    d. Windows, mirrors, picture frames

    e. Light switches

    f. Any newly damaged areas

    g. Objects moved from their original location

    h. Toilet handles

    i. Wall above the toilet

    j. Thermostats

    k. Under furniture that has been moved (framing)

    l. Garage door openers

    m. Anything else that appears to have been handled

3. Interior examination

III.   Cautions

1. Before entering room, look for shoe prints using oblique lighting.

2. DO NOT touch light switches.

3. Handle doorknobs as little as possible.

4. Check overhead (ceilings).

The following items should be considered during the interior examination:

Alarms on or off?	
Auto lighting systems on or off? What is time set for?	
Is doorbell operational?	
Make/model of garage door opener?	
Locks on doors locked? Operable? Describe the type of locks.	
Locks on the windows locked? Operable? Describe the type of locks.	
Position of curtains/drapes? Check field of vision in and out?	
Light switches on/off? Operable? Bulbs operable?	
Lights on/off?	
Streetlights visible?	
Heating A/C setting on/off? List the unit type and inside temperature.	
Check fireplace/stove for destroyed evidence.	
Check calendar/bulletin boards for date shown and any dates of significance.	
Check phone machine for messages.	
Check clocks/watches. Are they working?	

Check time set/alarm set.	
Is radio/TV on or off? What channel or station?	
Check auto timer on electric appliances.	
Document contents of pet bowls.	
Is toilet running?	
Is there evidence of any vandalism/graffiti (cult activity)?	
Feces? (Human? Composition?)	
Document items apparently out of place.	
Document any items apparently missing. Look for dust-free areas.	
Check weapons/cartridges (jammed auto, stove-pipe, safety on or off, round chambered, etc.).	
Search for bullets and bullet holes.	
Cover cartridges with plastic cup for protection.	
Check blood splatters/stains. Degree of coagulation?	
Is there evidence of illicit drug use? Are there any leads to suppliers?	
Are there any odors (food, tobacco, solvents, gas, etc.)?	
Are the beds made/unmade? Are there any electric blankets on or off? What are the settings? Are the linens soiled? Seize for trace evidence!	
Are there any wet or dry stains on sinks/bathtubs?	
Have any toiletries been recently used?	
Seize used towels/washcloths for trace and biological evidence.	
Is the bathroom carpet/floor wet?	
Search for prescription medicines. Document type and doctor names. Seize and process for prints.	

Open and photo video closet/cabinet.	
Is food cooking or being prepared?	
Log and compare to stomach contents.	
Is the stove on or off? Time on?	
What are the contents in the microwave? Is timer set?	
Is the table set? Are dishes dirty?	
Check the glasses outside cabinets or dirty glasses for finger-print or trace evidence.	
Photo and document contents in trash can.	
Examine the contents in ashtrays.	
Any signs of a party?	
Examine books for hidden items and underlined passages.	
Examine bookcases for items hidden behind books.	
Examine behind appliances for hidden items.	
Examine cameras. Have film developed.	
Examine magazines for interests and dates.	
Examine newspapers for dates and underlined passages.	
Examine mail. Document senders.	
Examine homemade audio/video tapes.	
Obtain handwriting samples through letters, schoolwork, etc.	
Examine bank statements.	
Examine credit card receipts.	
Examine personal phonebooks/diaries.	
Examine typewriter ribbons.	
Examine/seize computer.	
Look for intended writings.	
Examine contents of vacuum cleaner.	
Examine wallet/purse of victim.	

Review the scene again in sunlight, near the time of occurrence. Note lighting conditions (shaded and lighted areas).

Observe regular (daily) activities occurring at the time of occurrence.

Is a Roadblock Necessary????

Outside Scene Examination	
Examine under windows for impressions and fingerprint evidence.	
Examine outbuildings.	
Examine wells.	
Examine driveways for tire impressions, oil, fluids, and debris.	
Is dew disturbed?	
Are any scrubs damaged?	
Examine glass on outside points of entry for fingerprints and biological evidence.	

Vehicle Scene Examination

What is the general condition/damage? Denote any fresh damage.	
Dirty or clean?	
Get soil sample from pedals!	
Is ignition key on/off?	
Check for fingerprint evidence.	
Are the wheel covers accounted for?	
Are all tires the same tread design, make, and model?	
Get soil samples and inked impressions.	
Condition of spare?	
Windows up or down?	
Manual or electric?	

Are the doors locked or unlocked? Manual/electric?	
Mileage/odometer:	
Trip meter:	
Radio on or off?	
Station:	
Tape player:	
License plate Number:	
VIN:	
Identify and obtain numbers of all decals and stickers.	
Check for sticker of last service date/place.	
Windshield wipers on or off?	
Heater or A/C on or off? Settings:	
Fuel gauge reading?	
Ensure that it is operable and drain the tank and measure contents (if applicable).	
Are the lights operable?	
Headlights low/high beams	
Taillights	
Front and rear turn lights	
Fog lights	
Brake lights	
Backup lights	
Map lights	
Interior lights	
Instrument lights	
Position of front seats?	
Position of rearview mirrors?	
Examine mirrors for fingerprints.	
Inventory entire vehicle.	
Remove trunk carpet for trace evidence.	
Vacuum entire vehicle, separating by quadrant.	
Check under the hood.	

1. Identify type and degree of any fluid leaks.___

    a. Vehicle information

Suspect	
Victim	
Witness	
Other	

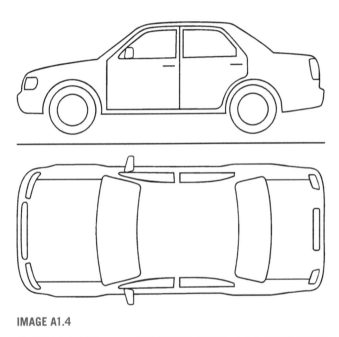

IMAGE A1.4

Year	Tag #	2-door
Make	VIN	4-door
Model	Color	

Evidence Process and Control Procedures

Ensure that all evidence is properly marked and packaged.
Establish a chain of custody.
Designate a searching officer to take charge of all evidence.
Photograph all evidence in its original position (in situ).
Record the position and location of all evidence on the crime scene sketch and the investigative notes.
Record the name of any officer or person discovering physical evidence and the location where it was recovered.

Initiate a Canvass

Initiate a canvass of the immediate area by assigning sufficient personnel to locate any witnesses or persons who may have information about the investigation.
Assign a coordinator to organize the canvass.
Provide canvassers with relevant information regarding the investigation so they can solicit information from potential witnesses or persons of interest. This may include photos of the scene or deceased if available.
Have officers check vehicles and record registration numbers of autos in the immediate area.
Require official reports from canvassers indicating:
Negative locations (locations with no results)
Locations that have been canvassed, indicating number of persons residing therein
Positive locations for possible follow-up and re-interviews

Statement of Witness That Discovered the Body

Name:	
D.O.B.	
Address (home/work):	
Phone(s):	
Employment:	
Relation to victim:	
Relation to suspect:	
How did you learn of the incident?	
When did you learn of the incident? Date/time:	
Who told you of the incident?	
Exactly what did they say?	
How did you approach the scene?	
How did you gain access to the scene?	
Was the window/door locked?	
Were the lights on?	
Which lights did you turn on?	
In which room did you find the victim? Which rooms did you transit to find that room?	
From exactly what location did you view the victim?	
In exactly what position was the victim (sitting, on back, face down, etc.)?	
Was the victim clothed? Did you cover the exposed portions of the victim's body?	
Did you attempt to revive the victim?	
How was the victim's position altered by your efforts?	
Did anyone else alter the victim's position? (Police/Fire/EMS)	
Did you straighten up or clean up anything?	
What weapons did you see? Describe them.	
Whom did you call after finding the victim? Catalog witness list.	
To whom have you spoken about this incident? Catalog witness list. Interview each.	
What did they tell you about it (rumors they heard)?	
Why did this happen?	

How did this happen?	
Did the victim make any statements? Who else was present?	
Who else did you see on the scene?	
Who else did you see as you approached?	
Who else did you see as you departed?	
Who do you think saw this happen?	
Please tell me of your whereabouts (at the time the crime is suspected to have occurred).	
Obtain FWAS.	
Do you mind being fingerprinted? <u>Do it immediately!!</u>	

Suicide: Investigation Considerations

NOTE: Even if death appears to be accidental or suicidal, it should **always** be handled just as you would a homicide!!!

Evaluation of the wounds:
Could the deceased have caused the injuries and death? _____
Was the person physically able to accomplish the act? _____
Are the wounds within reach of the deceased? _____
Are the wounds grouped together? _____
Is there more than one cause of death? _____
Describe the nature and position of the injuries: _____
Are there any hesitation marks? _____
Psychological state of the victim:
Obtain a background of the victim from family and friends. This includes medical as well as social information.
Were there any warning signs indicated by the victim? (See section on recognized warning signs.)
Were there any recent deaths in the family?
Is there any indication of a recent upset or stress?
Did the victim leave any notes? (Obtain a handwriting sample thru letters, schoolwork, etc.)
Did the deceased have any close personal relationships, any close friends, etc.? Obtain FWAS!
Any prior mental disease or defect:
Has the deceased been under any professional treatment? _____
Has the deceased ever attempted suicide in the past? _____

Has anyone in the family ever committed suicide? _____
Was the deceased a heavy drinker? _____
Was the deceased on any medications? _____
Was there a history of drug abuse? _____

Recognized Warning Signs and Extreme Danger Signs in Suicides
Warning signs:
A change in sleeping habits, followed by sadness_____
A change in eating habits—weight loss or lack of appetite_____
A lack of interest in sex—a loss of sex drive _____
A sudden drop in grades or school attendance—students _____
A loss of interest in work—adults _____
Loss of interest in favorite activities, hobbies, sports_____
Loss of interest in friends and family/isolation _____
A preoccupation with death, or unusual interest in art or music dealing with death _____
Loss of interest in personal hygiene and appearance _____
Involvement with drugs, including abuse of alcohol _____
Extreme danger signs:
Sudden positive mood swing following a depressive period. After deciding on suicide, many individuals experience a relief that manifests as joy or euphoria._____
Giving away prized possessions _____
Speaking of life in the past tense_____

Autoerotic Fatalities (Accidental Asphyxia)

Investigative Considerations

Autoerotic deaths are deaths that result during solo sex-related activities.
The following question should be considered:
Is the victim nude or sexually exposed?__
If the victim is a male, is he dressed in feminine attire? __
Is there evidence of masturbatory activity? _____
Are sexually stimulating paraphernalia present (vibrators, dildos, other sexual fantasy aids or pornography, etc.)? ____
Is bondage present (ropes, chains, blindfolds, etc.)? _____
Are the restraints interconnected? _____
Is there protective padding between the ligature and neck? _____
Is there evidence of infibulation? _____

Is there evidence of fantasy (erotic literature, diaries, fantasy drawings, etc.) or fetishism? ___
Are there any mirrors or other reflective devices present? _
Is the suspension point within reach of the victim? _____
Is there evidence of prior such activities (abrasions or rope burns on the suspension point, photographs, etc.)? _____
Is there a positioned camera? If so, seize videotape or film. _____
Does the victim possess literature dealing with bandage, escapology, or knots? _____
Is there any indication of suicidal intent? _____

Release of the Death Scene

CRITICAL DECISION: Authorities should hold onto the crime scene as long as possible in the event that further process, investigation, or review becomes necessary as additional information becomes available.

1. Do not release the scene prior to the completion of the canvass and any interviews of witnesses or interrogations of suspect(s).

2. Note the telephone numbers of any phones at the scene.

3. If the scene is to be abandoned temporarily during certain investigatory procedures, provide for the continued crime scene protection during the absence of investigators.

4. Before leaving the crime scene, look over the entire area from the perspective of the defense counsel to make sure that you have "covered all the bases."

5. Gather all materials used in the crime scene processing, such as film packs, Polaroid negatives, flash bulbs, notes, tape, evidence, containers, etc.

   a. Remove these materials from the scene for destruction and disposal at another location.

   b. Utilize large plastic garbage bags at the scene for disposal of materials generated during the search.

****It is important to note that the extent of the crime scene search can be ascertained by the examination of these types of materials if they are left behind at the scene by the authorities.

Release of the Crime Scene

Complete the crime scene checklist while at the scene during the processing phase. Carefully review the process and make sure you complete each step. **Tip:** Put yourself in the shoes of the public defender and the prosecutor when observing a crime scene. What information would they need?

| Crime scene released on _____/_____/_____ |
| at _____ hours |
| Crime scene released per: |
| Det. _____ |
| ID #____ |
| By: _____ |
| To who: _____ |
| Secured from the scene at _____ hours |

Body Diagrams

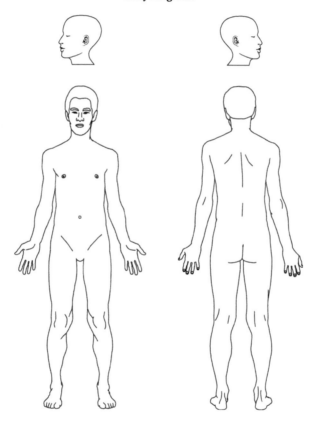

IMAGE A1.5

Photographic Log

Roll #: _____   Date taken: ____/_____/_____   Photographer: _____Color: _____   B&W: _____

Exp. #	Item and location	Flash	Aperture
1			
2			
3			
4			
5			
6			
7			
8			
9			
10			
11			
12			
13			
14			
15			
16			
17			
18			
19			
20			
21			
22			
23			
24			
25			

Photographic Log

Roll #: _____ Date taken: ____/_____/_____ Photographer: _____ Color: _____ B&W: _____

Exp. #	Item and location	Flash	Aperture
1			
2			
3			
4			
5			
6			
7			
8			
9			
10			
11			
12			
13			
14			
15			
16			
17			
18			
19			
20			
21			
22			
23			
24			
25			

Additional Note/Rough Sketch:

Appendix 2: Investigation & Intelligence Acronyms

ACTIC Arizona Counter Terrorism Information Center

AOR Area of Responsibility

ATF Bureau of Alcohol, Tobacco, & Firearms

ATIX Automated Trusted Information Exchange

BJA Bureau of Justice Assistance

C3 Command, Control, and Communication

C3I Command, Control, and Communication Information

CALEA Commission on Accreditation of Law Enforcement Agencies

CAP Common Alerting Protocol

CDC Centers for Disease Control and Prevention

CFR Code of Federal Regulations

CHRI Criminal History Record Information

CICC Criminal Intelligence Coordinating Council

CI Confidential Informant

CIA Central Intelligence Agency

CII Act Critical Infrastructure Information Act

CITCS Criminal Intelligence Training Coordination Strategy

CJIS Criminal Justice Information Services

CODIS Combined DNA Indexing System

COMINT Communications Intelligence

COMPSTAT Computerized Statistics

CONOPS Concept of Operations

COOP Continuity of Operations Plan

COPS Community Oriented Policing Services

CP Community Policing

CTTWG Counter-Terrorism Training Coordination Working Group

CUI Controlled Unclassified Information

DEA Drug Enforcement Administration

DHS U.S. Department of Homeland Security

DIA Defense Intelligence Agency

DISA Defense Information Systems Agency

DNA Deoxyribonucleic Acid

DOJ U.S. Department of Justice

DTO Drug Trafficking Organization

EPIC El Paso Intelligence Center

EUROPOL European Agency for Law Enforcement Cooperation

FAQ Frequently Asked Questions

FBI Federal Bureau of Investigation

FEMA Federal Emergency Management Agency

FI Field Interview

FinCEN Financial Crimes Enforcement Network

FOIA Freedom of Information Act

FOUO For Official Use Only

FR Facial Recognition

FTTTF Foreign Terrorist Tracking Task Force

GISWG Global Infrastructure/Standards Working Group

GIWG Global Intelligence Working Group

Global Global Justice Information Sharing Initiative

Global JXDM Global Justice XML Data Model

GPS Global Positioning System

GXSTF Global XML Structure Task Force

HEAT Help End Auto Theft

HIDTA High Intensity Drug Trafficking Areas

HIFCA High Intensity Financial Crime Areas

HSAC Homeland Security Advisory Council

HSIN Homeland Security Information Network

HSOC Homeland Security Operations Center

HSPD Homeland Security Presidential Directive

HUMINT Human Intelligence

IACA International Association of Crime Analysts

IACP International Association of Chiefs of Police

IADLEST International Association of Directors of Law Enforcement Standards and Training

IAFIS Integrated Automated Fingerprint Identification System

IALEIA International Association of Law Enforcement Intelligence Analysts

IC Intelligence Community

ICE U.S. Immigration and Customs Enforcement

ICAP Integrated Criminal Apprehension Program

ICSIS Integrated Convergence Support Information System

III Interstate Identification Index

ILP Intelligence-Led Policing

IMAP Intelligence Mutal Aid Pact

INFOSEC Information Systems Security

INTELUNIT Intelligence Unit

INTERPOL International Criminal Police Organization

IRTPA Intelligence Reform and Terrorism Prevention Act of 2004

ISAC Information Sharing and Analysis Centers

ISE Information Sharing Exchange

ITWG Intelligence Training Working Group

JABS Joint Automated Booking System

JICC Justice Intelligence Coordinating Council

JTTF Joint Terrorism Task Force

LAWINT Law Enforcement Intelligence

LECC Law Enforcement Coordinating Committee

LEEP Law Enforcement Enterprise Portal

LEIN Law Enforcement Intelligence Network

LEIU Law Enforcement Intelligence Unit

LEO Law Enforcement Online

LES Law Enforcement Sensitive

LINX Law Enforcement Information Exchange

MAGLOCLEN Middle Atlantic-Great Lakes Organized Crime Law Enforcement Newtork

MAP Mutual Aid Pact

MASINT Measurement and Signature Intelligence

MATRIX Multistate Anti-Terrorism Information Exchange

MOCIC Mid-States Organized Crime Information Center

MOU Memorandum of Understanding

NASINT National Security Intelligence

NCIC National Crime Information Center

NCIS Naval Criminal Investigative Service

NCISP National Criminal Intelligence Sharing Plan

NCJA National Criminal Justice Association

NCSD National Cyber Security Division

NCTC National Counterterrorism Center

NDA Non-Disclosure Agreement

NDIC National Drug Intelligence Center

N-DEx Law Enforcement National Data Exchange

NESPIN New England State Police Information Network

NGIC National Gang Intelligence Center

NIBRS National Incident Based Reporting System

NICS National Instant Criminal Background Check System

NIJ National Institute of Justice

NIMA National Imagery and Mapping Agency

NIPP National Infrastructure Protection Plan

NIST National Institute of Standards and Technology

NJTTF National Joint Terrorism Task Force

NLECTC National Law Enforcement and Corrections Technology Centers

NLETS The International Justice and Public Safety Information Sharing Network

NMEC National Media Exploitation Center

NNFC National Network of Fusion Centers

NSA National Security Administration

NSI Nationwide Suspicious Activity Reporting Initiative

NSIS National Strategy for Information Sharing

NTAC United States Secret Service National Threat Assessment Center

NTC National Tracking Center (ATF)

NTER National Threat Evaluation and Reporting Program

NW3C National White Collar Crime Center

OASIS Organization for the Advancement of Structured Information Standards

OC Organized Crime

OCA Original Classification Agency

OCDETF Organized Crime Drug Enforcement Task Force

OEP Occupant Emergency Plan

OJP Office of Justice Programs

OPCOM Open Communication

OPSEC Operational Security

OS Open Source

OSIN Open Source Information

OSIS Open Source Information System

OSS Office of Strategic Services

PII Personal Identifiable Information

RCIC Rockland County Intelligence Center

REMSEN Remote Sensing

RFI Request For Information

RFS Request For Service

RICO Racketeering Influenced Corrupt Organization

RISS Regional Information Sharing Systems®

RMIN Rocky Mountain Information Network

RMS Record Management System

ROCIC Regional Organized Crime Information Center

SAR Suspicious Activity Report

SARA Superfund Amendments and Reauthorization Act

SATINT Satellite Intelligence

SBU Sensitive But Unclassified

SCI Sensitive Compartmented Information

SCIF Sensitive Compartmented Information Facility

SHSI Sensitive Homeland Security Information

SIGINT Signal Intelligence

SLTLE State, Local, & Tribal Law Enforcement

SLTT State, Local, Tribal, & Territorial

SME Subject-Matter Expert

SOA Service-Oriented Architecture

SOP Standard Operating Procedure

STG Security Threat Group

STIC Statewide Terrorism Intelligence Center (Illinois)

STTAC State Terrorism Threat Assessment Center (California)

TEW Terrorism Early Warning Group

TFC Tennessee Fusion Center

TFO Task Force Officer

TLO Terrorism Liaison Officer

TRP Threat Review and Prioritization Process

TRS Terrorism Research Specialists

TS Top Secret

TSA Transportation Security Act or Transportation Security Agency

TSC Terrorist Screening Center

TTIC Terrorist Threat Integration Center

UNYRIC Upstate New York Regional Intelligence Center

UCR Uniform Crime Reports

URL Uniform Resource Locator

USC United States Code

USCS United States Customs Service

US-CERT United States Computer Emergency Readiness Team

USP3 United States Public-Private Partnership (formerly DHS's HSIN-CI)

VCTOF Violent Gang and Terrorist Organization File

VICAP Violent Criminal Apprehension Program

VIN Vehicle Identification Number

VPN Virtual Private Network

WMD Weapons of Mass Destruction

WSIN Western States Information Center

XML Extensible Markup Language

Glossary

10-print card: the generic fingerprint card used to identify or compare fingerprints of a person. Generally, the 10-print card is taken after someone is arrested or to submit for identification purposes.

28 C.F.R. Part 23: a federal regulation that provides law enforcement guidance on the implementation standards for operating multijurisdictional intelligence systems funded by the federal government under the Omnibus Crime Control and Safe Streets Act of 1968.

active listening skills (ALS): listening with the goal of understanding the speaker by providing full attention.

admission: a statement or acknowledgment, typically from a suspect, that can be proven as factual.

alibi: an excuse or defense of a person's whereabouts at the time of an alleged act.

analysis: extent to which data is collected from law enforcement and the community on elements, contributors, and past responses to the problem.

arson: the act of damaging or trying to damage real estate or personal property via fire.

assault: the intentional or reckless cause of bodily injury or to cause reasonable fear of imminent bodily harm to another.

assessment: extent to which the response(s) is evaluated for effectiveness to eliminate the problem and adjust responses accordingly.

asset forfeiture: civil proceeding that allows law enforcement to seize assets of drug dealers or traffickers.

body language: nonverbal communication a person's body exhibits through movement or gestures. This movement can be conscious or nonconscious communication throughout the body, including eyes, posture, body, and limbs.

Brady material: any material that can be considered favorable to the defendant; also known as discovery material.

burglary: the unlawful entry of a structure or motor vehicle to commit a theft or felony.

classified: a uniform system for classifying, safeguarding, and declassifying national security information, including information relating to defense against transnational terrorism, to ensure certain information be maintained in confidence to protect citizens, U.S. Homeland Security, and U.S. interactions with foreign nations and entities.[1]

---

1 David L. Carter, Selections from "Law Enforcement Intelligence," *Law Enforcement Intelligence: A Guide for State, Local, and Tribal Law Enforcement Agencies*, pp. 436, 438, 441-442, 444-447. Copyright © 2022 by David L. Carter. Reprinted with permission.

closed-ended questions: questions that required the interviewee to respond with short answers, like a yes or no.

coercion: the practice of persuading someone to do something by using force, threats, or promises.

collation: the act of collecting, reviewing, and cataloging intelligence to determine if it is valuable to an investigation.

collection: the identification, location, and recording/storing of information, commonly from sources that include human or technology (data entries), for entry into the intelligence cycle for the purpose of meeting a defined tactical or strategic intelligence goal.

confession: an acknowledgment of guilt in a crime.

confidential: see "classified."

cognitive interviews: interview methods used by law enforcement to help victims or eyewitnesses recall specific memories from crime.

community policing: a system where law enforcement work in and become familiar with a local area or neighborhood so they may develop collaborative relationships with community members. In doing so, they may work with the community to prevent crime.

corroborate: confirm or give support to (a statement, theory, or finding).

crime analysis: the collection and analysis of information from crime scenes and other sources to provide law enforcement with actionable strategies and increase operating efficiency of the department.

criminal enterprise: a group of people who share common purpose of engaging in criminal conduct, with a recognizable structure or hierarchy, and with criminal purpose to engage in significant criminal activity.

crime trend: an identifiable change in a selected crime or crime type within a defined timeframe and/or area geographic in nature.

criminal intelligence: "the end product (output) of an analytic process that collects and assesses information about crimes and/or criminal enterprises with the purpose of making judgments and inferences about community conditions, potential problems, and criminal activity with the intent to pursue criminal prosecution or project crime trends or support informed decision making by management."[2]

criminal investigation: the collection of information and/or evidence to identify, arrest, and subsequently convict suspected offenders involved in criminal activity.

culpable negligence: negligence that involves careless or reckless disregard.

custody: police detention or arrest that deprives a person's freedom to leave.

---

2 Carter, D. (2022). *Law enforcement intelligence: A guide for state, local, and tribal law enforcement agencies* (3rd ed.). U.S. Bureau of Justice Assistance. https://bja.ojp.gov/sites/g/files/xyckuh186/files/media/document/Law_Enforcement_Intelligence_Guide_508.pdf

customers: an agency, investigator, analyst, or a group that may receive an intelligence product.

dark web: a specialized website that is encrypted, hidden, or only accessible through special software and allows users to be anonymous or untracked.

data: raw information containing facts or measurable variables used as a basis to reason, for discussion, or calculation.[3]

debrief: a discussion about a completed event or mission.

denial: any statement by the suspect that contradicts the truthfulness of an allegation relating to a specific crime.

deoxyribonucleic acid (DNA): a set of molecules in the human body that is unique to each individual person. DNA can be collected from blood, hair, skin cells, and other bodily fluids.

dissemination: the distribution of analyzed intelligence that uses specific processes and formats to provide those with the need to know of information to accomplish their intelligence needs or goals.

dying declaration: a statement from a mortally injured person who believes they are about to die.

euthanasia: the practice of intentionally ending a life to relieve pain and suffering.

evidence: any material (physical, court exhibit, or testimony) used to prove a crime was committed.

false confession: a claim that someone was responsible for a crime they did not commit.

field interview: questions that require the interviewee to respond with more than a yes or no and provide some detail or particularity.

first formal statement (FFS): the first statement given by a person being interviewed.

formal written adopted statement (FWAS): the first statement by a person being interviewed that is documented in writing and adopted by the interviewee as their formal statement.

forensics: use of scientific methods or techniques to process the investigation of criminal activity.

forensic interview: an open-ended conversation conducted by a trained professional, commonly a child psychologist, or child specialist with a child that is not leading and related to possible traumatic events that the child may have experienced or witnessed.

fusion center: the collaboration of two or more law enforcement agencies that provide resources, information, technology, and expertise in one location, which focus on and maximize each other's capabilities to prevent, detect, and respond to criminal and terrorism activity throughout multiple jurisdictions.

homicide: the killing of a human being by another human.

honesty: fairness and straightforwardness of conduct.

---

3   David L. Carter, Selections from "Law Enforcement Intelligence," *Law Enforcement Intelligence: A Guide for State, Local, and Tribal Law Enforcement Agencies*, p. 438. Copyright © 2022 by David L. Carter. Reprinted with permission.

hot spots: identified locations (places or areas) where criminal activity is elevated or as increased over a period of measured time.

hypothesis: an initial assumption or educated guess to be proven or disproved through analysis and/or an investigation.

identity theft: knowingly obtaining, possessing, buying, or using the personal identifying information of another without consent or knowledge of the person.

incest: sexual activity between family, including blood relatives and, in most states, relatives by marriage, stepfamily, adoption, or lineage.

information: data compiled, analyzed, and/or disseminated in an effort to anticipate, prevent, or monitor criminal activity.[4]

integrity: doing the right thing even when it's not the most popular decision by adhering to sound moral and ethical principles; being honest and trustworthy.

intelligence: a product resulting from the collection of information and/or raw data on suspicious activity or people that has been evaluated for authenticity and credibility related to identifying criminal activity.

intelligence gap: an unanswered question relating to criminal activity or a threat of criminal activity or national security.[5]

intelligence-led policing: a law enforcement collaborative philosophy that starts with information gathered at all levels of an law enforcement agency that is analyzed to create actionable intelligence products for an improved understanding of their operational environment, which assists in making administrative and investigative decisions.

intelligence products: "reports or documents that contain assessments, forecasts, associations, links, and other outputs from the analytic process that may be disseminated for use by law enforcement agencies for prevention of crimes, target hardening, apprehension of offenders, and prosecution."[6]

intelligence sharing: law enforcement's capability to collaborate with federal, state, and local agencies, as well as the private sector, to disseminate intelligence, information, data, and/or knowledge.

internalized false confession: a false confession that is obtained when the subject has a gap in memory, self-doubt, and no independent recollection of the crime but confessed based on information provided to them.

interrogation: a detailed suspect interview when the subject is in custody and the interview is directed toward a specific crime.

interview: a noncustodial fact-seeking discussion.

---

4 https://en.wikipedia.org/wiki/Criminal_intelligence

5 David L. Carter, Selections from "Law Enforcement Intelligence," *Law Enforcement Intelligence: A Guide for State, Local, and Tribal Law Enforcement Agencies*, p. 442. Copyright © 2022 by David L. Carter. Reprinted with permission.

6 Carter, D. (2022). *Law enforcement intelligence: A guide for state, local, and tribal law enforcement agencies* (3rd ed.). Bureau of Justice Assistance. https://bja.ojp.gov/sites/g/files/xyckuh186/files/media/document/Law_Enforcement_Intelligence_Guide_508.pdf

latent print: an impression of ridged skins, also known as friction ridges, from human fingers, palms, and soles of the feet that is not visible without being processed by powder or chemical.

manslaughter: the unlawful killing of another without specific intent or culpable negligence.

Miranda warning: a warning given by law enforcement to criminal suspects that advised them of their constitutional rights against self-incrimination and a right to have an attorney present during questioning.

modus operandi (MO): an offender's pattern or method of operation to commit a crime.

motive: the reason or purpose a person commits a crime.

need to know: the need to obtain information to execute official responsibilities.

nonverbal communication: communication of information through channels other than written or spoken words. Also see "body language."

omission: a statement that can be proven to be a lie or something intentionally left out that's supported by evidence contrary to the statement.

open-ended questions: questions that require the interviewee to respond with more than a yes or no and provide some detail or particularity.

operational intelligence: intelligence that is actionable as it relates to long-term threats and used to create proactive and preventable responses. Operational intelligence is used in complex criminal investigations that typically involved multiple law enforcement agencies.

patent print: an impression of ridged skins, also known as friction ridges, from human fingers, palms, and soles of the feet that is visible without being processed by powder or chemical.

personal crime: any offense or crime against an individual or persons.

planning: the preparation for future law enforcement operational situations, estimating agency requirements or needs and resources needed to address the know problem(s), and creating strategies to solve the problems.

privacy (information): "the assurance that legal and constitutional restrictions on the collection, maintenance, use, and disclosure of personally identifiable information will be adhered to by criminal justice agencies, with use of such information to be strictly limited to circumstances in which legal process permits use of the personally identifiable information."[7]

privacy (personal): "the assurance that legal and constitutional restrictions on the collection, maintenance, use, and disclosure of behaviors of an individual—including his/her communications, associations, and transactions—will be adhered to by criminal justice agencies, with use of such information to be strictly limited to circumstances in which legal process authorizes surveillance and investigation."[8]

---

7 Carter, D. (2022). *Law enforcement intelligence: A guide for state, local, and tribal law enforcement agencies* (3rd ed.). Bureau of Justice Assistance. https://bja.ojp.gov/sites/g/files/xyckuh186/files/media/document/Law_Enforcement_Intelligence_Guide_508.pdf
8 Carter, D. (2022). *Law enforcement intelligence: A guide for state, local, and tribal law enforcement agencies* (3rd ed.). Bureau of Justice Assistance. https://bja.ojp.gov/sites/g/files/xyckuh186/files/media/document/Law_Enforcement_Intelligence_Guide_508.pdf

proactive: anticipating or stepping in front of a known law enforcement issue, problem, and/or crime by collecting information and data.

problem-oriented policing: a process in community-oriented policing that involves identifying a problem within a community, addressing the problem by solving it through analyzing crime and disorder, and reassessing the response to adjust strategies to maintain effectiveness.

processing: sifting through collected raw data to determine what is most valuable to the mission.

proffer: a legal binding contract that allows the accused to be questioned about their crime without it incriminating the accused as long as they abide by the terms of the contract.

property crime: a criminal offense that involves theft, larceny, burglary, or arson and does not involve violence.

props (for interview/interrogation): material used to give an appearance that there is more meaning or purpose than there actually is.

purge (records): the removal and/or destruction of records that usually occurs after an allotted time period because they are either deemed to have no further value or serve no legitimate law enforcement interest.

pyromaniac: a person who sets fire to objects because of uncontrollable impulses or excitement to watch the fire burn.

qualitative (methods): "research methods that collect and analyze information that is described in narrative or rhetorical form, with conclusions drawn based on the cumulative interpreted meaning of that information."[9]

quantitative (methods): "research methods that collect and analyze information that can be counted or placed on a scale of measurement that can be statistically analyzed."[10]

quota: a fixed or required minimum or maximum number of a particular item.

rape: the penetration, without consent of the victim, of any body part (vaginal, anal, or mouth) by a sex organ from another human.

raw data: "data collected by officers or analysts not yet subjected to the intelligence process; thus, it is not intelligence."[11]

reevaluation: an assessment or review of intelligence within the intelligence process to assess the value of information or intelligence output.

reliability: asks the question, "Is the source of the information consistent and dependable?"[12]

---

9 Carter, D. (2022). *Law enforcement intelligence: A guide for state, local, and tribal law enforcement agencies* (3rd ed.). Bureau of Justice Assistance. https://bja.ojp.gov/sites/g/files/xyckuh186/files/media/document/Law_Enforcement_Intelligence_Guide_508.pdf
10 Carter, D. (2022). *Law enforcement intelligence: A guide for state, local, and tribal law enforcement agencies* (3rd ed.). Bureau of Justice Assistance. https://bja.ojp.gov/sites/g/files/xyckuh186/files/media/document/Law_Enforcement_Intelligence_Guide_508.pdf
11 International Association of Law Enforcement Intelligence Analysts. (2012). *Law enforcement analytic standards* (2nd ed.). U.S. Department of Justice. https://bja.ojp.gov/sites/g/files/xyckuh186/files/media/document/law_enforcement_analytic_standards_04202_combined_compliant.pdf
12   David L. Carter, Selections from "Law Enforcement Intelligence," *Law Enforcement Intelligence: A Guide for State, Local, and Tribal Law Enforcement Agencies*, p. 445 Copyright © 2022 by David L. Carter. Reprinted with permission.

right to know: legal authority to obtain the information being received pursuant to court order, statute, or decisional law.

robbery: the intentional or knowingly taking of property (theft) from another person or place by use or threat of violence, force, or fear.

rapport: an emotional or interpersonal connections, understanding, and feeling of trust between people.

secret: "a classification applied to information, the unauthorized disclosure of which reasonably could be expected to cause serious damage to the national security that the original classification authority is able to identify or describe."[13]

sensitive compartmented information (CSI): "classified information concerning or derived from intelligence sources, methods, or analytical processes that is required to be handled within formal access control systems."[14]

solvability factors: determining factors related to a criminal investigation that can provide leads or information about the crime and who is involved.

spoof: a method of trickery used in phone calls where the spoofer uses a legitimate phone number that shows on caller ID but calls from a private phone number other than the one listed. Spoofers use phone application to change the appearance of the phone they are calling from the disguise their actual number to deceive the person they are calling.

statistical analysis: the process of collecting and using numerical information or data to identify patterns or trends as it relates to criminal activity.

strategic intelligence: "an assessment of targeted crime patterns, crime trends, criminal organizations, and/or unlawful commodity transactions for purposes of planning, decision making, and resource allocation; the focused examination of unique, pervasive, and/or complex crime problems."[15]

subject matter expert (SME): a person who has extensive knowledge, skills, and/or understanding related to a specific subject.

tactical intelligence: intelligence provided to law enforcement agencies so that they can develop strategies that stop and prevent oncoming imminent threats.

theft: the unlawful taking, carrying, leading, or riding away of property from the possession or constructive possession of another without the effective consent of the owner, thus depriving the owner of said property.

---

13 U.S. Senate Select Committee on Intelligence. (n.d.). *Legal resources*. https://www.intelligence.senate.gov/laws/national-security-information#:~:text=(1)%20%22Top%20Secret%22,damage%20to%20the%20national%20security

14 Computer Security Resource Center. (n.d.). *Sensitive compartmented information (SCI)*. National Institute of Standards and Technology. https://csrc.nist.gov/glossary/term/sensitive_compartmented_information

15 Carter, D. (2022). *Law enforcement intelligence: A guide for state, local, and tribal law enforcement agencies* (3rd ed.). Bureau of Justice Assistance. https://bja.ojp.gov/sites/g/files/xyckuh186/files/media/document/Law_Enforcement_Intelligence_Guide_508.pdf

third-agency rule: an agreement whereby a source agency releases information under the condition that the receiving agency does not release the information to any other agency—that is, a third agency.[16]

top secret (TS): a classification applied to information, the unauthorized disclosure of which reasonably could be expected to cause exceptionally grave damage to the national security that the original classification authority is able to identify or describe.[17]

trauma-informed interview: an interview technique where interviewers recognize trauma induced victims by building rapport and using open-ended questions to provide traumatized victims the opportunity to a better opportunity to recount.

unclassified: information that does not require safeguarding or dissemination controls.

Uniform Crime Reporting Program (UCR): statistical data generated by the FBI for law enforcement that is derived from reported criminal offenses to law enforcement agencies.

validity: asks the question, "Does the information actually represent what we believe it represents?"

victimology: the study of a victim, their trends or patterns, social status, and interacts that may develop leads and/or motives to a criminal investigation to link the victim to an offender.

voluntariness: state of being free without constraint.

voluntary false confession: an intentional false statement to law enforcement without pressure.

working copy: a copy of digital media, such as a video, audio, or photographs, that is used for review and may be modified or enhanced for investigative purposes.

---

16   David L. Carter, Selections from "Law Enforcement Intelligence," *Law Enforcement Intelligence: A Guide for State, Local, and Tribal Law Enforcement Agencies*, p. 447. Copyright © 2022 by David L. Carter. Reprinted with permission.
17   David L. Carter, Selections from "Law Enforcement Intelligence," *Law Enforcement Intelligence: A Guide for State, Local, and Tribal Law Enforcement Agencies*, p. 447. Copyright © 2022 by David L. Carter. Reprinted with permission.

Index

Printed in the USA
CPSIA information can be obtained
at www.ICGtesting.com
LVHW071437140824
788162LV00019B/119